Research for
**tomorrow's schools:**
*Disciplined inquiry for education*

Report of the Committee on Educational Research of

the National Academy of Education
*lt)*

# Research fo

## *Discipline*

James S. Coleman, Johns Hopkins University

Lawrence A. Cremin, Teachers College, Columbia
University

Lee J. Cronbach, Stanford University

John I. Goodlad, University of California, Los Angeles

Calvin Gross, University of Missouri, Kansas City

David M. Jackson, Midwest Regional Educational
Laboratory

Israel Scheffler, Harvard University

Patrick Suppes, Stanford University

# tomorrow's schools:

## *inquiry for education*

## Lee J. Cronbach and Patrick Suppes

### *editors*

The Macmillan Company

Collier-Macmillan Limited, London

A publication of the

NATIONAL ACADEMY OF EDUCATION

THE MACMILLAN COMPANY
COLLIER-MACMILLAN CANADA LTD., TORONTO, ONTARIO

Printed in the United States of America

*The sources of educational science are any portions of ascertained knowledge that enter into the heart, head and hands of educators, and which, by entering in, render the performance of the educational function more enlightened, more humane, more truly educational than it was before.*

John Dewey

# *Foreword*

IT IS INCREASINGLY APPARENT that the development of modern nations depends heavily upon the creation of knowledge and its application to agriculture, industry, medicine, and other fields. Recognition of this need has resulted in public support for research and development relating to public services, including education. But, currently, confusion about the nature of research in education and its potential contributions to education and schooling seriously interferes with constructive efforts to create and use relevant knowledge. The need for more adequate understanding led the National Academy of Education to appoint a Committee on Educational Research and to commission it to study the issues and publish its conclusions. This volume is the report of the Committee.

The National Academy of Education was founded in 1965 under charter from the Board of Regents of the State of New York, "to promote scholarly inquiry and discussion concerning the ends and means of education, in all its forms, in the United States and abroad." The Academy serves as a forum for conversation, debate, and mutual instruction, for the communication of accurate information and informed opinion, and for the stimulation of fruitful research. When requested, it counsels public and private agencies.

Academy members are selected by the process usual in such organizations. Each member is a scholar whose works are judged by the other members to be substantial, penetrating, and relevant. The Academy, which elects investigators with established reputations whose work is judged by colleagues to be disciplined inquiry of a high order, forms but a small part of the community of investigators. Because only a few members are elected each year and because a person will ordinarily not be elected on the basis of a single major piece of work, many able investigators, particularly younger ones, are not members at this time. The Academy has not elected to membership persons who make their contribution to education through means other than scholarly inquiry, because the primary basis for judging qualifications for membership is published works.

The diversity of membership is suggested by the list of its sections: History and Philosophy of Education, The Politics, Economics, Sociology, and Anthropology of Education, The Psychology of Education, and The Study of Educational Practice. Members include some who have been identified as students of education throughout their careers, and some whose chief professional identifications have been with fields such as economics, philosophy, or psychology, but who have studied educational problems. The educational topics on which individual members have conducted studies span the whole spectrum of education. Leadership methods of the school administrator, political organization of federal agencies relating to education, motivation of high school students, teaching methods for mathematics in the primary grades, clarification of the objectives of education, analysis of the financial support for education and its economic return to the nation—these are but samples.

Because the Academy membership represents both a wide range of disciplines and a similar diversity of educational topics on which investigations are conducted, an Academy group can draw upon a broad base of scholarship for study and deliberation. Hence, it is in a position to form a committee that can deal comprehensively with the nature of educational research and its contributions to the development of education.

Under the leadership of Lee J. Cronbach and Patrick Suppes as Co-chairmen, the Committee has examined this subject for two years, and this report is the result of their work. Although this report has been read and criticized by the members of the Academy in its draft stage, its final form is the Committee's statement and stands on its own merits. The Academy as a whole was not asked to endorse the report. This kind of statement must be worked out through long study and discussion and its wording represents the common understanding that develops from this effort. It has added importantly to the knowledge and views of the members who were not part of the Committee. We hope that the readers will find this report helpful in clarifying the history, goals, and current status of educational research.

*Ralph W. Tyler*
PRESIDENT
NATIONAL ACADEMY OF EDUCATION

CONTENTS

# *Preface*

THIS IS A CRITICAL TIME in education. There is a call for innovative practice, and a call for research that will point out productive paths to follow. The Academy therefore proposed to develop a report that would help the educational community make effective use of research and scholarship. A committee of members of the Academy and nonmembers was appointed to prepare a statement putting the research enterprise into perspective. The committee was directed to proceed as rapidly as possible, in view of the timeliness of the subject. A thorough study, carried out by a staff over a period of some years, would produce deeper insights than appear in this report. The Committee acknowledges financial assistance provided by the Carnegie Corporation of New York.

The reader may find it helpful to know something about the collective background of the Committee. While this report is not without bias, an interesting diversity of biases entered our discussions. Of the nine members, seven are or have been professors of Education, and six hold or have held professorships in departments in the arts or sciences. Counting past and present roles of its members, the Committee contains two sociologists, two philosophers, a historian, two psychologists, and two statisticians; a director of a laboratory developing computer-assisted instruction, two laboratory-school principals, two deans of university Schools of Education, a director of a regional laboratory for educational research, and a metropolitan school superintendent. Members have done classroom teaching at all levels. Several members have served on panels or councils of government agencies including the U.S. Office of Education, the National Institute of Mental Health, and the National Science Foundation.

The Committee was aided by Academy meetings at which members and guests reviewed their own programs of investigation or examined current policies and organizations for research. The Committee was also able to draw on a number of recent investigations of and symposia on the research enterprise and its organization. Because the reader interested in our topic is likely to find these related investigations of value, we have provided in an Appendix an annotated bibliography prepared by David C. Berliner of the University of Massachusetts, who has also assisted the Committee in many other ways.

These extended citations make it unnecessary to describe within the body of this report the sources on which we have drawn. The typical investigation of the research process has collected limited information about a particular type of organization. We attempt to go beyond this, to an integrated picture of the entire research enterprise as it relates to education, with special attention to the diversity of functions to be performed and the needed variety of institutional arrangements and policies.

This report is addressed primarily to decision-makers. It is they who must understand the scholarly process if society is to make the best use of its expanding investment in education. In the United States, significant decisions are made at many levels and in many localities. Within the federal government we expect our remarks to be pertinent to Congressional committees and to officials in several departments and independent agencies. We speak to administrators and policy makers at the city and state levels who have a role to play in setting up and using research organizations. Our report bears also on the day-to-day planning of these men, insofar as they seek to base educational programs on ideas from the research community. We address ourselves to the directors of the nation's private foundations, great and small, whose strategically placed grants have at times touched off educational revolutions. We hope to interest also the thoughtful laymen who, through their service on school committees, their writings in the public media, and their conversations with each other, provide the base of community support and healthy criticism without which professional educators cannot provide good service.

Within the scholarly community, we speak to university presidents and deans, directors of research laboratories, and professors. Few individuals in the academic community have an adequate picture of the service it can and should render to education. Even many of those engaged in research are so preoccupied with technical puzzles that they may have little perspective on the social process that will eventually put their ideas into action. We make no attempt to discuss directly the research of other nations or international collaboration in research. Problems requiring serious investigation exist everywhere, and research enterprises to cope with them are in various stages of development all over the world. We hope that our remarks will assist our foreign colleagues (who are represented in the Academy by a number of distinguished associate members) to review their own research processes and institutions.

# Aims, origin, and basic concepts of this report

IN THE UNITED STATES, demands upon education have reached an unprecedented peak. More children are enrolled in school and attend for more years than at any other time or place in history. Outside the school there is an equally vast educational enterprise serving adults through mass media, community mental-health agencies, and training programs for workers and executives.

The public demands not merely more education but also considerably better education. No longer can the schools merely certify the children of families with high educational aspirations, so that they can move into a comfortable station in life. Now at one end of the social spectrum there is a demand for professional workers and managers who can accelerate scientific, economic, and social progress, who will be creators more than practitioners. The young people who are asked to take on these roles are insisting on the invention of instructional methods that will match their energies and independent spirit. The older form of education—transmitting facts and rules of thumb, and issuing a lifetime certificate of professional competence —has no validity in a world where social goals, communication patterns, and even scientific theories are changing constantly. At the other end of the social spectrum, the school is asked to instruct the children from homes where there is no educational tradition and no preparation for responsible intellectual effort. The nation, speaking through its local and national leadership, is calling for the invention of new educational methods that will wipe out the cultural depression of the inner city. The older form of education, designed to educate only those motivated to learn from printed symbols, ready to conform to authority, and prepared to work for distant rewards, has no validity in a culture that wants and needs to educate everyone.

Educational reform does not come easily or instantly, as the example of curriculum reform in mathematics shows. Sustained efforts to rework the school mathematics curriculum, aligning it with the modern thinking of mathematicians and child psychologists, have been going on for decades. Radical new instructional materials were well into the experimental stage in the early 1950's, and their influence is now found to some extent in every American classroom. Yet the reforms have not truly succeeded. An International Study [1] that compared the mathematical achievements of adolescents in various countries showed that American students have a proper understanding of the nature of mathematics as a growing field of knowledge, but find mathematics more alien and uninteresting than students in several other nations. Few of even the best American students have the desired skills in mathematical reasoning. Hence the process of invention, trial, partial success, attempts to reformulate the problem, and then further invention must continue for a long time.

So great is the enthusiasm for education, and so yeasty the ferment of change, that expectations are somewhat unrealistic. Minor alterations in procedures and materials can do some good. Providing more teachers and better facilities is certainly wise. But with the need to teach learners who do not respond to the old methods and to reach goals that the schools have not previously worked toward, there will be few immediate breakthroughs. The recent attempt to solve the problem of the lower-class child through quickly organized preschool programs is a case in point. The teachers had to proceed on their best guesses as to what tactics would truly give these children a "headstart" toward school success. The assumptions in some centers were diametrically opposed to those of others.[2] While adequately controlled estimates of the success of these initial efforts are not available, the general impression is that they were disappointingly ineffective. There were gains in intellectual skills, according to before-and-after tests, but the children given the special help did not maintain their momentum as they moved into the regular school. Hence investigation continues into the possibilities of designing better preschool programs and into the possibilities of following the initial push with some school program that will augment rather than diminish the pupil's momentum.

Educational leaders rightly expect the scholar to help in reshaping and revitalizing educational institutions and policies. The scholar is well equipped to provide many things education needs: dispassionate criticism; identification of missed opportunities and emerging problems; a fundamental understanding of the learning process; clarification of the institutional structure of education; invention of procedures; and painstaking elaboration of each rough preliminary idea into a detailed and practical method. Finally, education needs dispassionate evaluation of each new procedure to make sure that it is educating as intended and to identify problems still unsolved.

The scholar is only one among many who contribute to the formulation of questions, answers, and proposals, but scholarly studies of education have on occasion produced major upheavals. Charles Sanders Peirce, a philosopher of the late nineteenth century, altered the traditional conception of knowledge. His influence, brought to bear by John Dewey, E. L. Thorndike, and others, did much to establish what is best in American schools today. Dewey, in founding the Laboratory School at the University of Chicago and later inspiring a force of adherents at Columbia University, generated fundamental changes in the elementary school. Thorndike provided the intellectual framework for a revolution in secondary education. Although not all the educational forms developed under these influences are in favor today, education has been permanently changed by the pragmatist principle that the school should foster the ability to solve problems rather than learning for its own sake.

A more recent example of the scholar's influence is the 1954 desegregation decision and the subsequent efforts to improve the condition of the Negro in America. More than a decade before the nation recognized the plight of the Negro, sociologists and other investigators were familiarizing themselves with the problems of the poor, tracing the sources of their handicaps in society, their feelings of rejection and self-depreciation. Sociological and psychological testimony based on these studies led the Supreme Court to declare (*Brown* v. *Board of Education,* 1954):

> Segregation with the sanction of the law, therefore, has a tendency to retard the educational and mental development of Negro children and to deprive them of some of the benefits they would receive in a racially integrated school system.[3]

Later studies of the intellectual and emotional restrictions on the child reared in the ghetto not only explained why such children were unprepared for the regular school, but suggested types of preschool experience, emotional as well as intellectual, that might compensate for limitations of the home. So the frontier of inquiry has now moved on to the testing of the various proposals.

The heightened demand for contributions from scholarship and research is seen in the increased financial support from public and private sources for studies related to education. It is seen in the attempts of school systems to organize research concerning their own operations and innovations, in the establishment of new laboratories for the study of education, and in the start of international collaborations intended to obtain comparative data helpful in policy formation. After a thirty-year period in which Schools of Education [4] considered systematic inquiry less important than professional training and service to nearby schools, numerous universities have started to revitalize their training programs for educational research. The demand for inquiry is seen in every project developing curriculum materials or new educational procedures, for these innovative enterprises are constantly turning up questions to which past investigations provide no adequate answer.

Thomas Sprat's words regarding the enthusiasm for science in the century of Bacon and Newton apply to today's educational research: "It has begun to keep the best company, refine its fashion and appearance and become the employment of the rich and great, instead of being the subject of man's scorn." [5] Different fields of investigation are cultivated in different generations, and the great advances in a field often come when it is the center of intellectual discussion. As our historical account in Chapter 2 will show, we have just come through something of a desert in educational scholarship. Around 1900, there was a short-lived concentration on education by men of genius. They brought about a transformation of the school. We appear to be on the threshold of another, we hope more lasting, concentration on the nature and conduct of education.

The most encouraging evidence that this demand for excellent research can be satisfied is the fact that investigators in traditional disciplines are turning to problems significant for education and already have made important contributions. The sociological studies of the Negro poor mentioned above are an example of this sort of work. The studies were conducted as part of the general mission of sociologists to understand their society. Only rarely were they carried out with funds earmarked for educational research; yet, when completed, they mapped out a territory that had to be understood by anyone planning education for the Negro child. This sociological work, and the psychological studies that have had such a strong influence on educational thought, are now joined by significant work in economics, political science, and history. For social scientists in those fields to recognize the significance of education is only to correct a long-standing oversight. Another more recent development is the growing interest in education among persons trained in such fields as operations research, statistics, and systems engineering. All of this activity, together with the substantial number of well-qualified investigators employed in educational systems and Schools of Education, demonstrates that there is now a diversified community of investigators at work.

A scholarly approach to education is facilitated by all the centralizing forces of the times. When there is a widely distributed curriculum in biology it is profitable to study in detail how it is working, whereas it would be spendthrift to inquire so intensively into the workings of a course of study used only in a single community. When computers are a routine aid in educational administration, investigators can be supplied easily with data that formerly could have been obtained only through troublesome special questionnaires. With the new resources and new morale of the educational research community, one can be optimistic that important findings will emerge.

But it is not at all certain that the full potential of the scholarly community will be realized. There are misconceptions about the nature of scholarly work and its relation to educational practice, and these misconceptions divert effort into unprofitable channels. The course of inquiry is shaped by the ways in which resources are allocated, research institutions administered, and educational innovations adapted. These forces encourage one set of studies rather than another, and so determine whether the results will be transient and minimal, or fundamental and far-reaching. There are disturbing indications that the label *research*, and funds originally appropriated for research, are sometimes applied to activities that are not properly classified as research—activities that are essentially promotional, or that confine themselves to casual trials of new ideas without systematic analysis and evaluation. As the research effort has expanded, policies for research administration have been enacted piecemeal to meet day-to-day emergencies. Some of these policies, if firmly imbedded in institutions, may impede the scholarly effort for a long time to come.

The work of the scholars is equally in need of review and redirection. The concern of some investigators for what is practically important has not been matched by an equal dedication to hard-headed reasoning, and the investigators with the highest intellectual standards have sometimes retreated to the study of problems that are more elegant than significant.

This document is an attempt, by a more or less representative group from the community of investigators, to present a balanced account of the potential contributions and the limitations of disciplined inquiry as a force toward better education.[6]

# The scope of this report

THE IDEAS that move education forward do not arise exclusively from research and formal scholarship. All manner of communications addressed to the educator, the government official, and the layman help to shape ideas of what the schools can and should do. Some of the communicators are scholars or popularizers of scholarly findings, but others are journalists, advertisers, political leaders, and, of course, the teachers themselves. In concentrating on the communications that flow from disciplined inquiry, we do not intend to belittle the influence of other sources.

Our concern is not restricted to what is conventionally called "educational research"; it ranges over all inquiry and reflective analysis relevant to education. Changes in educational aims and practices originate in diverse areas of scholarship. Modern instructional technology derives from studies of cats in puzzle boxes and of salivating dogs. Modern school administration is to some extent a descendant of Frederick Taylor's time-and-motion studies of industrial production lines. Conversely, scholarship that is self-consciously "educational" may have profound influence on noneducational concepts, so much so that its origin in educational inquiry is forgotten. Father Ong defends the thesis that both the scholastic inquiries in the medieval university and the great Renaissance studies of such men as Erasmus were fundamentally oriented toward the improvement of education.[7] Nor is it difficult to trace a line of descent from the educational writings of Rousseau to current views on the family and the community.

There have been reports similar to ours, and other reports are currently in preparation. A landmark is *The Scientific Movement in Education* produced by the National Society for the Study of Education in 1938.[8] At the close of the first great period of vigorous investigation of education, the leaders of the era reflected on what had been accomplished since 1900 in the study of all aspects of education from handwriting to school finance. A briefer statement, somewhat similar in character, was published at the same time by a committee of the American Council on Education.[9] The reports are useful accounts of the accomplishments and aspirations of educational research at a time that, in retrospect, proves to have been a high-water mark. Neither, however, attends to the organization of research nor to the conditions that cause significant investigations to flourish.

Among more recent discussions, perhaps the first to strike out along new lines was a 1958 proposal by a committee organized by the National Academy of Sciences–National Research Council.[10] Their proposal of a centralized research institution concerned with education, comparable to the Clinical Center of the National Institutes of Health, fell on deaf ears. It is significant that the report was sponsored by the agency that most nearly speaks for the scientific community in the United States. For this agency to point to the accomplishments and potential of disciplined study of education was a large step beyond what might be interpreted as self-congratulatory writings by persons making a profession of educational research. The report, questioning the basis on which research has been organized, opened discussion that reverberated through subsequent papers, symposia, Congressional hearings, and informal meetings. One prominent committee report of the decade came from the Panel on Educational Research and Development of the President's Scientific Advisory Committee (1964).[11] This Committee celebrated curriculum reforms in science, mathematics, and other subjects, which had been accomplished by bringing together experienced educators, specialists in a subject-matter field, and substantial financial support. Many of the curriculum teams proceeded artistically, on a trial-and-error basis, to produce instructional materials in fresh styles and with fresh content. The PSAC report does not seriously concern itself with the scholarly investigation of education. It does, however, echo the NAS–NRC report in calling for a new central organization to cultivate innovations in education.

Most recently, the suggestion for a central agency took a different form in a recommendation from a study group of the Committee for Economic Development.[12] Their proposal is not for an operating agency but for a planning and review agency. The many institutional changes of the past decade have created a different scene from that in which the NAS–NRC and PSAC recommendations evolved. The 1968 CED proposal conceives of an independent non-governmental agency, something legally akin to the Corporation for Public Broadcasting. While we would encourage thoughtful attention to the CED proposal, we have not had the opportunity to make the detailed study of their proposed machinery that would warrant a more specific comment.

Another recent report having considerable relevance is a staff study made for the Committee on Government Operations of the House of Representatives. This gave considerable attention to education within a general inquiry concerning the usefulness of federally supported social research. For convenience we shall refer to this as the Reuss report, Congressman Henry Reuss being the chairman of the sponsoring subcommittee. The report compiles facts, source papers, and opinions on many topics of concern to us. The covering and summary sections of the report were prepared by Harold Orlans, a sociologist. The following passage from Orlans' discussion of educational research is especially pertinent:

Plainly, the critical questions which remain to be resolved during the next few years concern the appropriate roles of universities; the many new nonprofit organizations created by government or private initiative and now engaged in educational research and development; and the vigorous new educational industry. All three sectors are competing for the same limited talent, money, and influence; and it will take an order of statesmanship not always in evidence to transform some of this competition into collaboration, and to turn the remainder to constructive channels.[13]

The symposia and reports of the past decade speak with increasing candor of the need for better intellectual and organizational approaches to research on education. There has been agreement, both within and without the ranks of educators, that systematic investigation has much to offer. Indeed, there is agreement that *massive, lasting changes in education cannot safely be made except on the basis of deep objective inquiry.* Until the early 1960's the appeal for suitable financial support dominated all other elements of the message. This appeal was answered with an alacrity that caught the research community unprepared, and its discussions soon focused on how the new resources might be used effectively. The Panglossian tone of the early reports on educational science has been replaced by a note of honest evaluation. The recognition that much educational research has been inadequate is nowhere more clearly expressed than in presentations by and to the educational community; most notably the symposia organized by the educational fraternity, Phi Delta Kappa.[14]

Our report has a marked historical flavor because we wish to place current policy decisions in a long perspective. Education is a complex system of institutions, slow to change. A specific innovation reaches its full effect through a lengthy evolutionary process in which it is supported by social forces and by other deliberate changes. This is as true for changes that stem from scholarly inquiry as for any others. To understand current inadequacies we need to recognize how we got to our present situation, what forces have operated to limit forward movement, and what momentum can be capitalized upon. Positive contributions made in the past indicate what sort of contributions scholarly work can make in the future; instances where research efforts were unprofitable or had unfortunate consequences can serve as a warning. An additional virtue of the historical emphasis is that one can examine with some detachment the activities of the previous generation, whereas a critique of current projects is bound to engage the partisanship of both writers and readers. Our stress on the past does not imply that what is going on today is of less importance, but we do consider ourselves better justified in claiming that a Dewey or a Pavlov had a striking impact on educational thought than in singling out the exceptional figures among our contemporaries.

We start with the premise that inquiry into educational matters is essential but extremely difficult. We therefore are particularly concerned with the impediments to excellence in educational research. To discover and propagate new mechanisms for conducting research and new research styles will require changed attitudes within the academic community. These must grow; they cannot be legislated.

# *Key concepts of the report*

## Disciplined Inquiry

In discussing disciplined inquiry and its relation to the improvement of education, we give no narrow definition to the term. Too many writers seem to limit the term "research" to quantitative empirical inquiry. While much has been and will be learned from social surveys, measurements, and controlled experiments, the study of education requires nonquantitative as well as quantitative techniques. Naturalistic observation, for example, has tended to fall into disuse, though it is a significant form of disciplined inquiry, as is illustrated by Newcomb's observations of the Bennington College community out of which emerged the ideas represented in today's "cluster colleges."

Inquiry is not restricted to the "scientific." Historical studies provide perspective on current proposals. An excellent case in point is the light cast on debates about public aid for church schools by scholarly studies on the origin and meaning of the first amendment to the Constitution. The philosopher adds to the clarity of educational discussions by helping in the statement and evaluation of goals and by sharpening educational theories. Logical analysis of the school's "subject matter" also can contribute to better instruction.

An inquiry generally sets out to answer a rather narrowly defined question. The specific findings of such inquiries are usually less important than the conceptualizations they generate.

Broadly applicable concepts raise the level of intelligence with which educational matters can be analyzed. There was a time, for example, when economists conceived of the economy as an occupational arena in which individuals competed for individual rewards; similarly, education was something the individual purchased as a personal capital investment. On the grand account, society's contribution to education was an expense item. In the economist's present view, individual abilities constitute a natural resource. Society reaps an economic reward when abilities are properly developed and deployed, and its educational outlay is a capital investment to be returned with interest. This conception has required planners to devise "manpower policies;" these in turn have raised the priority assigned to education in both the advanced and the developing nations.

CRITICAL PROCESSES Disciplined inquiry has a quality that distinguishes it from other sources of opinion and belief. The disciplined inquiry is conducted and reported in such a way that the argument can be painstakingly examined. The report does not depend for its appeal on the eloquence of the writer or on any surface plausibility. The argument is not justified by anecdotes or casually assembled fragments of evidence. Scholars in each field have developed traditional questions that serve as touchstones to separate sound argument from incomplete or questionable argument. Among other things, the mathematician asks about axioms, the historian about the authenticity of documents, the experimental scientist about verifiability of observations. Whatever the character of a study, if it is disciplined the investigator has anticipated the traditional questions that are pertinent. He institutes controls at each step of information collection and reasoning to avoid the sources of error to which these questions refer. If the errors cannot be eliminated, he takes them into account by discussing the margin for error in his conclusions. Thus the report of a disciplined inquiry has a texture that displays the raw materials entering the argument and the logical processes by which they were compressed and rearranged to make the conclusion credible.

It is easiest to see the meaning of "discipline" when a study arises strictly within one of the established academic fields such as mathematics or sociology. In each such field there has evolved a consistent system of concepts, techniques, and critical questions, together with a prescribed form for presenting completed arguments. Each has a style well suited to investigate a certain range of problems. But disciplined inquiry can scarcely be mapped into the traditional disciplines, as disciplines themselves evolve.

Subdisciplines branch off within a field, and new hybrid disciplines emerge. Even fields that now have a tradition were new disciplines, or not accepted as disciplines at all, a century ago; this is true of genetics, psychology, even history. Just the past few years have seen new departures: quantitative studies in history, mathematical studies in sociology, and a psychology that uses the computer instead of the animal as an analogue to man. There is an attempt to develop an all-purpose form of disciplined inquiry under such a label as operations research, where the effort is to find a way of asking and answering questions that will generate insight into and control over virtually any complex process.

Disciplined inquiry does not necessarily follow well-established, formal procedures. Some of the most excellent inquiry is free-ranging and speculative in its initial stages, trying what might seem to be bizarre combinations of ideas and procedures, or restlessly casting about for ideas. There was nothing systematic, for instance, in Ventris' procedure for breaking the code of the Mycenaean script Linear B; the style of the inquiry was one of following hunches. But there was discipline in the checking of the hunches and in organizing the report so that any qualified reader could accept or reject the argument. Binet's inquiry into intelligence was not greatly different. He had some vague ideas about the nature of intellect, but the indicators whose possible usefulness he explored ranged from rote memory to palmistry. His success came both from this openmindedness and from his relentless self-criticism, together with his convincing exposition of the reasons for the scale he finally proposed.

Not all the writings of academic men are scholarly reports. The person who completes a systematic inquiry will perhaps prepare an account of it in a freer style for the general public or for policy-makers. Such general writings may offer views on aspects of education the scholar has not studied intensively. They may extrapolate beyond the relatively limited conclusions strictly warranted by his research. Though essays, polemics, and statements of belief are outside the category of disciplined inquiry, they too can be important. In such writings the academic scholar speaks as a citizen joining the discussions of the community. He wins adherents by persuasive language, like any lawyer or executive who addresses the same audience. His specialized studies have given him a special perspective and, one hopes, some wisdom. His general writings are likely to offer fresh ideas. But a society that regards these essays as the academic man's chief work will not care properly for the headwaters from which the stream of ideas flows.

It is scarcely necessary to remark that not all conclusions of disciplined inquiry are true. Each investigation is limited by its methods, and the consensus of the best-informed members of a discipline is limited by the state of the art. In the most traditional academic fields conceptualizations and theories are continually being debated, and even factual conclusions are altered from time to time.

A disciplined inquiry does have an internal consistency that requires colleagues to take the findings seriously, even when they disagree with them. A scholarly report is considerably more than a printout of speculations, preconceptions, and wish-fulfilling observations. It nourishes thought. Indeed, the fact that it invites and rewards close examination is the mark of worthy inquiry. The detail of the argument, whether it is describing methods of data collection or the derivation of practical recommendations, is lucid, specific, and pertinent. With such a presentation there is something to learn from *explication de texte*, whereas in an undisciplined discussion the summary message is all that can be taken seriously.

The success of academic men in breaking old intellectual molds and inventing fresh concepts results from the fact that they value the process of inquiry at least as much as they value its fruits. They are trained in specialized techniques of observation and analysis. Instruments to refine the judgment of the observer, statistical models to weed out chance effects, mathematical models, canons of documentation, and formal criteria of acceptable definition, constitute the technology of inquiry. But far more fundamental to disciplined inquiry is its central attitude, which places a premium on objectivity and evidential test.

DISCIPLINE IN EDUCATIONAL INQUIRY    Studies of education can share fully in this attitude. Anyone undertaking educational research can hold himself to the highest standards of careful observation and systematic reasoning. Admittedly, social processes are complex and ever-changing, and can rarely be experimentally controlled or comprehensively observed. Studying a classroom is at least as difficult as studying a hurricane. Even so, given sufficient effort, talent, and self-discipline, systematic inquiry can be expected to give a far more dependable explanation than will come from casual reflection upon casual observations.

Our interest is not confined to encouraging inquiry that advances one of the traditional disciplines. There are important studies to be done that will simultaneously increase knowledge about an aspect of education and understanding about a basic problem in a discipline such as sociology. There are worthwhile analyses to be made of practical educational situations, where techniques of one or more disciplines are employed solely to serve the educator. Other needed educational studies can scarcely be identified with any particular discipline. An example is the construction of the *Taxonomy of Educational Objectives*.[15] The work was rigorous and subject to disciplined criticism. Though it was influenced by psychology, psychometrics, and philosophy, the statement of the problem and the critical questions applied were to some extent unique. Studies of education often have to assemble their own method and rationale, using bits and pieces of statistics, economics, philosophy, etc. to construct a suitably controlled inquiry.

This diversity implies that there is no uniform "method of educational research," and indeed each of the numerous textbooks on how to do educational research is a potpourri. This diversity presents serious problems in the preparation of research workers. The graduate faculty in Education must have extremely varied backgrounds if the faculty is to contain at least one individual well qualified in each important method of inquiry and criticism.

## Conclusion-oriented and decision-oriented inquiry

In the absence of well-understood categories, discussion of the contribution and promotion of various kinds of inquiry is not easy. An enthusiast for an investigatory activity affixes to it whatever label is likely to win favor from his particular audience at a given time. The popular labels "basic research" and "applied research" seem especially hard to employ precisely. It is extremely difficult to tell whether a research study is basic or applied: the cross-fertilization of peas by a curious monk does not differ in its operations from a cross-fertilization carried out on the plantings of a seed company in the hope of direct profit. Storer [16] decided that the main difference between the two approaches to inquiry is the proposed audience:

> Basic research is that which is carried out by a scientist who hopes his findings will be primarily of interest to his scientific colleagues, while applied research is intended to produce findings which will be of greater interest to the investigator's employer or to the lay public.

Marvin Reagan [17] offers the Storer quotation, and a dozen others, to show that the ambiguity of the basic-applied distinction obscures policy recommendations in any field. And when writers use it to categorize studies all of which are significant for education, it becomes extraordinarily troublesome.

Inquiries do need to be categorized, as a rhetorical device to point up contrasts between kinds of study that affect the school in different ways or that flourish in response to somewhat different environments. A distinction of this sort has to be taken lightly, however, for not only are there borderline cases, but a single program of investigation may cross the dividing line as the work progresses. The categories we use emphasize not the topics under study or the motivations of the investigators, but the conditions under which the studies take place.

We propose to distinguish *decision-oriented* from *conclusion-oriented* investigations.[18] In a decision-oriented study the investigator is asked to provide information wanted by a decision-maker: a school administrator, a governmental policy-maker, the manager of a project to develop a new biology textbook, or the like. The decision-oriented study is a commissioned study. The decision-maker believes that he needs information to guide his actions and he poses the question to the investigator. The conclusion-oriented study, on the other hand, takes its direction from the investigator's commitments and hunches. The educational decision-maker can, at most, arouse the investigator's interest in a problem. The latter formulates his own question, usually a general one rather than a question about a particular institution. The aim is to conceptualize and understand the chosen phenomenon; a particular finding is only a means to that end. Therefore, he concentrates on persons and settings that he expects to be enlightening.

The conclusion-oriented investigator is free to reframe his questions as he goes along, taking advantage of each partial insight to redirect his inquiry. Seaborg [19] has said,

> If the investigator is not free to make radical changes in his program or to pursue some unexpected question which has arisen in his work and which excites his curiosity as to why and how, the program is probably not too basic.

We would use the term "conclusion-oriented" rather than "basic," because this freedom for exploration and self-direction can be present in research on (e.g.) practices in school administration or on the effects of educational television—topics that many people would not consider basic.

Freedom is present in a decision-oriented inquiry to only a very limited degree. The investigator can decline the commission. He can recommend that the decision be made without the proposed study, on the ground that the study would not be valuable enough to repay its cost. He can seek to persuade the decision-maker that the wrong question is being asked, and that some different inquiry, perhaps one that will be much slower to arrive at an answer, will be a wiser undertaking. But unless such negotiations cause the decision-maker to sponsor a frankly conclusion-oriented and openended inquiry, the investigator undertakes to deliver an answer to the practical question, more or less on a stated schedule. He is not free to wander down interesting bypaths or to burrow into deeper questions, if that will delay telling the decision-maker what the latter wants to know.

Because of borderline instances our distinction can be puzzling. Two side comments may contribute to greater clarity. First, we acknowledge that often conclusion-oriented research is also commissioned; but the sponsor has a very different understanding of the research than the decision-maker who asks for direct help. Commissioning a conclusion-oriented study is like commissioning a composer to produce a symphony. One does not assign the theme, the key, or the mood; one asks only that he spend the resources on composing for the orchestra rather than on writing songs or writing an autobiography. When a School of Education appoints a research professor, it expects him to do research that can be seen as potentially interesting for education but it does not lay out the questions he is to answer. A slight extension applies to the mission-oriented agency that sponsors conclusion-oriented research. The head of the agency may need to direct the total program so that delivery dates for certain products are met, and yet he may engage investigators to do wide-ranging studies on topics within the agency's area of concern. The classification as conclusion-oriented or decision-oriented applies to a type of study, not to a program or an agency.

The conclusion-decision dichotomy has only a weak correspondence to the basic-applied distinction. Decision-oriented research no doubt is applied. Conclusion-oriented research, however, may also be concerned directly with educational institutions and instructional activities, and in that sense it too may be "applied research." We are not alone in recognizing that some studies of practically important matters should properly be categorized as basic or conclusion-oriented. We note that Frederick Seitz, as President of the National Academy of Sciences, spoke of *"true basic scientific* research of a pure *or applied* nature" (italics ours) in contrast to that spent for "engineering development, testing, and evaluation in preparation for possible production." [20]

The distinction between decision-oriented and conclusion-oriented research lies in the origination of the inquiry and the constraints imposed by its institutional setting, not in topic or technique, nor in the interests held by the investigator. The investigator in a decision-oriented study contracts to deliver the information that a particular school officer, program planner, or curriculum developer has requested. Once the decision-oriented study is undertaken, the investigator is expected to stay with the plan until he has a report on the question selected for study.

The conclusion-oriented study is not planned with an eye to a definite and useful result. The main benefit is in the unforeseen ideas it adds to society's intellectual capital. Hence the gain from a line of work can be judged only after the study has been completed and interpreted. The faith is that with a good many studies in progress, some of them will generate conceptual advances significant enough to offset the cost of the whole enterprise. As Lederberg has put it in testimony before a Senate Committee,

> It is fair to say that society exploits the poetic fascination that motivates many academic scientists, eventually capitalizing on applications that no one could have foreseen. It may even be that research work loses rigor and sharpness of focus if the research worker himself is too sensitive to the unpredictable implications of what he is doing.
>
> It is important that such utilities be discovered as soon as they can be useful. This discovery, though, is a function of a whole community of basic and applied scientific effort. To place the burden [of practical justification, in advance] on individual projects would be the surest possible way of stifling the most creative and the least predictable advances in scientific understanding.[21]

The conclusion-oriented investigator does not promise to answer a particular question by a particular date. Pressure from a donor or superior to do so reduces him to the status of a technician for the duration of the study.

We warn the reader against reading a value judgment

into our distinction. Neither type of inquiry is preferred over the other. The two have distinctive functions, but each needs the stimulus of the other, and neither alone can do the needed job. T. R. McConnell has put it well:

> Experience in other fields has shown that many processes intervene between research and production. . . . There is abundant testimony that the flow from research to development and innovation is neither unidimensional nor unidirectional. At any stage in the process the researcher, the developer, or the evaluator may have to cope with unanticipated variables. Furthermore, "feedback" occurs at various stages of the research-development-evaluation continuum. One stage enriches others; one phase may require adaptation in previous ones, or even an entirely new start.[22]

A particular set of data might be collected with either decision-making or conclusion-drawing in view. A decision-oriented study very often plays a role in the development of broad conclusions. An example is the study *Equality of Educational Opportunity*,[23] conducted for the U.S. Office of Education under a mandate from the Congress. The mandate circumscribed the questions to be asked about the education of minorities, the procedures to be used, and the time schedule for completing the report. The report placed the Congress and the Administration in a position to review their legislative plans. Being thus constrained, the study did not collect the data or follow the research strategy that might have appealed to a scientist seeking primarily to understand the effects of segregation and other differences among schools. The data are good enough, however, that sociologists and educational specialists have started to re-examine them in an effort to extract general conclusions. In addition to studying the published tables and summaries, these investigators are making further tabulations of the original data and trying to enrich the interpretation by direct observation in schools. Questions suggested by the survey inevitably lead to more direct, more intensive studies, some of them decision-oriented and some conclusion-oriented.

Conclusion-oriented research is intended to have a general significance, whereas decision-oriented research is designed for its relevance to a particular institution at a particular time. Occasionally the "institution" is a sprawling one, as in the study mentioned above, on how minorities fare within the American school system as a whole. Most decision-oriented studies, however, have a local reference; it is not their aim to be suggestive for other institutions. The conclusion-oriented study, even when carried out in a single setting, is intended to produce broadly applicable concepts and generalizations.

Thus Newcomb studied Bennington to gain insight into civic education in general. The specific data on Bennington were only incidental to the broader concepts reported, and if the investigator had been forced to move to a different setting he still could have carried on his study. In the decision-oriented study, however, the setting studied is of central interest and transferrable insights, while welcome, are not the aim. Because of its specificity, the decision-oriented study is likely to be carried out by an employee of a school system or another operating agency. Because of its generality, the conclusion-oriented study is normally directed by a university professor or a member of a research laboratory. But this is not a necessary division of labor. A case can be made for a certain amount of conclusion-oriented, publishable research carried out in school systems; this can contribute to the professional thinking of all who participate. And the scholar who joins a decision-oriented investigation comes to see his specialty differently in this value-laden context; the experience can make his subsequent thinking richer and more realistic.

Because conceptualization is the aim in conclusion-oriented work, the results are likely to be relevant to many human activities. A finding that adds to the base of knowledge about education is likely to add to knowledge about other social institutions. It is not especially important to decide whether a study is or is not directly concerned with education. What is vital is that the knowledge be developed with the encouragement and assistance of any of the agencies whose mission could eventually profit from such knowledge.

TYPES OF DECISION-ORIENTED STUDY   We find it useful to distinguish two kinds of decision-oriented research: (1) operational or institutional research; and (2) product or developmental research. The former is illustrated by the typical work of a research bureau in a city school system, the latter by the work of investigators developing programmed instructional materials for sale to schools. Operational studies are conducted in universities, state educational systems, national agencies such as the Joint Commission on Mental Health in Children, and various other private and public agencies of all sizes. Product research includes not only development of text materials but also the design and evaluation of school buildings and equipment, visual aids, and systems for administrative control such as scheduling by computer.

Operational research is obviously decision-oriented. The research office in the school system or the institutional research office in a university establishes routine procedures for monitoring certain aspects of the system, and uses them to identify trouble spots deserving administrative attention (e.g., drop-out rates for various schools and various types of students). The office also conducts *ad hoc* studies of questions that arise in administrative planning—for example, of the ways district lines could be redrawn to improve racial balance.

*The role of each study is to provide the decision-maker with information, not to tell him what to do.* The study gives an organized account of relevant facts, and may forecast the probable outcome of each of the possible alternative actions. The choice of action is the responsibility of the school executive rather than the investigator; only the executive or his advisory board is in a position to weigh the political, economic, and educational aspects of the choice. Decision-oriented "product research" is part of an effort to develop an educational procedure that can be followed systematically in the future, ordinarily in many localities. Such product research is often called "development." Too often, especially in education, the word "development" refers simply to the construction of some procedure or material on the basis of general notions as to what will be effective. Deliberate inquiry, however, is an essential component in true developmental research. This inquiry is directed, first, to collecting information needed to design the product; then to testing the pilot versions in order to identify and explain remediable faults, and eventually to appraising the final product.

For the sake of completeness, we mention one type of inquiry that does not fit neatly into either the conclusion-oriented or decision-oriented category. This is the routine, continuous collection of facts that is often called social accounting. The best-known example of this is the United States census, which compiles facts thought likely to be useful for many different purposes. More mundane examples of social statistics are the compilations of data on enrollment and faculty salary for American schools and colleges. Studies of this sort produce data banks to which persons with diverse questions may turn. Some of them will use the facts as a basis for decision and some will use them in pursuing general conclusions. Although we shall not discuss this type of research at length, its social function is obvious.

NOTES

1. Husén, Torsten (ed.), *International Study of Achievement in Mathematics*. New York: Wiley, 1967.

2. Hess, Robert, and Roberta Bear (eds.), *Early Education: Current Theory, Research, and Action.* Chicago: Aldine Publishing Co., 1968.
3. *Brown v. Board of Education,* 347 U.S. 483, 74 Supreme Court 686, 98 L. Ed. 873, 1954.
4. In this report we adopt the convention of capitalizing Education when it refers to a faculty or subdivision within a university and of capitalizing School when we refer to (e.g.) a School of Education. Because much of our discussion refers to schools and to education in their general usage, capitalization for this special use will eliminate some possible confusion.
5. Sprat, Thomas, *History of the Royal-Society of London, for the Improving of Natural Knowledge.* London: Royal Society, 1667.
6. We acknowledge with thanks the comments of various individuals on drafts of this report, particularly those of participants in a seminar at Stanford University during the summer of 1968.
7. Ong, W. J., *The Barbarian Within and Other Fugitive Stories.* New York: Macmillan, 1962.
8. Whipple, Guy M. (ed.), *The Scientific Movement in Education.* 37th Yearbook, National Society for the Study of Education, Part 2, Public School Publishing Co., Bloomington, Ill., 1938.
9. *Educational Research: its Nature, Essential Conditions, and Controlling Concepts.* Washington, D.C.: American Council on Education Studies Series 1, Vol. 3, No. 10, 1939.
10. National Academy of Sciences—National Research Council, *Psychological Research in Education.* Washington, D.C.: The Academy, 1938.
11. *Innovation and Experiment in Education.* Report of the Panel on Educational Research and Development of the President's Science Advisory Committee. Washington, D.C.: Government Printing Office, 1964.
12. *Innovation in Education: New Directions for the American School.* Committee for Economic Development. New York: The Committee, 1968.
13. *The Use of Federal Research in Federal Domestic Programs.* Committee on Government Operations. Washington, D.C.: Government Printing Office, 1967.
14. Banghart, F. W. (ed.), *First Annual Phi Delta Kappa Symposium on Educational Research.* Bloomington, Ind.: Phi Delta Kappa, 1960; Collier, R. C., Jr., and S. M. Elam (eds.), *Second Annual Phi Delta Kappa Symposium on Educational Research: Research, Design, and Analysis.* Bloomington, Ind.: Phi Delta

Kappa, 1961; Guba, E., and S. Elam (eds.), *Sixth Annual Phi Delta Kappa Symposium on Educational Research: The Training and Nurture of Educational Researchers.* Bloomington, Ind.: Phi Delta Kappa, 1965.

15. Bloom, B. S. (ed.), *Taxonomy of Educational Objectives I: The Cognitive Domain.* New York: Longmans Green, 1956; Krathwohl, D. R., and others (eds.), II. *The Affective Domain.* New York: McKay, 1964.

16. Storer, N. W., *Basic Versus Applied Research: The Conflict Between Means and Ends in Science.* Cambridge: Harvard University Press, 1964.

17. Reagan, Marvin D., "Basic and Applied Research: A Meaningful Distinction?" *Science*, Vol. 155 (1967), pp. 1383–1386.

18. Tukey, J. W., "Conclusions vs. Decisions," *Technometrics*, Vol. 2 (1960), pp. 423–433; Merton, Robert B., "Basic Research and Potentials of Relevance," *The American Behavioral Scientist*, Vol. 6 (1963), pp. 86–90.

19. Seaborg, Glenn T., in *Federal Research and Development Programs.* Select Committee on Government Research. Washington, D.C.: Government Printing Office, 1964, Part 1, pp. 65–73.

20. Seitz, Frederick, *ibid.*, pp. 56–65.

21. Lederberg, Joshua, "Some Problems of Instant Medicine," *Saturday Review*, Vol. 50 (March 6, 1967), pp. 66–70.

22. McConnell, T. R., *Research or Development: A Reconciliation.* Chicago: Phi Delta Kappa, 1967. P. 30.

23. Coleman, James, and others, *Equality of Educational Opportunity.* Washington, D.C.: Government Printing Office, 1968.

**2**

# American scholars and educational progress 1855-1958

A SURVEY OF THE EVOLUTION of educational research in the United States during the past century should illuminate its traditional strengths and limitations, and its prospects for further service. The research enterprise is still young and conceptions of its ideal nature and character have changed repeatedly. We shall concentrate on inquiries made by self-styled educational research workers, because to look at all disciplined inquiry relevant to education would be to survey not only the emergence of the social and behavioral sciences, but also many aspects of more general humanistic scholarship.[1] We shall devote little attention to studies by historians and philosophers of education because, as Schools of Education gradually allowed such studies to fall into neglect, they came to be excluded from the so-called "scientific movement in education."[2] We shall redress the balance in Chapter 3, however, by examining two specific lines of nonempirical inquiry and their impact on educational thought and practice. Finally, we shall confine our discussion to the United States. European thought had a profound impact in America prior to 1900, but in the twentieth century there have been only occasional instances of international collaboration and communication in educational inquiry. Happily, there seem to be significant new stirrings in our own time; and indeed, some fresh and able leaders in the developing nations, asking searching questions about education in novel settings, may shortly become a major source of new lines of inquiry.

Our survey will be divided into three somewhat arbitrary periods: the first, from 1855 to 1895; the second, from 1895 to about 1938; and the third, from 1938 to 1955. The years since 1955 appear to have opened a new era in the history of educational inquiry and reform. It was about 1955 that the federal government began to assume a more central role in education, and there was a resurgence of interest in educational problems among scholars outside the ranks of educational specialists. It has seemed to us better to fit these later events into the description of the present state of affairs that extends through our report, to deal with them as a living present that can be shaped rather than to embalm them as past history.

The first period, which we date from the appearance of Henry Barnard's *American Journal of Education* in 1855, marks the beginning of self-conscious scholarship in American education: it was prescientific, resting largely on the German ideal of *Wissenschaft* or systematized assembly of knowledge, and closer in spirit to history and philosophy than to science. The second period dates from the 1890's, that remarkable decade that began with the publication of William James' *Principles of Psychology* and that witnessed the establishment of the National Society for the Scientific Study of Education (1895), the founding of the Laboratory School at the University of Chicago (1896), and the appearance of Joseph Mayer Rice's "The Futility of the Spelling Grind" (1897) and of Edward L. Thorndike's *Animal Learning* (1898). It was a period of vigorous empiricism, with emphasis on the quantitative measurement of educational effectiveness. Psychology provided the chief models for both conclusion-oriented and decision-oriented research. The third period dates from the 1930's, a decade that saw the beginning of the Eight-Year Study, the launching of *The Social Frontier*, and the publication of two landmark documents on the state of educational research, the NSSE Yearbook on *The Scientific Movement in Education*, and the ACE report on *Educational Research*. At this point decline set in. In the years after 1938 writings on education were more often works of contention than of scholarship, disciplined reports received little attention from educators, and much that was labeled research consisted of communal activities intended to stimulate individual teachers to change their practices.

# Education emerges as a field of study
# 1855–1895

EDUCATION became a topic of continued and serious scholarship in the mid-1850's. To understand how radical this development was, one need only recall the character of American schools, of writings on education, and of professional training at that time. Writings on pedagogy were scattered. There was little reflection on the aims and content of education. Relatively few persons made teaching a life work. Training of teachers was largely a matter of demonstration and apprenticeship, in addition to coverage of the lessons the novices would soon be repeating to their own classes. The profession, seen more as schoolkeeping than as schoolteaching, was accorded little status. The primary qualification for a teaching post was good moral character. People believed in education, but inquiry into its means and ends was at best speculative, and at worst, the simple codifying of common sense.

## Henry Barnard: The Journal and the United States Office of Education

It was into this situation that Henry Barnard projected the *American Journal of Education* as a periodical "devoted exclusively to the History, Discussion, and Statistics of Systems, Institutions, and Methods of Education, in different countries, with special reference to the conditions and wants of our own." Beginning in 1855, Barnard made the *Journal* a repository of educational information from all ages and places—the United States, Europe, Canada, Latin America, even India and Persia.[3] He presented biographies of educators, translations of classical documents, pedagogical exercises, hints to teachers, model lessons, and treatises by philosophers and psychologists. Barnard gathered, systematized, and published the materials for a "science of education," thereby giving teachers and policy-makers convenient access to the wisdom of ancient and modern times in the fields of their concern.

Barnard wanted to transform education from a haphazard practice into an enterprise regulated by the best available thought. In educational history and philosophy, he was partial to German scholarship, devoting hundreds of pages of the *Journal* to translations of Karl von Raumer's monumental *Geschichte der Pädagogik*. In educational psychology, on the other hand, Barnard tended to ignore the rising experimental investigations of Lotze, Fechner, and Wundt in favor of Pestalozzian formulas and the Scotch commonsense precepts of his friend, William Russel. Barnard vastly expanded the purview of American educators, forcing them to contend with unfamiliar aspects of their own traditions. Beyond this, he exerted a direct reformist influence by presenting ideas, information, and materials favoring a more humane pedagogy, a more utilitarian curriculum that gave greater recognition to scientific and technical developments, and more effective governmental administration of education.

Barnard, as much as any man, was instrumental in the creation and early shaping of the federal Bureau of Education, the present United States Office of Education.[4] As early as 1854 he proposed that the Smithsonian Institution or some other agency appoint an official to "devote himself exclusively to the 'increase and diffusion of knowledge' on the subject of education, and especially of the condition and means of improving Popular Education. . . ." Others similarly favored having a federal bureau concerned with educational scholarship, as is evidenced by E. E. White's influential presidential address before the National Association of School Superintendents in 1866. When "An Act to Establish a Department of Education" was finally passed in 1867, the first section echoed Barnard by defining the chief purpose of the new Department (later called a Bureau, and then an Office) as one of "collecting such statistics and facts as shall show the condition and progress of education in the several states and territories, and of diffusing information respecting the organization and management of schools and school systems, and methods of teaching."

It would appear that the collection of statistics on enrollment, expenditures, and similar practical matters loomed large in what schoolmen hoped for from the agency. Not so with Barnard, whose primary interest was a serious consideration of the nature and quality of education. Taking office as the first Commissioner of Education, he looked forward to the preparation of a lengthy series of official reports containing accounts of educational experiments, statistics of national school systems, discussions of educational reform and reformers, biographies of great teachers—in short, a vast expansion of what he had originally envisioned as editor of the *Journal*. He seems literally to have spent his term of office nurturing plans for such lines of work, holding himself in readiness for Congressional resolutions calling for special reports on the purposes and potentialities of education. The resolutions never came. Unable to persuade Congress of the importance of his plan, Barnard gave up the Commissionership after three years, and returned to his home in Hartford to give himself fully to the *Journal*.

His departure was no doubt hastened by Congressional discontent. The Congress, composed of men of action, had expected the new Department to plunge forcefully into the business of setting up a new educational system for the just-freed Negroes of the South, and when Barnard failed to satisfy this demand, his annual appropriation was reduced each year. Here is an early instance of the conflict between the political leader's demand for prompt action and the scholar's insistence on taking the long view that continues to plague federal efforts to improve education. As Commissioner John J. Tigert later reflected on Barnard's fall from Congressional grace,

> In fulsome speeches it had been proclaimed . . . that the Department of Education would exert a powerful influence to enlighten the mass of ignorance in the Nation, particularly among the freedmen of the South. Two years passed, and the Commissioner of Education with his three clerks had failed to cause the enlightenment of four million freedmen or to show any appreciable reduction in the sum total of ignorance in the country at large. It was disappointing to the enthusiasts, and the reaction had its natural effect.[5]

President Andrew Johnson appointed as Barnard's successor a Commissioner—John Eaton—who had been active in the administration of Reconstruction agencies, who got on famously with the Republican Congressional leaders, and who did embark on an activist program. Eaton was willing to reduce the scholarly mission of the Bureau to a passive watch-standing, but he strongly developed the program of collecting statistics and overcame the reluctance of local schoolmen (already protesting federal "meddling") to fill out factual report forms for Washington. Years later, William T. Harris said of him in a gracious reminiscence:

> General Eaton was the true founder of this Bureau, in the sense that he established as the chief work of this Bureau, the annual collection of statistics by means of statistical schedules, which were sent to all institutions and all general officers to be filled out and returned to the Com-

missioner from year to year. In this way he trained educators to keep original records of their operations and made
these operations available for analysis and comparison.[6]

Eaton was succeeded briefly by a nonprofessional, Nathan-
ial H. R. Dawson, who was Commissioner for three years.
Under Dawson, the inquiry function of the Bureau was
institutionalized in a Division of Statistics, and a number
of qualified men were commissioned to prepare historical
and descriptive accounts of higher education in their re-
spective states.

## William T. Harris as Commissioner
## of Education

In 1889 William T. Harris, a rare combination of
scholar and administrator, left the superintendency in St.
Louis to succeed Dawson as Commissioner. The sheer force
of Harris's personality and intellect, coupled with the almost unanimous support he enjoyed from the educational
profession, gave the Bureau a stature during his tenure that
it did not achieve again until recent times. Here was a man
who could found the first learned philosophical journal in
the English-speaking world and also serve as a practicing
school administrator. His work was phenomenal in range,
size, and significance; nothing other than Barnard's matches
it in its time. Even Nicholas Murray Butler, who prided
himself on knowing all the major personalities of his era,
placed him squarely in the first rank:

> It would be quite impossible to overstate the ability, the
> learning or the commanding intellectual influence of Doc-
> tor Harris. To my thinking, his was the one great philo-
> sophical mind which has appeared on this side of the
> Atlantic. In addition to his philosophical learning and

power, he had a most extraordinary gift of very simple exposition and it was this which gave him his power over the teaching profession. Doctor Harris could stand up before an audience of any kind of teachers or principals and expound in the simplest language profound philosophical ideals and ideas, and so shape, in accordance with those ideals and ideas, the conduct of the thinking and action of those who heard him.[7]

The French scholar Gabriel Compayré was fond of noting that although the idea of a centralized ministry of education was anathema to Americans, Harris managed as United States Commissioner to exercise through intellectual and moral suasion an influence many a Minister had been unable to exert even with direct power.

Under Harris, the systematic inquiries of the Bureau expanded in directions Barnard would have prized: historical, comparative, and philosophical. What Harris accomplished for his generation was to focus public and professional attention on the great philosophical and sociological questions that must be examined systematically if a society's educational system is to reflect its most deeply held values. Policy, Harris argued, must be based on the criticized memory of the race, not on the dictates of the most powerful, or the most recent, or the most popular. He used the publications of the Bureau much as Barnard had used the *American Journal,* to bring together the relevant, historical, philosophical, and sociological materials from the nations of the West for American educators to confront and consider.

Harris' influence derived from his personal force rather than from the Bureau and its activities. The Bureau remained its old mild self while a boom-town enthusiasm inspirited educational matters elsewhere. Perhaps this had something to do with Harris' educational convictions as well as his administrative style: subsequent generations have criticized him as a conservative who emphasized effort rather than interest in the schoolroom, and formal learning rather than useful learning in the curriculum. In any case, his influence seems to have reached a peak during the middle 1890's, and then declined rapidly. By the time his one major book, *Psychological Foundations of Education*, appeared in 1898, Harris was 63; and his potential audience was already attending to the newer psychologies of James, Hall, and Dewey.

## Other sources of leadership

During this formative era of the United States Office of Education, there was also a quickening of state educational activity, as annual reports became regularized, educational journals were launched, and a professional community began to develop among career educators.

Reports from state education officers were especially influential in the communication of educational ideas. In the absence of substantial historical studies of these reports, we are limited to a few impressions. Some states proceeded more rapidly than others in data gathering, with New York and Massachusetts certainly in the lead in 1855. There was an interchange of ideas between the states, through the reports themselves and through discussion of them in the growing number of state educational journals. And it is clear that the national data collection initiated by Barnard and Eaton had a stimulating and disciplining effect on state efforts to keep track of their school systems.

Although social accounting in education was thus well launched, there seems to have been a complete absence of disciplined research on the quality of education. There were changes in course content and teaching method, to be sure, but these innovations were commonly offshoots from some theory that commanded enthusiasm. Thus, for example, the American Pestalozzians began in the 1840's to work out an elementary-school curriculum based on the principles of object-teaching and warm attention to the child. The American Herbartians after the 1880's made similar use of their own chosen doctrines. These efforts at application can be criticized for their lack of skepticism and reference to hard data, but by nineteenth-century standards of educational leadership they were advances. If nothing else, they challenged educational tradition and so introduced the questioning mood that became dominant in the 1890's.

In the first period of educational leadership in America, the style was collection, collation, and dissemination of facts. Just as the curriculum of the time contained a large element of knowledge for its own sake, so Barnard and Harris, and General Eaton with his burgeoning statistics, seem satisfied that diffusion of information would in itself produce sounder management of schools. Similarly, the curriculum reformers were engaged primarily in the popularization of ideas that seemed to come largely from European sources. American educators, of course, debated the various proposals for change in the schools, but systematic analysis and testing of proposals came to the fore only at the very end of the period. What native theorizing there was seemed not to go beyond speculation, of the genre of Harris' Hegelianism.

# The heyday of empiricism

## 1895-1938

THE 1890's brought a sweeping change in the intellectual orientation of American society. An unprecedented consciousness of national power, an emerging urban industrial society, and the sudden adoption of science as the source of truth set the stage for a questioning of tradition in every form. It was an age of quickening interest in the scientific exploration of social and natural phenomena and of high hope concerning the social benefits of such exploration. It was an age of scientific enthusiasm not only among scholars, but also among the lay audiences that devoured the popularized science of such magazines as *The Forum, Popular Science Monthly, The Saturday Evening Post,* and *The World's Work;* it was an age of heady optimism based on the widely held belief that science had won the day, and now had only to transform the world. Not surprisingly it was also an age when education became a matter for scientific investigation, controlled experiment, and rational reform: Thorndike and other psychologists drew practical recommendations from studies of learning; Franklin Bobbitt and other curriculum-makers revised courses of study on the basis of systematic observations of contemporary society; and George Strayer and other administrators formulated policy recommendations founded on quantitative analyses of school performance. And all made common cause with a generation of practical-minded schoolmen seeking answers to Herbert Spencer's insistent question, "What knowledge is of most worth?"

This period is of special significance for this report because it demonstrates much of what research can accomplish at the same time that it reveals how institutions and philosophies can circumscribe those achievements. A number of the significant contributions of the period can be mentioned briefly, with fuller details on some to be given later. Perhaps most important was the widespread acceptance of pupil accomplishment as the fundamental test of the educational program. This change, replacing argumentation from *a priori* principles with an appeal to evidence, made it possible to banish misconceptions and to narrow the ground of controversy. Many an ancient claim was exploded—most notably, the belief that the pupil who grinds away at an academically difficult subject is sure to develop his intellectual powers. A substantial beginning was made toward a psychological analysis of each school subject. A technology for the measurement of aptitude was developed. And penetrating inquiries were made regarding the nature and development of mental health and character.

Gains were not confined to the psychological aspects of education. Decisions about curriculum that had formerly been settled by pronouncements from committees came more and more to rest on careful assessment of the manpower needs of society and of the tasks persons in various roles actually perform. Matters long taken for granted were freshly examined; certain grammatical expressions roundly condemned in the schoolbooks were found to be commonplace and accepted in the actual speech and writing of cultivated persons, and hence "usage" supplemented grammar as the basis of courses in English. And certain demonstrated facts led to new reflections on educational policy—for example, the finding that the income of an adolescent's family had more to do with his attending college than his ability, and the related finding that he was far more likely to attend a college if one were located near his home.

The journalistic exposés of Joseph Mayer Rice pictured

the machine that was the American school in the 1890's: syllabi and textbooks prescribed the course of study; the responsibility of the pupil was to master the material that would appear on examinations; the responsibility of the teacher was to assist the pupil to that mastery, relying principally on incessant drill and unreflecting discipline.[8] Four decades later the 1938 Yearbook of the National Society for the Study of Education could point to an almost wholly new curriculum, with an elective system that spanned dozens of school subjects; to a range of instructional methods that embraced laboratories, field trips, visual aids, and school libraries; to consolidated high schools offering vocational as well as academic curricula; to vocational guidance programs and diagnostic services directed by school psychologists; to school buildings designed for educational efficiency and built to high standards; and to enormous advances in the preparation, style of work, and salaries of teachers.

Educational improvement in the later nineteenth century had come largely from the requirements of the American democratic experiment, though it had been leavened by pedagogical ideas of European philosophers. Better schooling in the earlier twentieth century grew out of the transformations wrought by industrialism, but it was profoundly influenced by the characteristically American psychology of William James and his pupils G. Stanley Hall and Edward Thorndike.

James and Hall, prominent equally in the academic world and as writers and speakers to the general public, stand at the dividing point between the first and second periods. James rejected the quantitative experimental techniques of the German laboratories, but he saw enough promise in an observational approach to the study of the mind to have founded his own experimental laboratory four years before Wundt's in Leipzig. Through his freshly written textbooks and lectures—many of them directed to teachers—James brought the problems of integrative, adaptive behavior to the fore, while the German psychologists and their more orthodox American disciples were doggedly tabulating isolated sensations. For all his ability to reason and his readiness to seek evidence, James' commonsense was the most prominent element in his writings. An example is this well-known passage from his *Talks to Teachers* that has profound relevance for this report.

> . . . you make a great, a very great mistake, if you think that psychology, being the science of the mind's laws, is something from which you can deduce definite programmes and schemes and methods of instruction for immediate schoolroom use. Psychology is a science, and teaching is an art; and sciences never generate arts directly out of themselves. An intermediary inventive mind must make the application, by using its originality. . . .
>
> Everywhere teaching must *agree* with the psychology, but need not necessarily be the only kind of teaching that would so agree.[9]

Hall's interests were even broader than James', though his curiosity and enthusiasm often seemed to outrun his self-critical discipline as a researcher. But Hall did gather data, and indeed was a pioneer in the fruitful application of the questionnaire method. His most lasting influence on American education was his inauguration of the child-study movement, which provided popular and scholarly support for efforts to liberalize the curriculum.

The turn of the century also witnessed the arrival on the educational scene of John Dewey, Thorstein Veblen, Paul Monroe, E. L. Thorndike, and Joseph Mayer Rice, to be followed soon after by Charles H. Judd, Lewis Terman, George Strayer, Ellwood P. Cubberley, and Franklin Bobbitt. From these men came trenchant social criticisms, new devices for data collection and analysis, and energetic surveys of school practice. They presided over the emergence of graduate study in Education, notably at Teachers College of Columbia University, at the University of Chicago, and at Stanford University. They set the patterns for the state, city, and university research bureaus that sprang up across the country, and for the laboratory schools that grew up on the model of the Dewey venture at Chicago.

Joseph Mayer Rice, the liberal muckraking pediatrician who made a career of school reform, is often credited as the founder of empirical scholarship in education. Inspired by the teaching he observed in Germany, he found himself appalled by the mechanical, nonreflective, noncreative character of American schools and set out to bring them into line with the new emphasis on interesting, reflective classroom activity that he had encountered abroad. Singling out the blight of endless rote spelling drills, he thought it would be a simple matter to collect facts to show that these could be reduced without loss, and thus persuade the authorities to release time to more intellectual activities. A large number of schools administered spelling tests of Rice's devising to some 16,000 students in the years 1895–1897, in a crude forerunner of today's National Assessment of Educational Progress. As Rice anticipated, the pupils' attainment on his tests bore no relation to the number of minutes per week their schools devoted to spelling. "The presentation of the results," Leonard Ayres wrote years later, "brought upon the investigator almost unlimited attack. The educators . . . united in denouncing as foolish, reprehensible, and from every point of view indefensible, the effort to discover anything about the value of the teaching of spelling by finding out whether or not the children could spell." [10] Rice, though a member of the National Education Association, was an "outsider" criticizing the profession, and there was no place of honor for such a man. The result was that Rice was disenchanted with the scientific movement almost before it was well under way. Reminiscing in the 1920's in a statement before a Congressional committee, Rice remarked: "I had covered the fundamentals in educational research to the point where further work would be for the most part matters of detail only. I then [in 1904] decided to quit." [11]

Although Rice found educators unready to acknowledge hard facts, the situation soon changed. The larger community was coming to be dominated by business ideals in which a favorable balance sheet was the only acceptable evidence of successful management. As Raymond Callahan [12] has documented, the educators were soon parodying the excesses of stopwatch management in industry, talking solemnly about return on investment per pupil and about the number of recitations in Greek that could be purchased for a dollar. The absurdity quickly infected instructional practice; if superintendents were to be judged by the number of pupils turned out per dollar, teachers were to be judged by the number of pupils they could pass on to the next grade. It soon became the practice to pass nearly every student each June, regardless of the quality of his schoolwork.

But quality was not always ignored. Rice had demonstrated that applying an objective test uniformly in many schools is sure to stir up educational debates, and soon there were scales for appraising achievement in handwriting, arithmetic, spelling, drawing, reading, and eventually, every other school subject. At the same time, intelligence testing was being developed. By 1918, Walter S. Monroe [13] could describe over a hundred well-regarded standardized tests of pupil performance. The tests served the iconoclasm of the new educational scholarship well. Thorndike's famous study, in which he concluded that the study of bookkeeping does just as much to develop testable mental ability as the study of Greek, was dynamite in the hands of the utilitarians who condemned the traditional academic education for doing nothing to prepare high school graduates for "useful work."

# Dewey and the promotion of innovation

A major event in the launching of the new era of inquiry was the establishment in 1896 of John Dewey's Laboratory School at the University of Chicago. "Practice schools" had been in operation since the first teacher-training institutions appeared before the Civil War; and "model schools" had grown up in the 1880's and 1890's in connection with the Cook County Normal School and Columbia's Teachers College. But while such schools may well have been models of innovation and excellence, they were not seriously concerned with inquiry. What was new about the Laboratory School was the explicit intention of using it to test hypotheses in practice.

Dewey had been a firm advocate of psychological research as a means of understanding education, but he had no hope that psychological studies alone would show what schools should do. As he said in an 1897 reply to critics of the child-study movement:

> Many of the criticisms proceed from a failure to draw the lines carefully between those aspects of child study which belong to the province of the scientific investigator and those which interest the educator. It takes time to develop scientific method, to collect and sift facts, and to derive theoretic conclusions. There is no more sense in attacking the scientific investigator in this line because he doesn't provide on demand usable recipes, ticketed and labeled for all pedagogical emergencies, than there would have been in attacking the early pioneers in electricity because they worked quietly in the laboratory upon seemingly remote and abstruse subjects instead of providing us offhand with the telegraph, telephone, electric light, and transportation.[14]

Dewey's School was an attempt to work out practical techniques; he was concerned with development and demonstration. For all the School's claim to be a laboratory, the papers emanating from its staff strongly suggest that the inspiring of emulation took precedence over inquiry. Many of the premises of the School's program were articles of faith from the outset. Thus, writing in the *University Record* in 1896, Dewey announced an intention to test the hypothesis that the school is a social institution. He touched on four more specific problems: how to bring the school into closer relation with the home and neighborhood; how to introduce history, science, and art so that they have significance in the light of the child's experience; how to obtain progress in reading, writing, and arithmetic as a by-product of other subjects and activities; and how best to demonstrate the benefits of individual attention secured by small groupings of children and large numbers of teachers.[15] In reading the voluminous literature of the School between 1896 and 1904, one is struck constantly by the problem of how to know when a hypothesis had been established. The continuing attempt to rationalize content and method was surely a contribution to education. Yet for all Dewey's pragmatism it is not clear that he was seeking objective evidence of the strengths and weaknesses of the new proposals.

The fact that this first well-led Laboratory School did not carry on disciplined inquiry and did not produce well-substantiated results is noteworthy because it presages the promotional emphasis and neglect of hypothesis testing that marked later laboratory schools. But it would be captious to criticize Dewey personally for what he did in those eight years. At that time the methods for testing educational hypotheses were little developed, and even James relied as much on anecdote as on research for his conclusions. Dewey founded the school as an act of faith, and his failure to develop a science of classroom experimentation is very likely attributable to the success of his proposals. His ideas had wide appeal and he was therefore deprived of the stubborn and articulate opposition that may push a man to collect solid evidence. Thorndike was more fortunate. His arguments regarding transfer opposed the interests of teachers of the classics and other subjects, and he was therefore pressed to elaborate his views and to amass evidence for them. If Dewey had been so pressed, he might have been more explicit on such matters as the significance of making learning purposeful rather than merely interesting, and the importance of subject-matter knowledge even in a progressive curriculum. Had he spelled out these concepts, the progressive movement might have been saved from ultimate self-caricature and collapse.

The laboratory schools were limited in their impact because many educators believed that they were too distinctive to serve as models for the majority of the nation's schools. Their advantages in the form of well-equipped facilities, superior teachers, and selected pupils were so apparent that what they demonstrated seemed irrelevant to ordinary institutions. Dewey spoke clearly on this matter in the early days of the Chicago venture:

> As it is not the primary function of a laboratory to devise ways and means that can at once be put to practical use, so it is not the primary purpose of the school to devise methods with reference to their direct application in the graded school system. . . . It is the function of some schools to create new standards and ideals and thus to lead to a gradual change in conditions.[16]

> There is a difference between working out and testing a new truth, or a new method, and applying it on a wide scale, making it available for the mass of men, making it commercial. But the first thing is to discover the truth, to afford all necessary facilities, for this is the most practical thing in the world in the long run. We do not expect to have other schools literally imitate what we do. A working model is not something to be copied; it is to afford a demonstration of the feasibility of the principle, and of the methods which make it feasible.[17]

Laboratory schools set up by universities in the wake of Dewey's success were vigorous for a time, and served as a showcase for new styles of teaching. Ultimately, however, many of them lost their internal vitality. The laboratory school of 1938 was often no more than a conventional private school benefiting the children of a university community. Some of the schools were released from their university connections, and few of them were still functioning as centers of educational development during the curriculum reform movement of the 1950's and 1960's.

# The Office of Education:
## a middle-aged bureaucracy

In school systems throughout the country, the gathering of facts became a thriving enterprise. But the U.S. Bureau, matured into middle-age, under the curse of resistance to federal influence in education and under pressures for economy, contributed little to the ferment. Under Commissioner Philander P. Claxton (1911–1921) there was a renewed burst of dissemination activity, proclaimed in terms recalling Barnard's original intentions. In his last report Claxton wrote:

> The bureau attempts, first, to serve as a clearing house for accurate and comprehensive information in respect to all educational agencies and all forms of education in the United States and all foreign countries, and to disseminate this information among school officers, teachers, students of education, and all others directly interested in any form of educational activity. In attaining this end the bureau does by far the larger and more important part of its work in the regular routines of daily duties at the offices in Washington. By means of letters of inquiry, questionnaires,

personal interviews, voluntary reports from school officials
and others, and studies of original documents, it gathers
facts and makes the information thus gained available to
the public in the form of pamphlets, bulletins, circulars,
and letters to the individuals and the press.[18]

The Bureau was thus a rather passive link in the communication circuit. We find a revealing hint about the character
of its scholarship in J. J. Tigert's complaint, upon taking
office as Claxton's successor, that because of a lack of funds
"many investigations are made and before funds are available to publish them they are out of date." Findings that
so quickly went out of date were obviously confined to
transient questions which, though worthy of study for
purposes of decision-making, rarely make much cumulative
contribution to knowledge.

Under Tigert and William John Cooper, the now-
renamed Office did produce major nationwide surveys of
land-grant colleges and universities, Negro higher education, secondary schools, teacher-training institutions, and
school finance. These were intended to rise above the file-
and-forget category, but any potentially influential conclusion they drew fell on the deaf ears of a nation preoccupied
with the Depression. In his definition of the role of the
Office, Cooper did place considerable emphasis on coordi-
nating and using "fundamental research," but without
resources he was unable to exercise leadership in this direction.

## Local surveys and local research bureaus

The fact-gathering and surveying that influenced
education in the early 1900's was primarily an attempt to
bring matters into the open for critical discussion. This aim

reflects the tendency of the Progressive political movement to regard exposure as a principal weapon against corruption, waste, and injustice. The survey became the prime method of detecting aspects of school administration and curriculum in need of reform. Surveys conducted before the turn of the century which relied on the impressions of a single observer were replaced by the systematic gathering of diverse data.

Surveys became a feature of local school management as teams of professors and experienced administrators from other communities came in to review the local scene. Such surveys were commissioned by superintendents who desired guidance, by other superintendents who wanted to initiate change and required ammunition for their campaign, and by lay critics who suspected that their schools were in need of reform. The most influential of the early general school surveys were undertaken in Boise, Idaho; Montclair, New Jersey; Baltimore (directed by the U.S. Bureau of Education, playing a new role); New York City; and in Cleveland, the famous survey of 1915–1916 directed by Leonard Ayres. Survey methods were applied to curriculum-making in the work of the Committee on the Economy of Time in Education, which was appointed by the NEA's Department of Superintendence in 1911, and which issued four major reports between 1915 and 1919.

Yet there were problems from the beginning with the conception of the school survey and its relation to reform. The term itself was borrowed from sociology, and used loosely by schoolmen to designate "careful factual studies of educational conditions and results together with constructive criticism of the findings." The rub, of course, lies in the definition of "constructive criticism," in the relationship between what is found to be and what is thought desirable. Too many surveyors, relentlessly quantifying, ended up measuring merely what was measurable, and confusing what is with what could be and ought to be. Furthermore, a movement that started out by featuring open-minded questioning soon found itself propagating new orthodoxies. Even before an innovative practice had proved itself in one school system, it was recommended to other systems, through survey reports and through university teaching by those who had served on the survey team. Despite the intention to use local facts as a basis for decision-making, the recommendations of survey teams proved to be remarkably alike in community after community.

However that may be, survey research carried an aura of irrefutable scientific authority; and many superintendents, determined to have its benefits on a continuing basis, set up research bureaus within their school systems. The mission of such bureaus is typified by the charge to the one established in Boston in 1914:

> . . . to promote educational efficiency and economy in administration and executive procedure in the school; to promote the investigation and professional study of school problems and the development of standards of achievement in the various subjects and grades of school work; to develop a system of promotion of teachers after appointment on the basis of merit; to conduct independent investigations . . . such as the workings of the child-labor law, retardation of children, elimination [dropping-out] of pupils in the high schools; to conserve the benefit of the testing work of recent years. . . .[19]

All this, with a staff consisting of a director and "such clerical help as may from time to time be necessary."

Callahan [20] points out that these bureaus, which were expected to contribute to school efficiency what the industrial engineer was contributing to industrial efficiency, missed one of the major elements of the Taylor approach to "scientific" management, namely, the use of a planning department "to develop the science of the job, which involved the establishment of . . . rules, laws, and formulas to replace the judgment of the individual workman." Monitoring or quality-control, outlined in the Boston mandate and in those of other cities, is important enough, but it is not the constructive function of finding better ways to perform school tasks.

Proposals that local schools conduct genuinely creative research were not lacking. We find Josiah Royce [21] stressing the merits of psychological studies and yet insisting that the university scientist, working part-time in a remote laboratory, could not come to grips with concrete school problems. Royce proposed that the school system hire a laboratory experimenter to work in the system as "a decidedly practical man" who would find out, through inquiry, "whatever it is possible and worthwhile for the teacher and the trained psychologist together to know concerning the mental states and processes present in the children of the schools of the city." The topics of investigation Royce went on to list included fatigue, the teaching of spelling, and the social psychology of "occasional student mutinies."

Nothing like this came to pass. The task of identifying principles upon which superior programs could be constructed fell by default to university professors, and schoolmen found themselves returning year after year to Schools of Education to find out "what research says."

## The humanities in decline

Throughout this period, inquiry was dominated by the empirical and the statistical. The analysis of the effects of instruction and the comparison of instructional methods were problems made to order for psychologists interested in applications of their new discipline. History and philosophy, on the other hand, did not thrive in this atmosphere. The most prominent work in the history of education was prepared by Ellwood P. Cubberley, a professor of school administration not trained as a historian. And the most prominent work in philosophy of education came from men far more interested in active policy-making than in systematic speculation or criticism. Even Dewey found less and less connection between his systematic activities as a philosopher and his policy-oriented activities as an educational statesman. The educational world was marching to the drummer of empiricism, and the subtle tones of humanistic scholarship were far too muted for the times.

Men educated in one tradition have only a sketchy understanding of the commitments and bases for judgment of the other tradition, and institutional structures have tended to foster rather than to break down this separateness. The schism dates back at least as far as the reign of Charles II when the physicist Robert Hooke stated the lofty purpose of the new Royal Society as

. . . to improve the knowledge of naturall things and all useful Arts, Manufactures, Mechanick practices, Engynes and inventions by Experiments (not meddling with Divinity, Metaphysics, Moralls, Politicks, Grammer, Rhetorick or Logick).[22]

Just such a schism between the things that are the scientist's and the things beyond his notice has characterized inquiry into education during its rapid growth in this century. This schism exists, despite the fact that the prevailing view of education must somehow merge partial glimpses obtained through many modes of inquiry, and despite the fact that "how to teach" questions of empirical inquiry cannot possibly be pursued independent of "what to teach" questions of normative inquiry.

When the scholarly approach to education was developing late in the nineteenth century, the leading figures (Harris, James, and Dewey in America; Herbart and

Spencer abroad) were skilled both in humanistic inquiry and in the emerging method of inquiry by systematic observation. As the "scientific method in education" came to be identified with quantification, with a doctrinaire behaviorism, and with formal experiments, educational research became entirely one-sided. As early as 1911, Paul Monroe [23] was lamenting the loss of respect for "the traditional method of logical investigation." A handful of scholars continued to study education from humanistic perspectives; there were fewer and fewer men able to ask the penetrating philosophical and historical questions about an educational problem as well as the empirical ones. Training for empirical research, whether in a School of Education or in one of the social sciences, has usually not included an adequate exposure to humanistic methods of inquiry. The scholar trained in the humanities learns to be critical of the empirical approach to social processes, but his exposure to empirical work is so slight that he cannot take proper advantage of its conclusions.

The problem is not just that there has been a lack of humanistic inquiry into education. The difficulty is that the problems that really matter can only be resolved by the joint and sophisticated use of humanistic and empirical methods. This is most especially true of problems of curriculum and instruction, but it is also true of all thinking that bears on policy.

The cultures are still isolated within educational scholarship, as is demonstrated by the virtual absence of learned societies or journals in which contributions of the two sorts encounter each other. We note two recent changes for the better: a broader dialogue within the Comparative Education Society, and a newly founded Division on History of Education and Historiography within the American Educational Research Association.

The empiricists who had started out to establish facts about methods of instruction gradually began to claim that their approach was also capable of determining aims. In

1906 Thorndike [24] had been content to claim that education would become efficient "in proportion as the leaders in education direct their choices of *methods* by the results of scientific investigation rather than by general opinion" (emphasis added). By 1916, however, Thorndike [25] was saying, "Control (of education) by public opinion and legislation is giving way to control by expert administrative boards at an increasing rate."

## Education separates from the arts and sciences

One manifestation of the emergence of education as a self-consciously independent profession was the sharp separation of Education from the arts and sciences that gradually developed in the years following 1905.[26] Before that time, a fairly warm spirit of cooperation had marked the relations between academic scholars and professional educators. If one takes the NEA as an example, men such as President Eliot of Harvard and President Gilman of Johns Hopkins worked closely with well-known superintendents of schools such as William B. Maxwell and with leading professors of Education such as Charles DeGarmo and Charles and Frank McMurray. That Butler could feel as he did about Harris, the most noted professional educator of his day, is indicative of the respectful cooperation.

The rift between the more pragmatically oriented educators and the more traditionally oriented academicians is dramatically conveyed by the same Butler who had waxed eloquent over his "vigorous and enthusiastic service" to the National Education Association from 1885 to 1905. After that date he complained that the organization, once a body of genuine educational leaders who were dealing with ideas and institutions, had degenerated into a large popular assembly dominated by a very inferior class of teachers and school officials whose main object appeared to be personal advancement.[27] However much personal conflicts may have led Butler to this harsh allegation, it was patently a reflection of two larger social phenomena: the popularization of schooling and the professionalization of teaching.

The universities responded to the demand for more and better education by establishing independent faculties of Education. Whatever they gained in the short run by way of vigorous attention to education must be weighed against the attenuation of the critical and independent influence of the disciplines. Pressed to advise the schoolman, the scholar in the Education faculty found himself encouraged to pontificate and to draw concrete, unrestricted conclusions about proper practice from investigations either too limited to produce dependable results or too broad to sustain a disciplined attack.

For various reasons, academic specialists in the arts and sciences turned their attention away from the educational aspects of their fields so that by 1940 the separation was nearly complete. There were exceptions, to be sure: Charles Merriam and Charles Beard in political science, William Waller and the Lynds in sociology, Merle Curti and Samuel Eliot Morison in history. But the professions of educational sociology, educational psychology, educational philosophy, and educational history became separated from the main body of their disciplines. Few scholars outside Schools of Education read and commented on works related to education. Dewey, for example, once stated that his best presentation of his general philosophy was *Democracy and Education*, but he complained that philosophers had remained unfamiliar with the book because of its title.

Educational research and the training of educational researchers became a specialty of professors of Education. Between 1897 and the 1920's, the leading professors of Education were recruited directly from the disciplines and remained leading figures in their academic fields. In the 1920's the influential chairs began to fall to the students trained by the first generation of Education professors. An educational sociologist, say, who had studied under one professional sociologist, and under a dozen professors of Education having other intellectual commitments, could not be deeply grounded in sociology. Moreover, he was likely to have been indoctrinated with some particular view of what "the new education" ought to be.

Equally enfeebling was a glorification of breadth that often made it respectable for a single professor of Education to serve as expert over the whole range of history, philosophy, sociology, and perhaps psychology as well. (The argument for integrative thinking may have been no more than a rationalization of the fact that the Education faculty of that time could not afford to hire men to cultivate each area.) Meanwhile, students recruited into Education courses were often more motivated toward benefiting people here and now than toward the pursuit of knowledge. Hence, the profession came to contain fewer men who challenged the current assumptions, and fewer "breakthroughs" occurred. If the quality of the best research did not decline, it failed to advance beyond the early models in the field.

As a result, the training of researchers declined seriously in quality. By 1941, T. R. McConnell[28] found himself obliged to restate a number of elementary propositions that should have been obvious to his colleagues in Education. Thorough knowledge of the relevant phases of the basic discipline, he insisted, is a prerequisite for any sound educational research: studies of school finance must rest on a sound understanding of all public finance; studies of educational growth must be based on an understanding of child development in general. But by the 1940's, few educational researchers were qualified along such lines, and most universities were granting research degrees to students in Education who had not taken a single graduate course in a field of the arts and sciences.

An accompanying phenomenon was the proliferation of doctoral dissertations in education, each purporting unconvincingly to be a genuine contribution to knowledge. Standards for these studies could not be maintained when every aspiring school superintendent and every faculty member in the myriad teachers' colleges was expected to earn a doctorate. This pressure, together with the desperate need during Depression years to keep seats in the lecture halls occupied, led many Schools of Education to become degree factories. The output of the better universities is nothing to apologize for; the published dissertations that constitute the Columbia *Teachers College Contributions to Education* were serious and well-supervised studies (though the problems were not always highly intellectual). The students who did these studies, however, were rarely committed to disciplined inquiry as a career and the studies were *ad hoc* rather than communications to colleagues with similar intellectual concerns. Few of the dissertations were stepping stones toward a higher understanding. The sheer volume of soon-forgotten dissertations in Education contributed to a general inability of the educational community to take educational research seriously.

# *Promotional activity supplants inquiry*

# 1938-1958

IN THE 1920's, much attention was given to research and measurement. Leading educators were confident that increasingly diligent fact-finding would continue to improve textbooks, pupil classification, teaching procedures, and administration. A decade later, disciplined inquiry was becoming less influential. From about 1938 to 1955, the remaining educational research workers were far removed from the main theatre of educational debate and action. Only recently has research again begun to make vigorous contributions to the mainstream of educational discussions.

Some of the reasons for the decline of research are obvious. In Depression years, institutions straining every resource to pay their faculties could not afford to maintain research bureaus or to lighten teaching loads. In the war years and after, institutions were too busy straining to find teachers to cope with exploding enrollments to think about improving the quality of education. The post-1945 rise in clinical psychology, in mental-health research, and in research on military training drew off many persons who before the war would have become research workers in education. But there were more profound reasons for letting research fade out, and for being slow to revive it.

The overenthusiastic educational scientism of the 1920's invited a negative reaction. Teachers felt threatened when standard tests were applied to their classes on an administrator's order. Administrators were threatened by external comparisons of one school with another on the basis of tests and cost statistics. Those who realized that a liberal education could not be captured in a net of true-false questions accused the testers of acknowledging only such educational values as their tests could measure. The reviewers of the scientific movement writing for the landmark *Yearbook* of the NSSE in 1938 pointed to disappointing limitations that had been discovered in the research approach, limitations that restricted the significance of many findings.[29]

## Opposition to standardization and tradition

More critical still, the leading professors of Education espoused a view antithetical to the earlier philosophy of research. The thinking from 1900 to 1930 was oriented toward standardization, the discovery of one best curriculum and teaching method for each field. The. job of research was to establish conclusions that would apply everywhere. The progressives, on the other hand, opposed standardization. Although few of the nation's schools adopted the progressive model (except as the ideas in time infiltrated conservative practices), and although the model was spelled out only for the elementary schools, the progressive theory dominated instruction in Schools of Education and dictated the content of educational discussions.

A tenet of curriculum development in this period was that students learned best when they studied matters close to their daily lives. The content of the curriculum therefore had to be worked out by local teachers to fit the local concerns of their particular pupils. Moreover, it was believed that teachers who took part in curriculum-making would teach better, because they would understand the aims better and be more enthusiastic about them. If there were no standard selection or sequence of topics, however, there would be no way of doing generalizable research on the learning of any school subject. A related doctrine emphasized democratic relationships among pupils, teachers, and administrators. The acceptability of a decision among all affected by it loomed larger than the objective merit of the decision, and again the usefulness of general principles was reduced.

Although writers on education in the early 1900's had been iconoclasts, bent on blasting the schools out of their comfortable ruts, their educational revolution had accepted the American social-economic system. The writers of the 1930's, on the other hand, were dedicated to reshaping the society. The new arguments emerged well before the Depression; they can be seen in words Dewey addressed to the Progressive Education Association in 1928. Speaking of "the attempt to determine objectives and select subject-matter of studies by wide collection and accurate measurement of data," he commented:

> If we are satisfied upon the whole with the aims and processes of existing society, this method is appropriate. If you want schools to perpetuate the present order . . . then one type of intellectual method of "science" is indicated. But if one conceives that a social order different in quality and direction from the present is desirable . . . quite a different method and content is indicated for educational science.[30]

As the Depression heightened the feeling among intellectuals that the economic system deserved to collapse, articulate educational leaders attempted to formulate an educational program that would bring about a better social order, drawing upon the economics of Veblen, the sociology of the Lynds, the legal analysis of Holmes, the history of Beard and Robinson, the ethics of Dewey, and the journalism of the *New Republic* and the *Social Frontier*. The leading disputants are well known: Kilpatrick, Counts, Bode, Brameld, and Hutchins, to name a few. It would be unfair to say that their efforts involved no disciplined inquiry, for they used contemporary styles and methods of social analysis, and at its best their dialogue was as scholarly as it was forthright. Moreover, they did substantially broaden the purview of educational research by bringing to bear disciplines that had not generally been considered relevant. But the polemics overshadowed the scholarship, and the positions educators argued for came to be founded more on loyalty to a camp than on independently formed conviction.

## Research activity as an agent of change

After the 1920's there was a gradual shift toward using research as an agent of change. The famous Eight-Year Study of the Progressive Education Association is a superior example. The study was initiated to determine whether subject-matter requirements for college entrance, which seemed to limit efforts to modernize high-school curricula, were justified. The investigators suggested that such requirements be abolished for graduates of a selected group of schools, proposing that for experimental purposes any recommended graduate of those schools be admitted to college no matter what subjects he had studied. They proposed to compare the success of these students with that of students who had fulfilled conventional requirements in equally good high schools. This study was an unprecedented cooperative effort between thirty high-school faculties and a large, well-led central "evaluation staff."

Although the study was carried out as planned, one

cannot escape the impression that the central question was of minor interest to the investigators and the educational community. The main contribution of the study was to encourage the experimental schools to explore new teaching and counseling procedures. A subunit of the research staff did carry out the systematic follow-up study and did report that the experimental students "were significantly superior" in college performance.[31] When the report appeared, critics[32] argued that one could only claim that the experimental procedures had done no harm to the student's future academic career; the design of the study, they said, was biased in favor of the experimental schools. The fact that little attention was given to this criticism itself shows that few persons cared at this time about a scientific foundation for educational policy.

The main enterprise of the evaluation staff was to assist teachers in examining their own work. The staff developed ingenious procedures for studying educational outcomes other than factual knowledge and skill, procedures that have left a lasting mark on educational research and educational objectives. The staff members worked with teachers of each subject in each school on an individual basis; yet in the end there was a rather remarkable concurrence between the "local objectives" arrived at in the schools and the measuring instruments the staff brought with them from Chicago. The data on student performance were used primarily by the teachers involved, rather than by administrators and school boards, and there was virtually no attempt to draw publishable conclusions from the data. As in Dewey's Laboratory School, there was an initial faith that the experimental schools were proceeding along the right line, and no urge to challenge the innovations.

The social reformers and the progressive educators were essentially crusaders, not open-minded inquirers. Facts were occasionally gathered to demonstrate the need for a social change that had already been judged desirable in advance, or to monitor an operation so as to modify its details. Insofar as the crusade continued into the late 1940's and 1950's its research stayed safely away from the aims and content of education; on that, minds were made up, and dissent was ignored. The topics left open for research were the personal relationships among teachers, among pupils, and between teachers and pupils, the psychology and sociology of individual differences, and the nature and character of the counseling process.

A teacher-training activity known as "action research" absorbed at least as much professorial effort as more conventional inquiry, and attracted far more attention in the schools. Guided by the Eight-Year Study and the pattern used by the late Kurt Lewin to alter housewives' food-buying habits during World War II, persons seeking to change instruction set up projects in local schools under the leadership of visiting university professors. The cooperating teachers would identify some suspected inadequacy in their local program, collect facts by means of fairly unsophisticated instruments, plan some change on the basis of the facts, carry it out, and collect follow-up data. The goal was to change the practices of the teachers. The leaders of "action research" were convinced that nothing could be gained from conclusion-oriented research, that a study done in one school could not, through communication of findings, influence what was being done in the next.[33] Because the studies were usually for local use, they were not subjected to the crossfire of discussion and competent criticism that is an essential part of disciplined inquiry and they cannot be judged as research. No doubt in some settings and under particular leaders the studies were truly self-critical, decision-oriented inquiries that directly improved the local program; no doubt in other instances the entire activity was a disguised method of manipulating teachers to move in certain approved directions.

## NOTES

1. See Merle Curti's *American Scholarship in the Twentieth Century*. Cambridge: Harvard University Press, 1953, which does treat this broad theme.

2. A few distinguished exceptions, such as Isaac Kandel and Paul Monroe at Columbia's Teachers College and Boyd Bode at Ohio State, should be noted.

3. Thursfield, Richard E., *Henry Barnard's American Journal of Education*. Baltimore, Md.: Johns Hopkins Press, 1949.

4. Carpenter, Harold F., Jr., "The First Eight Commissioners of Education," *The Graduate Review*, Stanford University, School of Education, Vol. 2 (1967), pp. 27–45.

5. Tigert, J. J., "An Organization by the Teachers and for the Teachers," *School Life*, Vol. 9 (1924), pp. 195–196.

6. Quoted by S. Jackson, in "Memorial address: John Eaton," *Proceedings and Addresses*. National Education Association, 1906, p. 288.

7. Butler, Nicholas Murray, *Across the Busy Years*. New York: Charles Scribner's Sons, 1939, Vol. 1, pp. 190–191.

8. Rice, J. M., *The Public-School System of the United States*. New York: The Century Company, 1893.

9. James, William, *Talks to Teachers on Psychology*. New York: Holt, 1920, pp. 7–11.

10. Ayres, Leonard P., "History and Present Status of Educational Measurements," in Whipple, G. M. (ed.), *The Measurement of Educational Products*. 17th Yearbook, National Society for the Study of Education, Part II, 1918, pp. 9–15.

11. Quoted by Graham, Patricia A., "Joseph Mayer Rice as a Founder of the Progressive Education Movement," *Journal of Educational Measurement*, Vol. 3 (1966), pp. 129–133.

12. Callahan, Raymond E., *Education and The Cult of Efficiency*. Chicago: Phoenix, 1964.

13. Monroe, Walter S., "Existing Tests and Standards" in Whipple, G. M. (ed.), *The Scientific Movement in Education*. 37th Yearbook, National Society for the Study of Education, Part II, 1938, pp. 71–104.

14. Dewey, John, "Criticisms Wise and Otherwise on Modern Child Study," *Proceedings and Addresses*, National Education Association, 1897, pp. 867–868.

15. Dewey, John, "The University School," *University Record*, Vol. 1 (1896), pp. 417–419.

16. *Ibid.*

17. Quoted in Dworkin, Martin S. (ed.), *Dewey on Education*. New York: Bureau of Publications, Teachers College, Columbia University, 1959, p. 90.

18. Claxton, Philander P., *Report of the Commissioner of Education for the Year Ended June 30, 1920*, pp. 88–89.

19. Chapman, Harold Benjamin, *Organized Research in Education, with Special Reference to the Bureau of Educational Research*. Columbus, Ohio: Ohio State University Press, 1927.

20. Callahan, *op. cit.*, p. 35.

21. Royce, Josiah, "The New Psychology and the Consulting Psychologist," *Proceedings and Addresses*, National Education Association, 1898, pp. 554–570.

22. Weld, Charles R., *A History of the Royal Society*. London: John W. Parker, 1848, Vol. 1, p. 146.

23. Monroe, Paul (ed.), *A Cyclopedia of Education*. New York: Macmillan, 1913, Vol. IV, pp. 61ff.

24. Thorndike, E. L., *The Principles of Teaching*. Syracuse, N.Y.: Maron-Henry Press, 1906, p. 257.

25. Thorndike, E. L., "Education for initiative and originality." *Teachers College Record*, Vol. 17, 1916, pp. 405–416.

26. Jones, Howard M., Frances Keppel, and Robert Ulich, "On the Conflict Between the 'Liberal Arts' and the 'Schools of Education,'" *The ACLS Newsletter*, Vol. V (1954), No. 2, pp. 17–38.

27. Butler, *op. cit.*, p. 86.

28. McConnell, T. R., "The Nature of Educational Research," in *The Conceptual Structure of Educational Research*. Supplementary Educational Monographs, No. 55. Chicago: University of Chicago, 1942.

29. Whipple, G. M. (ed.), *The Scientific Movement in Education*, *op. cit.*, esp. pp. 71, 89, 323ff.

30. Dewey, John, "Progressive Education and the Science of Education," quoted in Dworkin, *op. cit.*, p. 119.

31. Chamberlin, Dean, and others, *Did They Succeed in College?* New York: Harper, 1942.

32. Chauncey, Henry, "Some Observations on Evaluation in the Eight-Year Study," *North Central Association Quarterly*, Vol. 15 (1941), pp. 258–264; Johnson, Helmer G., "Weakness in the Eight-Year Study," *School and Society*, Vol. 63 (1946), pp. 417–419.

33. Shumsky, Abraham, *The Action Research Way of Learning*. New York: Teachers College, 1958, p. 94.

**3**

# Some chains of significant inquiry

AFTER THE HISTORICAL SURVEY in Chapter 2, we now present a few extended examples of the interplay between inquiry, theory, and practice. We have chosen not to single out investigators for glorification or criticism, but rather to illustrate chains of inquiry. These examples show that each man's work is both linked to the times in which he lived and modified by his successors. Each decade contributes both insights and distortions to the practice and thought of the next. The chains chosen for illustration are concerned with mental tests and pupil classification, the philosophy of pragmatism as the root of major curriculum reforms, learning of arithmetic, and views on the politics of education generated by historical studies.

# Mental tests and pupil classification

THE RELATIONSHIPS between knowledge, conceptualization, and practice are well illustrated in the mental-testing movement, in which scientific work has moved steadily forward for a century. Because objective and reproducible techniques are the heart of the movement, an investigator is almost always able to confirm the findings of predecessors. Because investigators in this field have insistently criticized each other's work, the inquiry has been better disciplined and the findings better substantiated than most other research treating educational matters. But excesses of interpretation have been as common here as elsewhere; perhaps more common, because a certain scientism has flourished in the field.

The prevailing view of differences among men changes over and over. What a given finding signifies depends upon who is interpreting it and, to a large degree, on the climate of opinion of his decade. When the prevailing thought accepts a competitive model of society, the mental test is a sort of tipsheet that helps decision-makers get their bets down on the likely winners.[1] When ultra-equalitarianism reigns, the mental test is condemned as being an instrument of favoritism and privilege. Mental tests and the findings based on them have influenced social thought, but equally the prevailing thought has influenced the tests—the choice of tests for development, the questions asked about them, and the uses to which they are put. Testing was the first full-fledged "educational technology," and its history suggests something of the likely successes and excesses of technologies now emerging.

## Evolutionary theory and
## the idea of "fitness"

The history of the testing movement must be traced back at least to 1859, to Darwin and the theory of natural selection. Previous biologists had seen a species as a collection of uniform organisms of a fixed type, and any variation among members of a species was simply a nuisance to their taxonomic efforts. Darwin saw species as internally heterogeneous and ever-changing, the membership of the species shifting toward a variety whose genes aid its members to survive in their particular ecology. Individual differences were thus brought to the center of the stage. The summary phrase "survival of the fittest" was quickly extended far beyond the scientific context in which Darwin had justified it. Victorian England was (religionists excepted) delighted with a "natural law" that seemed to explain why man should dominate all other species, to place a halo of inevitability on the white man's worldwide dominion, and to provide doctrinal support for laissez-faire competition. Evolutionary thought soon permeated the prevailing view of man.

Darwin's key idea that "fitness" consisted of the potentiality for adapting to a particular environment, however, was soon lost. Darwin himself contributed to the confusion by seeing evolution as a process that "perfects" individual organs and so leads to superior species. It is a short step to thinking about the superior individuals among mankind, upon whom progress most depends. Galton envisioned the use of mental tests to select Civil Service employees, with the idea that leadership would thus be placed in the hands where it rightfully belonged.

Half a century was to pass before such testing became a reality; and it was the lack of fundamental knowledge about intellectual performance that caused delay. Galton himself started a massive program of pioneer research cutting across the nascent sciences of anthropology, genetics, statistics, and psychology. He tested thousands of subjects to obtain rudimentary descriptive facts on variation in human abilities. His tests ranged from the whistle that produces sounds too shrill for most ears to hear to the test of "imagery" in which persons recall and describe the morning's breakfast table. Like other psychologists of his day, he gave primary attention to elementary processes such as reaction time and ability to discriminate among weights, believing that the isolation of such elements was the key to understanding intellect. In France, Germany, and the United States, others were pursuing this search for elements in an equally diffuse manner.

Over and over, the tests for simple functions gave discouraging results; they had little or no relation to each other or to practical success. The few investigators who included complex intellectual tasks in their experiments were no more successful, until Binet in the 1890's made the study of complex processes his main concern. He too proceeded speculatively, ranging as far afield as palmistry in his search for clues; but he eventually concluded that tests of attention, reasoning, and above all of judgment show the correlates expected of a measure of intelligence. Only when he had reached this understanding was psychology ready to help in educational decisions. The Paris schools asked Binet to aid them in deciding which of their nonlearners were mentally defective and which were capable but needed to be stimulated. Binet accepted, and turned to developing an educationally useful product. The tests of Binet and Simon were a success because they offered a controlled, impartial, repeatable procedure to replace an impressionistic evaluation. The tests were adapted for use in all advanced countries, and similar tests applicable to groups evolved between 1910 and 1920.

The passage of decades between the first glimpse of what mental tests could do and their emergence as practical educational tools seems to have been inevitable. If energy, intelligence, and resources—substantial for that time—were needed, Galton had them. Yet he and dozens of others struggled with no direct success. Attempts to apply testing practically before the completion of Binet's studies caused a backlash, for the early tests did not correlate with practical success. As a result, many psychologists concluded that the whole line of inquiry was a waste of time. If there had been no Binet, some other man of a matter-of-fact cast of mind would have attained to his conception of intelligence. Any such success would have been an outgrowth of the extended exploration by many investigators which clarified the problem, formulated a style of inquiry, and, just by keeping the idea alive, attracted further investigators to the field.

## Mental tests in American schools

Those American psychologists closest to education, notably the students of Thorndike and Hall, moved to exploit Binet's breakthrough. American schools quickly adopted the tests. In fact, although the Stanford-Binet Scale and Army Alpha date only from 1916, by 1922 the National Society for the Study of Education had produced a volume summarizing experience with practical use of mental tests in schools. If the new tests truly measured intelligence (and few doubted that they did), the schools could well be enthusiastic. Here was a truly democratic device for identifying the talented to whom much encouragement should be given, and for identifying the slow learners who would only be frustrated by demands that they keep up with the normal classroom pace. Terman showed that the tests corresponded with other evidence of school success and success in life, and challenged school practices that were holding some children to a fifth-grade curriculum when their test performance matched that of normal children several grades ahead. The schools came to accept the IQ as an index of what could be expected of the child, the child with a high IQ being marked for success, and the "subnormal" IQ indicating a child who needed to be protected and trained for an undemanding job.

Few areas within education reflect so well the character of disciplined inquiry. Each step toward our present concepts has been hotly, but usually rationally, contested. Critical studies at the turn of the century cut down the claims for nonintellectual tests of perceptual speed and sensory discrimination. In the 1930's there was a similar hardheaded objection to the popular message that mental ability of average preschool children can be raised by special schooling. The message was perhaps right in its intuitions but totally unsatisfactory in terms of substantiation at that time. The 1930's saw also the launching of the critical *Mental Measurements Yearbook*,[2] in which specialists exposed each new test and its attendant claims to searching examination. Theory about individual differences has been slow to develop because leaders in test research have used mathematical and psychological disciplines to the exclusion of the philosophical. What, after all, is worth measuring? There has been a lack of social perspective. But disciplined the testing movement has truly been.

As evidence accumulated it largely supported the views with which Galton had started. Ability is general, in the sense that children superior in one complex task tend to excel in others. Ability does have a strong hereditary component, judging from follow-up studies of twins reared in distinctly different environments. And mental ability is constant to a degree, judging by the consistency from year to year of the rank order of test scores among school-age children. It is small wonder that the IQ came to be regarded as the long-sought index of fitness to survive, to lead, and to be educated.

THE TEST AS A SELECTIVE DEVICE   Tests came to determine the pupil's fate rather than merely to forecast it. The movement started with Galton's intent to select persons for special responsibility, and the group test burst on the American scene as a device to select men for training as officers. Soon the tests were being used to decide who should be accepted into college, who should be encouraged to take the college-preparatory subjects, and who, in the elementary school, should go into the "fast section." Personnel psychologists developed technical procedures for validating tests, the essential question being how well the rank on the test agreed with the person's rank on the end-of-training measure of accomplishment. By this standard of predictive accuracy, the mental test performed excellently. The highest scorers did tend to do best in college. The bright students, encouraged to move through school ahead of others of like age, generally made fine records and rarely seemed to be harmed by the acceleration.

The external critics of mental testing have raised many objections to the way the tests were applied, but none of these implies a disagreement with the scientific conclusions of the 1920–1940 period. The faults lay in the applications. Some were mere stupidities, as when an early tester assigned the young Jan Masaryk to an institution for the retarded because, as an immigrant from Czechoslovakia speaking little English, he earned a Binet score below 70. Some reflected narrowness of perspective, which elevated the IQ to disproportionate prominence and disregarded motivation, flexibility, and other characteristics of the child. Some were perhaps a consequence of the commercialization of tests;

certainly many tests were published without adequate formative research. As tests came to be judged primarily by their ability to predict subsequent grades, tasks for which the school gave direct training began to dominate test content to the exclusion of the tasks requiring judgment and fluid intelligence that had been the original *raison d'être* for mental tests. Among older students, no doubt, past achievement predicts future school achievement more strongly than do tests that do not rest on school learning. But the shift of mental test content away from abstract reasoning is simply an illustration of the distortion that occurs whenever a narrow standard is used to evaluate a product.

HANDICAPS OF THE GHETTO CHILD   The most severe criticisms of mental testing in education center on the possibility that the tests deny opportunity to children from poor environments. All testers agree that any measure reflects the pupil's present abilities as developed by his experiences. As early as the 1922 NSSE *Yearbook*, Colvin, speaking for the psychological profession, italicized the statement: "We never measure inborn intelligence; we always measure acquired intelligence, but we infer from differences in acquired intelligence, differences in native endowment when we compare individuals in a group who have had common experiences . . ." [3] This recognition that experience is needed to develop intellectual performance pervades the professional literature, but this observation at the abstract level has often been forgotten in concrete application of tests. The testers were sanguine in assuming that nearly all schoolchildren have had the experience necessary for successful test performance. The past three decades, however, have brought cultural influences increasingly to attention. The child from a poor home may have little encouragement to persist in a difficult problem, to work for a delayed or symbolic reward, to criticize his own answers, or to develop verbal and numerical concepts. If, in addition, he belongs to a mistreated minority that must "learn its place," he will very likely fail tasks, set by an authority figure, that he would accomplish in a non-threatening social situation.

The schools can scarcely be criticized for inferring that a poor child who does badly on tests will do badly in school. This is adequately supported by follow-up studies. The schools can be criticized, however, for accepting the predicted poor performance as inevitable. Schools have too often shunted low-scoring children into slow sections and into noncollege curricula with the closed verdict that "you can't expect anything more from them." This is more likely to happen to the lower-class child, white or Negro, than to the middle-class child whose parents will complain if they feel that their child is being downgraded. In a sense the school organization and curriculum have been biased against the lower-class child, simply because they assume a background of motivation and intellectual development more typical of middle-class homes. The more the mental test embodies the same demands, the more likely it is to be a valid predictor. If it is to be assumed that the "biased" school system will continue in the same manner, the realistic forecasts made by the test enable the school to fit its demands to the pupil so that all concerned experience minimal frustration. But tests used in this way help to make the biased system function and so perpetuate it.

On the favorable side, it must be said that tests served the cause of equal opportunity by demonstrating the very great overlapping of the test-score distributions of ethnic groups. Children of Oriental parentage in California typically have performed as well as white children, and in the North, Negro children do about as well as white children in the same social class. Regardless of averages, the plain finding that there are thousands of ghetto children with IQs in the range 120 and above is a powerful stimulus to efforts to bring good education to the inner city. Whatever ambiguity attends the low test score, a high IQ is always a sign of a pupil who merits stimulation and encouragement.

## Unified intelligence: a concept under attack

Much of the most interesting research on mental tests has been concerned with Galton's initial presupposition, later accepted by Binet and Terman, that intellect is a unified, general ability. Tests that did not agree reasonably well with the Stanford-Binet and similar general measures were discarded (except for some special abilities that seemed directly relevant to an occupation, such as the tonal discrimination tests used to appraise one element in musical talent). The construct of "general ability" has been repeatedly challenged.

At one point a leading investigator, L. L. Thurstone, went so far as to argue that the usual test is nothing more than a melange of independent abilities to reason with numbers, words, geometric diagrams, etc. His conclusion derived from his finding, in tests of several hundred college students, that each test content selected different persons as superior. His later investigations brought him back to agreement with the mainstream of studies that showed consistent positive correlations among the several abilities. The initial finding of zero correlations was explained as owing to the atypicality of selected college students. The reconsideration of this result, however, still left agreement that number tests, for example, agree more closely with each other than with the remaining tests. The general factor was joined by a constellation of lesser abilities, each presumed to be important in a restricted class of tasks. The mapping of this constellation continues, because researchers subsequent to Thurstone have fragmented some of the original abilities and added others. The critical question for the educator is not the list of abilities but the importance of each of them.

## Test profiles in college selection

To illustrate the slippery path from hypothesis to practice, we may concentrate on the use of ability profiles to select and advise college students. As early as 1923, less than a decade after the first group test appeared, Thurstone had assembled a test to be used in admitting, classifying, and guiding college freshmen that had the sponsorship of the prestigious American Council on Education. Thurstone chose six subtests dealing with language and three concerned with mathematical and abstract reasoning, and recommended that the student's entire profile of nine separate points be interpreted in reaching a decision about him. Over the years the number of tests was reduced. Finally only two scores, linguistic and quantitative, were offered for interpretation. The test in this form continued as the principal test for American college students until the middle 1950's when it was supplanted by the Scholastic Aptitude Test of the College Entrance Examination Board.

Thurstone's reason for reporting multiple scores, in place of the single IQ of other tests, was his conviction—years in advance of major research on that matter—that the subtests measured largely different things and therefore that the profile of ups and downs could and should be interpreted. What validating research was used to justify this practical recommendation? Essentially none, beyond the compilation of correlations to show that the tests, separately or together, did indeed predict grade averages. Any interpretation of this profile that a counselor or admissions officer might make rested on only his intuition. Here is another of those attractive ideas rushed into educational practice without hard examination. To be sure, some of the tests, such as Arithmetic Reasoning, were obviously and directly interpretable; but there was no similar basis for deciding what significance a Number Series test (4 6 9 11 14 . . .) might have, except as incorporated into a total score. Thus the fate of students was shaped for a generation by a test whose total score had been validated as a predictor but whose part-scores had no verified meaning.

Only in the late 1940's was the problem of profile validities directly examined. The most direct confrontation and the most disturbing evidence came from the authors of the Differential Aptitude Tests (which has been generally regarded as among the best profile measures for high-school use). Published in 1947, this test offered eight scores covering abilities that, separately, had seemed relevant to vocational success (e.g., clerical speed, mechanical comprehension, numerical reasoning, etc.). Different scores were expected to forecast success in different courses and occupations. When the authors collected follow-up data to determine whether the tests did indeed correlate as anticipated, the results frequently contradicted the prevailing intuitive notions. The test of Space Reasoning had nothing in particular to do with success in geometry in most schools. Success in language courses was predicted in a reasonable manner by the Verbal test, but the test of Numerical Reasoning often predicted just as well. The test that forecast success in one school was a nonpredictor in another; so great was the variation that, for geometry, almost every test in the battery took its turn as best predictor in one school or another. With this result before them, a group of college counselors went back to the older ACE test, and reached the same conclusion. The correlation of the L or Q score with marks in a given course ranged from high to low in different colleges; often L correlated higher in those courses where commonsense had said that Q was most relevant. It follows that a good fraction of the advice based on profile differences between 1923 and 1955 had been in error. If nothing else, these thorough inquiries made all users of profiles more cautious. The tale is one more warning against full-scale application of an intuitive idea or a technique derived from research, prior to adequately skeptical field trials.

Here the story branches: There is a practical epilogue and a theoretical epilogue. As for the practical, the main outcome of the troublesome validation studies was a proper insistence on local decision-oriented studies to determine what aptitudes are critical for the local course of study in, for example, Mechanical Engineering (and the various jobs to which graduates flow). Carrying out such studies to help the local counselor make reliable use of test profiles has been a common duty of institutional research workers in colleges.

The very fact that success in Mechanical Engineering depends on different things in different colleges and in different types of work within the profession undercuts the naive proposal to select those generally fittest. As Darwin's theory clearly implied, fitness depends on the environmental demand. A student sure to survive at one college is a risk at another. College selection is a matter of guiding youth into the right institutions, rather than just a process of skimming off the cream. Although this wisdom may appear obvious, it is a radical change from the prevailing view of the past century. An aspiring technology is embarrassed to discover that the result found in one locality cannot be duplicated in another, because of local conditions. If there is no standard formula for test interpretation, the test developer has merely provided the counselor a set of do-it-yourself tools to help him start his own local research.

## Test technology in the service of the individual

It is possible that test technology, by admitting the true complexity of its task and responding accordingly, can cope with variation. This is most strikingly shown in a recent project of the College Entrance Examination Board. It has long been known that a student's success depends on the college he chooses; variations in standards, in the competition, and in the instructional emphasis will make some colleges hard for him and others easy. The only way to move from vague advice on college choice to a precise statement of chances for success is to collect systematic follow-up data and reduce them to an intelligible form. This process is reflected in a College Board handbook, placed in the hands of high school counselors, which reports factually on each cooperating college. A fine example of decision-oriented research, this report states, regarding the Scholastic Aptitude Test, such facts as the distribution among persons accepted, and the distribution among students who survive the first year of college. Comparing his score to data in the handbook, the student can see what his personal chances are in his preferred college.

The Board carries this innovation a long step further in a pilot study being conducted in Indiana, using records collated from virtually every college in the state. The guide [4] now undergoing trial is designed for use by the student and his family. The student is shown how to make the small computations that combine his subtest scores on the SAT with his high school marks so as to predict the grades he will earn at any college. Because colleges make different demands, the various tests take on different weights from place to place. Thus, a technological procedure, based on carefully tabulated experience, supplants stereotypes and student gossip regarding colleges, curricula, and test scores. The student is free to apply, with his eyes open, to a favored college where his chances are only fair, or, if he prefers, to select a less demanding school where he is likely to survive. Accurate facts thus become an aid in entirely personal decisions. Under such a plan we may hope that a larger proportion of youth will complete college than when, using irrelevant criteria, the student was likely to pick a college whose teaching emphasis did not fit his aptitudes.

An additional by-product of conclusion-oriented research is the guide's descriptions of the "climates" of colleges, which differ from the usual catalog claim that the college possesses all possible virtues. A questionnaire devised on the basis of several years of research by Pace and Stern is administered to present students in the college, who check as true or false such statements as "Students here talk a lot about politics and world affairs." From the compiled results, the college may be described as having much or little emphasis on the contemporary, much or little personal exchange between students and faculty, etc. Publishing these "worm's eye" views of the college gives data to the prospective applicant that he would otherwise not have until he has committed himself and enrolled. The whole purpose of the Indiana study is to enable the student to match himself to the college. The data compilation is entirely technological, but his decision about where to apply is entirely individual.

The theoretical inquiries lead in much the same direction. They attempt to find out why the relevant aptitudes vary from course to course. The inquiry has now made clear that those interested in guidance have been asking the wrong question in judging a test by its general predictive power. Whenever the school aims to educate all pupils rather than just to select a few, tests are useful only to help choose an instructional method for the individual. This means they must forecast the difference between his probable achievement levels in two courses. A test that measures a general ability will predict level of success in both treatments but will not predict the difference. Needed for this type of decision is a test relevant to one treatment and not the other. This new rule of thumb overthrows the traditional canons of choosing tests, canons that derive from Galton himself and that are appropriate enough when selection for a fixed environment is the only aim. The new formulation came out of mathematical research on information theory and statistical decisions. To the extent that the earlier strategy of test research favored the survival of general predictors, it has weeded out any test relevant only to some styles of instruction and not others. The new research strategy should lead—though perhaps only after another two decades of exploration—to special-purpose aptitude measures quite unlike those that satisfied the former demands.

Any technology is designed to optimize some index, single or complex. To swallow whole a technology without examining philosophically and technically the index that directs its growth is to guarantee error. The critical attitude alone does not guarantee that every unsuitable index will be detected and improved upon, but nothing else makes wise use of technology conceivable.

The evolution of ideas on testing began in a study of natural history, developed through pioneering work on anthropology and genetics. It has recently been set on a new track by a type of mathematical research. Psychology and sociology have been even more prominent. What would better document the case that educational thinking profits from the "pure" disciplines?

# The philosopher and the concept

# of knowledge

PHILOSOPHY INFLUENCES practice by its continuous effort to raise fundamental conceptions to a reflective level, to clarify their import, and to submit them to critical examination. As an example of philosophical work, we shall discuss certain features of the thought of Charles Sanders Peirce, founder of the philosophy of pragmatism and a philosopher of the first magnitude. The selection of Peirce for discussion needs explanation, for Dewey was clearly the most directly influential of the pragmatists, particularly in educational and social thought. Yet it is particularly important to see in the more remote and abstruse work of Peirce the germ of later applications in pragmatism generally. For he strongly influenced Dewey and others through the force of his ideas, and without thought to application. Without Peirce, it is hardly possible, indeed, to conceive of the later applications of pragmatism in the form in which they became widespread and influential.

Charles Peirce was born in Cambridge, Massachusetts, in 1839, the second son of Benjamin Peirce, professor of mathematics and astronomy at Harvard, and in his day America's foremost mathematician. Peirce graduated from Harvard in 1858, and held several posts with the U.S. Coast and Geodetic Survey from 1861–1891. During the 1860's he gave occasional lecture courses on logic and the history of science at Harvard, and for five years held a logic lectureship at the Johns Hopkins University, but he never obtained a permanent university position. Despite his lack of university backing, he influenced such eminent philosophers of his day as Josiah Royce and William James and achieved a certain fame through his philosophical papers and his articles on physics, astronomy, and the theory of measurement.

Aside from his decisive influence on James and Dewey, and on the philosophy of pragmatism generally, Peirce is of interest because of his pioneering work in bringing scientific conceptions and attitudes to bear on philosophy, and in making explicit and defending "the laboratory habit of mind." His contributions to symbolic logic, to the theory of probability, induction, and measurement, to the philosophy of logic and symbolism, to the theory of definition and the analysis of belief—all are motivated by an overriding concern with clarifying the relevance and implications of scientific logic for critical thought and action. In terms of his notion of scientific logic, Peirce criticized not only classical rationalistic philosophy, but also nineteenth-century romanticism and positivism, proposing *logical method* as a unifying conception applicable not only to science but to life. For Peirce the essence of a general education was to be found in this conception of a general logical method that emphasizes the clarity of concepts and critical reasoning, the method being exemplified in modern scientific practice. In elaborating his conception, he developed an explicit formulation of what are now widely recognized as elements of scientific thought: a rejection of the idea that findings can ever be certain and final, an emphasis on probability and hypothetical reasoning, a conception of operational definition, a public notion of science as a community of investigators, a problem approach to inquiry, and a view of axioms as tentative assumptions to be tested in experience.

Translated into educational terms, many of these emphases are recognizable and familiar in pragmatic notions of schooling: the attempt to link thought and action, the effort to structure teaching around problems, the rejection of the quest for certainty and the corresponding effort to develop probabilistic modes of reasoning, the emphasis on publicly available evidence, and the primary stress on methods of arriving at knowledge rather than on the knowledge already stored up. Note that Peirce's motivations were primarily theoretical and philosophical; he himself did not translate his key notions into educational applications. Nevertheless, his general concern with modernizing our logical conceptions turned out to have significant, if indirect, effects on educational thinking and practice.

## Knowledge as the fruit of problem-solving

We cannot undertake to review the various facets of Peirce's philosophy; but, to indicate the nature of his work, we shall sketch some of his general lines of argument against the rationalistic view of knowledge exemplified, in particular, by Descartes. Descartes (1596–1650)—who, in freeing himself from authoritarianism, founded modern philosophy—had counseled adoption of a method of radical doubt. His aim was to achieve certainty and his method was deductive. Construing knowledge after the model of a mathematical system, he wanted to start with clear, distinct, and hence indubitable premises accessible to introspection, and then to move with deductive certainty step by step to an indubitable conclusion. His conception of science was that of a chain of linear reasoning resting upon a foundation invulnerable to doubt, the whole chain as strong as its weakest link. Descartes' starting point was his own indubitable existence, given immediately in the fact of his own conscious thinking: "Cogito ergo sum."

In his paper "Some Consequences of Four Incapacities," Pierce argues that "modern science and modern logic require us to stand upon a very different platform from this." [5] Radical doubt is an impossible method, he argues, for inquiry can never wipe the slate clean in order to start with foundations that are truly certain. "We must begin with all the prejudices which we actually have when we enter upon the study of philosophy. . . . Let us not pretend to doubt in philosophy what we do not doubt in our hearts." We begin always in the middle of things, taking for granted a whole mass of assumptions while we test the particular one that is thrown into doubt.

Doubt, he urges, cannot be produced at will by following a philosophical maxim. It is an active state of irritation, not the mere absence of belief. In inquiry, thought struggles to pass from real doubt to belief, a latent state of readiness or habit that sets us to act in selective ways in the future. Inquiry never starts afresh but operates with assumptions while it focuses upon genuine issues in doubt, defining a problem. The researcher takes for granted a variety of theories, laws, and factual assumptions in the process of testing some view that is the core of the issue presently in doubt. Afterwards, should one of his prior assumptions be itself put in doubt, he may appropriately set himself to testing that one. But he cannot throw all his beliefs into doubt simultaneously and to claim to do so is self-deception.

Nor, argues Peirce, can certainty be found in the individual consciousness. "Metaphysicians will all agree that metaphysics has reached a pitch of certainty far beyond that of the physical sciences—only they can agree upon nothing else," he writes. If one contrasts the sciences, in which men do come to agreement, theories are in a state of suspension until agreement is reached, whereupon—though the theory is known not to be a final one—the issue of certainty becomes idle. The relevant criterion is then not the subjective conviction of the individual consciousness, but the agreement of disciplined minds in the community of scientific investigators, an ineradicably public criterion which is built into scientific modes of thought. There is, in fact, no possibility that certainty will be found through introspection, for all thinking is inherently symbolic and general as well as hypothetical, "all knowledge of the internal world" being derived "by hypothetical reasoning from our knowledge of external facts."

Finally, the Cartesian conception of linear deductive reasoning from indubitable foundations is to be rejected in favor of the weaving together of a circumstantial fabric from many different strands. "Philosophy," writes Peirce, "ought to imitate the successful sciences in its methods, so far as to proceed only from tangible premises which can be subjected to careful scrutiny, and to trust rather to the multitude and variety of its arguments than to the conclusiveness of any one. Its reasoning should not form a chain which is no stronger than its weakest link, but a cable whose fibers may be ever so slender, provided they are sufficiently numerous and intimately connected."

The whole Cartesian conception of knowledge is thus rejected. The ideal of certainty is replaced by that of fallible hypothetical assumptions, the notion of radical doubt replaced by the selective doubt that focuses upon a well-defined problem, the conception of indubitable axioms replaced by provisional assumptions, the idea of subjective individual conviction replaced by public agreement within the informed community, and, finally, the notion of linear thought replaced by that of circumstantial reasoning. We have here a thoroughgoing attempt to make explicit the operative canons of modern experimental science, to oppose them to classical rationalism, to justify them and make them generally available, and to bring philosophical conceptions into line with them.

In "How to Make our Ideas Clear" (published, significantly, in *Popular Science Monthly* for January, 1878), Peirce offers a special critique of rationalistic criteria of *clarification*, which supplements the arguments we have just considered. Rejecting the Cartesian appeal to the clearness and distinctness of ideas as determined by introspection, Peirce also argues that abstract definitions are radically insufficient from a scientific standpoint.

The highest grade of clarification, for Peirce, is a form of what has since become known as "operationism," a tying of ideas both to actions and to their observable effects by means of an if-then rule or "habit." To develop the meaning of an idea, "we have, therefore, simply to determine what habits it produces, for what a thing means is simply what habits it involves." Given an idea, we need to consider what effects would ensue from specified operations upon its referent. "Our conception of these effects is the whole of our conception of the object."

## Educational aims suggested by the pragmatic view

This summary brings us to the significance of Peirce's ideas to education, for his doctrine of meaning has an obvious message for those who would explain concepts to children. Familiarity is not enough, nor is mere verbal definition—a theme memorably amplified in James' *Talks to Teachers*. The idea needs to be concretely related to the child's actions and his expectation of consequences ensuing therefrom. This requires, in turn, opportunities for him to act and to observe the consequences of his action in a purposive context. Here is the theoretical germ of the familiar Deweyan emphasis on meaning as the perception of relations between action and consequences. Here is the root of the "progressive" idea that teaching needs to be carried out in purposive units of action, so that subject matter takes on meaning as mediator between purposive action and observable result.

In Peirce's conception of inquiry initiated by real

doubt, we have, furthermore, a major source of the problem theory of teaching, the theory that genuine thought is elicited only in the effort to overcome a genuinely felt difficulty, and that teaching should therefore be organized around problem units relevant to the situation of the students. Moreover, Peirce's conception of beliefs as habits orienting us to the future makes it evident that beliefs are always in principle subject to the test of further experience. It provides a source of the Progressive emphasis on the tentative character of beliefs and on the notion that genuine inquiry provides its own intrinsic discipline. For the overcoming of doubt by attainment of belief is continually subject to the observable check of future experience. Educationally, the ideal discipline is to be conceived not as externally imposed by adults, but as flowing from the very process of meaningful inquiry in which solutions to real problems are sought.

It is important to note again that the educational suggestions inherent in Peirce's ideas were not developed by him, nor did they emerge originally from any direct intent to influence schooling. The initial motivation was theoretical, and the main goal was to spell out the general import of actual scientific standards and practices for a modern theory of knowledge. Abstract formulations such as those of Peirce nevertheless take on an autonomous life and enter into the pervasive social and intellectual climate of the educator and other thoughtful men. They filter into textbooks and explanations, they subtly alter the teacher's attitudes and conceptions of the task of schooling, and they form the basis for further philosophical criticism and interpretation, which in turn have their effects on what the school tries to do and how it proceeds. Though they do not directly address themselves to issues of practice nor provide the basis for technological development, these abstractions exercise long-run practical influence in channeling the reflective attitudes of men, attitudes which, after all, determine the uses to which technology is put.

Pierce, of course, came centuries after the initiation of modern empirical science, but he was contemporary with the beginnings of modern social and behavioral sciences, and the pragmatic viewpoint exercised significant influence on these sciences. Investigations of social problems, by such men as Quetelet and Galton, and of certain aspects of behavior, initiated by Fechner and Wundt among others, were well under way. But the methods used were almost entirely observational, descriptive, correlational, and narrowly empirical. Peirce and his successors stressed action rather than passive observation, and in psychology, education, and the biological sciences, experimental intervention came to be seen as the scientific method *par excellence*. Intervention in the larger social community can rarely be controlled, and experimentation has therefore played a minor role in sociology and political science. But even in such domains, and indeed in the area of social policy proper, pragmatists stressed the need to be critically alert to the consequences of social action, so that we may be prepared to learn from experience whatever it can teach us. The range of critical intelligence is not to be restricted to the scope of controlled experiment, but suitably expanded so as to facilitate application to the whole realm of human conduct.

Peirce's theoretical ideas thus constituted a genuine influence on the growth of the whole series of proposals that came to be known as progressive education and that, in their more practical formulations, have become a well-accepted part of today's prevailing view of education.

# Thorndike's impact on the teaching

# of arithmetic

UNTIL this century, arithmetic was taught orally, for the most part. Arithmetic texts were aimed at a public already educated in the algorithms of arithmetic, and were, almost without exception, like treatises in elementary mathematics. The verbal formulations had the style characteristic of late Greek mathematics, which meant that they were almost impossible for the uninitiated to understand. Development of a concept followed the sequence definition, rule, illustration, proof, and finally, examples for practice. This logical development often makes good sense for advanced portions of mathematics, but it makes no sense as a way of introducing young students to arithmetic. Already in the nineteenth century, the mathematician Augustus DeMorgan strongly advocated that instruction begin with the working of a problem and proceed to infer the rule after considering several examples. But DeMorgan's work was not really aimed at the elementary-school child; his presentation nearly always continued into an algebraic treatment of the topic.

Even in the oral teaching that predominated throughout most of the nineteenth century, the teacher often gave out impossible definitions and rules that pupils were to copy into an exercise book and to apply. Here is an example of such a definition written out by an 11-year-old boy in 1817. "Inverse proportion is when more requires less, and less requires more. More requires less is when the third term is greater than the first, and requires the fourth term to be less than the second. And less requires more is when the third term is less than the first, and requires the fourth term to be greater than the second." [6] Such obscurities fully justified the opinion on which Florence Yeldham remarks, in her book on the teaching of arithmetic through 400 years: "The nineteenth century ended with an opinion fairly generally expressed that arithmetic was the least liked of all school subjects." [7]

A major reform was instituted early in this century. Recent years have seen severe criticism of the teaching of arithmetic as it took place in this country from 1920 to the middle 1950's, and there have been radical changes toward a "new mathematics." This critical discussion has lost sight of the character and quality of the changes made in the years just after 1900. The most influential figure during this period was Edward L. Thorndike; his ideas on the teaching of arithmetic constituted a pedagogical revolution as far-reaching and as important in the history of the teaching of mathematics as the current curriculum reforms. Moreover, it is fair to say that Thorndike's proposals were more thoroughly based than these recent ones on ideas about learning, and that they involved a much more serious effort to derive changes from what was thought to be a correct theory of how students learn concepts and skills. The recent reform in mathematics curriculum has aimed to redress an imbalance created by the Thorndike revolution. The emphasis in the past decade has been on the content of the mathematics curriculum, not on the psychological aspects of how it should be taught and how students learn it. The pendulum is beginning now to swing back to a more serious consideration of the learning of students and the principles that guide that learning. For this reason it is particularly timely to analyze Thorndike's work as an example of how theory can affect pedagogical practice.

Thorndike's work included general research on psychology, represented in part by his three-volume *Educa-

*tional Psychology* (1913, 1914), a simpler treatment of these topics in a single volume (1924), and *The Principles of Teaching* (1906); the application of his general psychological theory to arithmetic, in *The Psychology of Arithmetic* (1922); and his own arithmetic textbooks (1917), which provided a model for subsequent authors.

## Principles of learning

Volume II of *Educational Psychology* was devoted to the psychology of learning. In it Thorndike attempted to work out what he considered the most significant and important consequences of his three fundamental laws: Readiness, Exercise, and Effect. Volume I had listed and described the tendencies of man as a species. Thorndike argued that there were connections or bonds, enormous in number, between stimuli furnished by the environment and the responses of which a man is capable. The subject of the second volume on learning was the analysis of the ways in which these initial tendencies can be modified by learning or experience. Before turning to a consideration of the three laws, it is important for us to note that Thorndike, unlike Locke and some other early British associationists, did not hold a *tabula rasa* theory of the mind. He asserts in numerous places in *Educational Psychology* that many of the connections between stimuli and responses are inherent in men, and are neither learned or modifiable through experience.

The Law of Readiness asserts that "when any conduction unit is in readiness to conduct, for it to do so is satisfying. When any conduction unit is not in readiness to conduct, for it to conduct is annoying." It should be apparent that this rather unusual language about conducting units is related to Thorndike's conception of connections or bonds. The primary point of the Law of Readiness is to emphasize the importance of a connection's being satisfying to the organism. Thorndike recognized with great clarity one of the central insights of behaviorism, that an account of learning cannot be successful if it does not include a concept of reinforcement or satisfaction.

The Law of Exercise is made up of two laws, one of *use* and the other of *disuse*. The Law of Use is that when a modifiable connection is made between a situation and response, the strength of the connection is increased, other things being equal. In other words, the strength of a connection between a stimulus and a response is increased whenever that response is given to the stimulus. The Law of Disuse states that when a modifiable connection between a stimulus and response is not employed for a period of time, then that strength of connection is decreased.

The Law of Effect, the most famous of the three laws, states that when a modifiable connection is made between a situation or stimulus and a response and it is accompanied or followed by a satisfying state of affairs, then the connection is strengthened; and if it is accompanied by an annoying state of affairs, it is weakened. To put it in slightly more modern terms, the importance of the Law of Effect is the relation it postulates between reinforcement and strength of conditioning.

It is also important to emphasize that Thorndike did not have an overly simplified idea of how connections are made and operate. He repeatedly stated that the connection is often compound and that each of the component connections has a different strength. He stressed that in educational theories of human learning, the primary subject matter is traits, functions, and units larger than the elementary connections. He perhaps did not realize sufficiently the difficulty of bridging the gap between elementary connections and complex school learning. The main examples analyzed in detail in Volume II of *Educational Psychology* concern learning to send the Morse Code, learning to type, and some of the elementary skills of arithmetic.

Thorndike was neither the first nor the only person to make this application of learning theory to simple skills, but he did it in the most systematic and extensive fashion. He also carried it through to bring the results directly to the attention of teachers and, perhaps most important of all, he formulated his scientific ideas clearly and explicitly. It is worth noting that almost no reference cited in *Educational Psychology* dates before 1890. There was a rapid and very active development of ideas during the twenty-year period extending from 1890 to 1910, and these are well embodied in Thorndike's systematic treatise. The very systematization of the material made disciplinary criticism possible and set the tone for the vigorous exploration of learning theory that has persisted now for sixty years. Even today, much psychological research is directed to puzzles and controversies that derive directly from Thorndike's formulations.

## The psychology of arithmetic

The general principles of learning worked out in *Educational Psychology* were already applied to arithmetic in some of the experiments Thorndike cited in Volume II. Not content with these illustrative cases, he went on to complete in 1920 a systematic work on the psychology of arithmetic, which was essentially a course of lectures he gave to elementary-school teachers and others at Teachers College. The high aims of this study and its radical new attitude toward arithmetic are best seen in the opening paragraphs of Thorndike's preface:

Within recent years there have been three lines of advance in psychology which are of notable significance for teaching. The first is the new point of view concerning the general process of learning. We now understand that learning is essentially the formation of connections or bonds between situations and responses, that the satisfyingness of the result is the chief force that forms them, and that habit rules in the realm of thought as truly and as fully as in the realm of action.

The second is the great increase in knowledge of the amount, rate, and conditions of improvement in those organized groups or hierarchies of habits which we call abilities, such as ability to add or ability to read. Practice and improvement are no longer vague generalities, but concern changes which are definable and measurable by standard tests and scales.

The third is the better understanding of the so-called "higher processes" of analysis, abstraction, the formation of general notions, and reasoning. The older view of a mental chemistry whereby sensations were compounded into percepts, percepts were duplicated by images, percepts and images were amalgamated into abstractions and concepts, and these were manipulated by reasoning, has given way to the understanding of the laws of response to elements or aspects of situations and to many situations or elements thereof in combination. James' view of reasoning as "selection of essentials" and "thinking things together" in a revised and clarified form has important applications in the teaching of all the school subjects.

This book presents the applications of this newer dynamic psychology to the teaching of arithmetic.[8]

In *The Psychology of Arithmetic*, Thorndike attempted an extensive analysis of the nature of arithmetic abilities, their measurement and their structure. Using his own experiments and those of others, he analyzed in detail the psychology of drills in arithmetic. He saw the psychological purpose of drill as being to strengthen the bonds between stimuli and appropriate responses. He held no overly simple view of the "stimulus," emphasizing not only the appropriate responses to basic facts but also the strength of bonds concerning the reasons for arithmetical processes. Because Thorndike is often thought of as encouraging drill and habit formation in arithmetic, it is worth emphasizing that he appreciated the desirability of students' having an understanding of the deductive theories of arithmetic and the mathematical basis of the algorithms they learned. What the pupil learns about deductive theory, he said, should "rank among the most rather than the least permanent of a pupil's stock of arithmetical knowledge and power." He pointed out also that when a student comes to understand the basis of arithmetic, he is then able to fill out particular fragmentary pieces that he may forget. As he puts it: "Details of *how* you arranged numbers to multiply might vanish, but the general reasons for the placing would be expected to persist and enable one to invent the detailed manipulations that had been forgotten." [9]

In analyzing drill in arithmetic, he moved from the general consideration of the strength of bonds to detailed and practical questions about the amount of practice and the organization of the various skills. He laid particular emphasis on the advantages of distributed practice (i.e., of spreading exercises of a certain sort over a period of time). He examined the actual distribution of practice in several textbooks, and considered how blunders might be avoided and how reasonable procedures might be instituted. His detailed proposals are more sophisticated psychologically than most current writings on methods of teaching arithmetic. In fact, as part of the swing of the pendulum mentioned earlier, the current textbooks for teachers on the teaching of arithmetic concentrate on mathematical content and spend little, if any, time on the psychology of student learning. In this respect, they resemble very closely the rationalistic texts of the eighteenth and nineteenth centuries.

## Teaching of arithmetic

To show the impact of Thorndike's ideas, we shall make some brief comparisons between arithmetic text-books in the 1920's and earlier textbooks. Typical textbooks illustrate the change in viewpoint and pedagogy. We may look first at a "post-Thorndike" textbook series, *Searchlight Arithmetics* by B. R. Buckingham and W. J. Osburn (1927). In the preface to their first book, they argue for thorough practice of component skills before more complex problems are introduced. They note:

> In this series of books every major topic has been carefully analyzed into units of difficulty. Each unit has then been presented separately so that the pupil may have but one new difficulty to master at a time. For example, . . . [difficulties in long division include] (1) estimating the quotient figure, (2) carrying in multiplication, (3) carrying in subtraction, and (4) zeros in the quotient. Two other conditions of difficulty have likewise been recognized. One is that division becomes more difficult as the number of digits in the divisor increases; the other is that the chance for error increases with the number of quotient figures the pupil has to obtain. Accordingly, the first section on long division presents none of these difficulties or presents them to a minimum degree; the second section adds a new point of difficulty; and subsequent sections introduce additional difficulties.[10]

In accord with Thorndike's emphasis on systematic drill, Buckingham and Osburn provide drill on number combinations according to a definite plan, with all essential number facts frequently repeated and well distributed. Brown and Eldredge (1925) likewise include special sections throughout their books devoted to systematic drill on difficult combinations.[11]

Thorndike insisted that transfer from one task to another does not occur unless the learning situations include noticeably similar elements which allow generalizations to operate. Much of *The Psychology of Arithmetic* is intended to describe ways of facilitating transfer in arithmetic, by appropriate placement of material and by emphasis on common elements in problems. His discussion of United States money and decimals is an interesting illustration of this doctrine. He urged that the topic of money be introduced very early, and used to facilitate later work with decimals. He remarks,

> The entire matter of long multiplication with integers and United States money should be treated as a teaching unit and the bonds formed in close organization, even though numbers as large as 900,000 are occasionally involved. The reason is not that it is more logical, or less scrappy, but that each of the bonds in question thus gets much help from, and gives much help to, the others. . . .
>
> The bonds involved in the four operations with United States money should be formed in grades 3 and 4 along with or very soon after the corresponding bonds with three-place and four-place integers. This statement would have seemed preposterous to the pedagogues of fifty years ago. "United States money," they would have said, "is an application of decimals. How can it be learned until the essentials of decimal fractions are known?". . . .
>
> The case illustrates very well the error of the older over-systematic treatment of the order of topics and the still more important error of confusing the logic of proof with the psychology of learning. . . .
>
> We need not be timid. . . . If we simply form the two bonds described above [the ability to operate with integers plus the two habits of prefixing and separating dollars from cents] and show by proper verification that the procedure always gives the right answer, the early teaching of the four

operations with United States money will in fact actually show a learning profit! [12]

For contrast, we turn to a text which appeared just before Thorndike's impact became evident. Although Byrnes, Richman, and Roberts had given problems using dollars and cents in Part One of their *Pupils' Arithmetic* (1912),[13] no systematic or formal introduction of these topics is given. In contrast, pennies enter on page 7 of the first book in the Brown-Eldredge series, and their complete introduction to United States money would be reached early in grade 2. Cents, dimes, nickels, quarters, half dollars, dollars, and the use of the period are included in this introduction. Byrnes, Richman, and Roberts teach decimals late in the fifth grade or early in the sixth; but there is no mention of United States money, and few problems in the initial section on decimals use monetary examples. When Brown and Eldredge discuss decimals (grade 6), they emphasize that decimals are used in referring to United States money, and point out that students have already been doing some problems using decimals. For example:

> You understand how to add and subtract United States money. This is, after all, only an application of decimal fractions. It is evident that $4.25 means 4.25 dollars, that $13.85 means 13.85 dollars. Since you can add and subtract United States money, so, too, you can add and subtract decimal fractions.[14]

In applying the principles of association and assimilation, Thorndike pointed out that in the schoolbooks of the early twentieth century desirable bonds were often neglected, and wasteful or harmful bonds encouraged. This can indeed be seen in turn-of-the-century arithmetic; later texts, published in the 1920's, show changes consistent with Thorndike's ideas.

One bond whose formation Thorndike encouraged is

that between operations on numbers and methods of checking or verifying the correctness of these operations. When the 1912 Byrnes primary texts for grades 1 through 3 demonstrate methods of checking, the student is not regularly asked to check his work, i.e., to use the connection. For example, after the procedure for checking subtraction is introduced, only 11 of the next 164 subtraction problems require the student to check his work. Instead, this section presents 106 combinations such as $11 - 2$, $21 - 2$, . . . . $82 - 6$, $92 - 6$, and asks the student to subtract at sight and memorize the result. Thorndike held that checking operations are valuable because they enable the student

> to find his own errors, and to maintain a standard of accuracy by himself . . . give him a sense of the relations of the processes and the reasons why the right ways . . . are right, . . . [and] put his acquisition of a certain power, say multiplication, to a real and intelligible use, in checking the results of his practice of a new power, and so instill a respect for arithmetical power and skill in general.[15]

For Thorndike, checking each subtraction would be of considerably more value than merely attempting to memorize the response to $72 - 5$ or $92 - 6$.

The passage just quoted also reflects Thorndike's desire to build a positive attitude toward arithmetic. He sharply criticized trivialities and absurdities in problems, ambiguous questions, etc. Again, his criticism is based on the principle of association: such problems build undesirable bonds.

> Bonds should not be formed between insignificant or foolish questions and the labor of answering them, nor between the general arithmetical work of the school and such insignificant or foolish questions. . . . Bonds should not be formed between a described situation and a method of treating the situation which would not be a useful one to follow in the case of the real situation.[16]

Numerous examples of such objectionable problems can be found in the texts of 1912 and earlier.

How many thumbs have 6 boys?

If a man can walk 9 miles in one day, in how many days can he walk 108 miles?

Count the number each of desks, seats, tables, chairs, and other articles of furniture there are in your class-room, and then find out how many pieces of furniture the room contains.

How many days in the year, leaving out December? [17]

Thorndike suggests that if a problem is given merely to test a principle or emphasize a fact, rather than to be of "direct service in the quantitative work of life," it is better simply to formulate it as a problem about numbers. In this connection note the following problem sequence from Byrnes:

1. Hudson discovered the Hudson River in ———; Fulton sailed the first steamboat on that river in ———. How many years between those two events?
2. Make up a similar problem about Washington and Columbus.
3. Do the same, using Washington and Lincoln.
4. Do the same, using Columbus and Hudson.[18]

Compare the sort of thing to be found in the 1925 book of Brown and Eldredge:

If 12 is ¼ of a number, what is the number?

I am thinking of a certain number. Half of the number of which I am thinking is 5. Tell me the number.[19]

Thorndike criticized the use of "rare and unimportant" words in verbal problems for the early grades, because difficulties in reading may block development in arithmetic.

Book One of the Byrnes text uses many words that later appeared on Thorndike's proscribed list of vocabulary to be avoided before the middle of the third grade: *election, bouquet, library, sprout, balance,* and *entertainment,* etc. The difficult words are italicized in the Byrnes text, to alert the teacher that an explanation will probably be needed. Thorndike criticized such a procedure, however, because it confuses the activities of a reading lesson with training in arithmetic. The 1925 Brown-Eldredge book is not entirely without difficult vocabulary items, but there are far fewer hard words and there is a noticeable attempt to use the same words repeatedly in word problems. Thus, a majority of verbal problems for the first year concern familiar objects: fish, rabbits, puppies, boys, girls, and various kinds of fruit. In contrast, in the older Byrnes book one finds many words such as *committee, insurance, charity, premises, installment,* and *treasury,* which are unfamiliar as vocabulary and difficult as concepts.

To take up one further point of contrast, we note that Thorndike urged that operations with large numbers should be introduced soon after the basic operations are taught. For example:

> Still surer is the need for four-, five-, and six-place numbers when two-place numbers are used in multiplying. When the process with a two-place multiplier is learned, multiplications by three-place numbers should soon follow. They are not more difficult than later. On the contrary, if the pupil gets used to multiplying only as one does with two-place multipliers, he will suffer more by the resulting interference than he does from getting six- or seven-place answers whose meaning he cannot exactly realize. They teach the rationale and the manipulations of long multiplication with especial economy because the principles and the procedures are used two or three times over and the contrasts between the values which the partial products have in adding become three instead of one.[20]

In line with this suggestion of Thorndike's, Brown and Eldredge introduce three-place multiplier and multiplicands in the fourth grade; later in the same year, they include multiplication of four-digit numbers by three-digit numbers. Buckingham and Osburn, too, introduce two-place multiplicands almost immediately after teaching of the multiplication operation.

It has been possible only to give indications of the profound influence Thorndike had on the teaching of arithmetic.[21] With the recent addition of more abstract mathematics to the elementary curriculum in mind, some people consider the whole problem of teaching arithmetic trivial and unimportant. However, arithmetic continues to constitute the bulk of the elementary-school mathematics curriculum. And the way arithmetic is taught today in schools throughout this country reflects Thorndike's influence more than any other. The profound character of this influence was well summarized by Gorman in a 1931 study of changes in the arithmetic curriculum between 1907 and 1930.[22]

It appears from the evidence given that in the majority of the cases just described the causes for changes in methods lie in the developments in educational psychology as applied to arithmetic. Practically all these changes appeared subsequent to the publication of the work of Thorndike on the psychology and methods of arithmetic.

It is not the mathematics of arithmetic that is fundamental to the teaching of arithmetic; most mathematicians today regard the subject as completely trivial from a mathematical standpoint. What is important is the way the subject is taught. Serious psychological studies at both the theoretical and practical levels of how children learn arithmetic, and attempts to analyze skills and concepts in the subject are certainly not trivial.

By contemporary standards for investigations of learning, Thorndike's theoretical formulation is imprecise and his analysis is not properly quantified. By the standard for developmental research this report advocates, the textbooks that tried to carry his ideas into practice were inadequately tested. Nonetheless, his work must be regarded as a major step in the illumination of practical problems of teaching by theoretical ideas. Indeed, the real criticism to be made is not directed to the scientific weaknesses of Thorndike's work but rather to the lack of substantial inquiry at the same theoretical and experimental level in succeeding decades.

# The politics of education: a legacy of historical inquiry

OUR NEXT EXAMPLE again bears on the role of humanistic scholarship in the development of educational thinking. A particular piece of scholarship, Frank Tracy Carlton's *Economic Influences upon Educational Progress in the United States, 1820–1850*, changed the way educators viewed the rise of the public school, and in so doing affected the way they came to conceive of and participate in the development of educational policy. Carlton, by sharply criticizing certain standard historical interpretations of his day, radically altered our forms of remembering, categorizing, and understanding the American education experience.

The standard interpretations of Carlton's day can be gleaned from the work of such early educational historians as Richard G. Boone, whose *Education in the United States: Its History from the Earliest Settlements* (1890), appeared in William T. Harris' influential International Education Series, and Amory Dwight Mayo, whose majestic history of the American common school from its colonial beginnings through the Reconstruction appeared in fourteen lengthy installments in Harris' annual reports as United States Commissioner of Education. Essentially, they run as follows, though we apologize for oversimplification: The colonists came from Europe bearing a variety of traditional ideas and institutions in the realm of education; hence, the early schools and colleges in the new world tended to resemble old world patterns. Among these patterns, the most noteworthy was the town school of Puritan

New England, which offered free, equal, tax-supported education to all who desired it. After the Revolution it became clear in state after state that the new republican society would need a revised form of education if it were to survive and succeed. In response to the need, a number of heroic figures—Horace Mann in Massachusetts, Henry Barnard in Connecticut, John Pierce in Michigan, Samuel Lewis in Ohio, Caleb Mills in Indiana—worked tirelessly and selflessly in the cause of public schooling. By the Civil War, their effort had borne fruit, and public education in the New England tradition had been widely accepted in the North, the West, and parts of the South. With the defeat of the South in 1865, that acceptance soon became universal.

Carlton undertook his critique of these standard interpretations as a graduate student at the University of Wisconsin. Born and educated in Ohio, he had attended the Case Institute in Cleveland (B.S., 1895; M.E., 1899) and had then taught for a time at the Toledo University Manual Training School. With the idea of preparing himself as a professor of physics, he enrolled for summer work at the University of Michigan and at Cornell; but physics proved a passing fancy, and he attended the summer sessions of 1902 and 1903 at the University of Chicago to work in Economics. In 1904 a fellowship brought him to Wisconsin, a university that was well on its way to becoming a renowned center of social science.

President Charles Van Hise had just assumed office on a platform of applying the fruits of systematic research to the rational solution of social problems; and the School of Economics and Politics, under the energetic leadership of Richard T. Ely, was already producing a steady flow of relevant materials. Ely had literally created the field of labor economics, and with his young associate, Thomas Sewall Adams, was publishing a brilliant succession of books, pamphlets, and articles. William A. Scott was undertaking pioneering investigations into the problems of public finance; Paul Reinsch was pressing forward incisive inquiries into the politics of colonialism; and John R. Commons, who had recently come from New York, was initiating studies that would culminate in the *Documentary History of American Industrial Society* and the *History of Labour in the United States.*

Carlton apparently worked under Ely, taking eight courses under the master himself, four with Adams, four with Reinsch, two with Scott, and one with Commons. One can only guess at how he happened upon his dissertation topic, though it is probable that the initial suggestion came from Ely, who had dealt with education in *The Labor Movement in America* (1886), and who was beginning, with Commons, to assign topics in connection with the projected *Documentary History.* In any case, by 1905 Carlton was well launched on his study; in 1906 he completed his work for the doctorate and won a professorship at Albion College; and in 1908 the dissertation was published under the title *Economic Influences upon Educational Progress in the United States, 1820–1850.*

## Economic interests as a force in educational policy

Carlton's thesis was forthrightly presented, extensively documented, and strikingly original. In place of the "great man" interpretation that had cast Mann, Barnard, Pierce, Lewis, and Mills as the prime movers in the public-school movement, Carlton portrayed the educational revival between 1820 and 1850 as one phase of a larger social development, contending that (1) "the tax-supported school system evolved out of heterogeneity of population, improvement in methods of production, the specialization of industry, the division of labor, the growth of factories and the separation of homelife from industrial occupations;" (2) the public school system was "the resultant of the conflict of interests—economic, social, religious, and racial—within the different states;" and (3) "the cities and the working classes were chiefly instrumental in placing our schools upon a tax-supported basis."[23] With respect to public policy for his own time, Carlton drew a clear moral: social forces, not altruistic leaders, had been and would continue to be the decisive factors in American educational progress. "If generalization is warranted by the data before us," Carlton counseled, "the conclusion is warranted that, in modern times, the trend of educational advance is determined by economic evolution. On the one hand, the student of educational problems, who is striving to improve the work of the public schools, must study the trend of industrial and social evolution; and, on the other hand, the political economist and social scientist must consider the economic and social significance of uniform advance in educational and industrial evolution."

For all its boldness and originality, Carlton's monograph elicited surprisingly little comment when it first appeared; one searches the learned journals in vain for anything more than passing notice. But the monograph did exert profound influence on subsequent scholarship. In 1910, John Commons and Helen Sumner gave the monograph unqualified endorsement in the monumental *Documentary History of American Industrial Society*; and eight years later, this endorsement was repeated in the *History of Labour in the United States*, which quickly established itself as the standard work in its field. Carlton himself restated his theses in *Organized Labor in American History* (1920), and in numerous other of his works in labor history and economics.

More to the point of our report, Carlton deeply affected the thought of Ellwood P. Cubberley, a Stanford professor of Education whose *Public Education in the*

*United States* (1919; revised, 1934) was a most influential work. Indeed, Carlton's impact on Cubberley must be judged decisive, not only with respect to the crucial matter of periodization, but also with respect to the seven cele- brated "battles" for free public education that have long been associated with Cubberley's work. At the very least, Cubberley borrowed from Carlton the idea of an "align- ment of interests" for and against tax-supported education; and he followed Carlton in relating these interests and ar- guments to the social, political, and economic changes that marked American life in the first half of the nineteenth century. Mann, Barnard, and the others still parade through the pages of Cubberley's book, but there is no mistaking the dramatic difference between Cubberley's interpretation and those that had come before: educational policy-mak- ing was now portrayed as a political process—a series of conflicts or battles—that took place within the context of a larger social evolution. Men still acted, but they acted as the representatives of social, religious, and ethnic interests. And the outcome of the battles was clearly conditioned by the social realities of the time.

## Effects on the thinking of schoolmen

The interpretation proffered by Carlton and Cub- berley gave American schoolmen in the 1920's, 1930's, and 1940's a much more sophisticated view of how American educational policy had been made in the past and how it was being made in their own time. In place of heroes, they were directed to political and social processes as the crucial factors in educational change, a shift that doubtless pre- pared them more effectively for the realities of their situa- tion. And in place of small-town America, they were directed to the cities, and more particularly, to the aspiring workingmen within the cities, as the source of much that was characteristic and distinctive in the idea and practice of universal public education.

Yet granted this, the interpretation of Carlton and Cubberley also served to put blinders on the schoolmen of the generation between the two world wars. For one thing, Carlton's conceptualization of political interest groups was at many points vague and incomplete. He included among those supporting public schools a category called "citizens of the Republic," and among those opposing public schools, a category called "taxpayers;" both categories, of course, so imprecise as to be worthless. Furthermore, Carlton tended to accept the public statements of the various interest groups at face value, and failed to look beyond to the behavior of these groups in elections and in legislatures. Had he done so, he would have found that the workingmen were less than consistent in their support of public schooling, while businessmen, who are not mentioned at all in the alignment of interests, were often in the vanguard of the movement.

Even more important, perhaps, was the use to which Cubberley put Carlton's analysis in arguing that the great battles for public education had been won, and that from the 1880's on, the primary problem facing Americans was to improve and refine their school system. Nurtured on this interpretation, many schoolmen of the 1940's and 1950's were simply at a loss to understand the criticisms of public education that came to the fore during the postwar era. Equipped with an inadequate version of the political history of American education, mistaking a particular coalition of interests that had won a particular set of nineteenth-century battles for some fictitious permanent coalition that had won some sort of epochal conflict for all time, they found themselves unable to comprehend the criticisms directed against them, and unable to muster the political strength they needed to defend their programs. Partly as a result, they ended up impugning the motives of their critics instead of responding to their charges.

Finally, there was the implicit Darwinism of the Carlton and Cubberley interpretation, which asserted that "in modern times, the trend of educational advance is determined by economic evolution." Had both men taken their argument seriously—and to do so would have raised grave questions about the significance of the great "battles" they so dramatically portrayed—they would have considered not merely the uniqueness of the American educational experience, but also its basic similarity to that of other industrializing nations. Had they done that, they might have equipped educators of the 1950's to realize that the educational crises of that era were the result neither of a conspiracy nor of a failure, but rather of the relentless pressure of a developing technology on the social ingenuity of men.

One can muse over whether all this might have been different had the historiography of American education been affected by the considerable advances in more general historiography during the 1940's and after. But that is not the sort of question historians can fruitfully tackle. In any case, there is no denying Carlton's central contribution to American educational scholarship. Ultimately, what he did was to offer the model for a serious political and economic history of American education at a time when the standard texts were portraying the public school as the gift of Mann, Barnard, and a half-dozen heroic contemporaries. The fact that Carlton did not write that history in an enduring form in no way negates the value of his effort. One can repudiate his rather crude economic determinism and still be instructed by his insistence on the inseparability of education and politics. One can criticize his pro-labor bias and still be persuaded that self-interest is at least as significant as altruism in reform movements. And one can reject the naiveté of his political analysis and still agree that such analysis is indispensable to an understanding of the nature of public education. Indeed, it is interesting to note that a good deal of present-day historical study is based on leads originally suggested by Carlton. And though the results of this work will probably differ markedly from his—at least two recent authors have rejected the conflict model completely, arguing that the broad American consensus on education in the nineteenth century was more significant than the conflicts—its very existence is testimony to the continuing fruitfulness of the questions Carlton asked and the approaches he ventured.

### NOTES

1. Young, Michael D., *The Rise of the Meritocracy 1870-2033: An Essay on Education and Equality.* London: Thames and Hudson, 1958.
2. Buros, O. K. (ed.); the first *Mental Measurements Yearbook* was titled "Educational, Psychological, and Personality Tests of 1933 and 1934." (*Rutgers University Bulletin*, Vol. 9 1935, No. 11.)
3. Colvin, Stephen S., "Principles Underlying the Construction and Use of Intelligence Tests," in Whipple, G. M. (ed.), *Intelligence Tests and Their Use,* 21st Yearbook of the National Society for the Study of Education, Part I, Chapter 2; pp. 11-44. Bloomington, Ind.: Public School Publishing Co., 1922, p. 19.
4. *Manual of Freshman Class Profiles for Indiana Colleges.* Princeton, N.J.: Educational Testing Service, 1965.
5. Peirce, Charles Sanders, "Some Consequences of Four Incapacities," *Journal of Speculative Philosophy*, Vol. 2 (1868), pp. 140-157.
6. Yeldham, Florence A., *The Teaching of Arithmetic Through 400 Years, 1535-1935.* London: Harrap, 1936, p. 129.
7. *Ibid.,* p. 130.
8. Thorndike, Edward L., *The Psychology of Arithmetic.* New York: Macmillan, 1922, pp. v-vi.
9. *Ibid.,* p. 115.
10. Buckingham, B. R., and W. J. Osburn, *The Buckingham-Osburn Searchlight Arithmetics, Book One.* Boston: Ginn, 1927, pp. vii-viii.

11. *Ibid.*, p. v; Brown, Joseph C., and Albert C. Eldredge, *The Brown-Eldredge Arithmetics*, *Grade* 5. Chicago: Row, Peterson and Co., 1925, p. 20 (for examples).

12. Thorndike, *op. cit.*, pp. 146–149.

13. Byrnes, James C., Julia Richman, and John Roberts, *The Pupils' Arithmetic, Primary Book, Part One*. New York: Macmillan, 1912. The two "Primary Books," *Part One* and *Part Two*, in fact begin at a third-grade level at the very least. *Part One* is certainly more difficult than present grade 3 texts in the elementary-school mathematics curriculum.

14. Brown, Joseph, and Albert C. Eldredge, *The Brown-Eldredge Arithmetics, Grade Six*. Chicago: Row, Peterson, and Co., 1925, p. 45.

15. Thorndike, *op. cit.*, pp. 81–82.

16. *Ibid.*, pp. 92–93.

17. White, Charles E., *Number Lessons, A Book for Second and Third Year Pupils*. Boston: Heath, 1899, pp. 22, 148; Byrnes, Richman, and Roberts, *op. cit.*, *Part Two*, p. 20; *Part One*, p. 39.

18. Byrnes, Richman, and Roberts, *op. cit.*, *Part Two*, p. 36.

19. Brown and Eldredge, *op. cit.*, *Grade* 5, p. 94.

20. Thorndike, *op. cit.*, p. 146.

21. It is worth remarking that Thorndike also made a thorough empirical study of the psychology of algebra and carried out what is probably the first systematic empirical investigation of the actual content of elementary textbooks in algebra, the way in which problems are distributed, concepts reviewed, and drill organized. It has not been possible to review here the total contents of *The Psychology of Algebra* (New York: Macmillan, 1923) but it is probably fair to say that in spite of its many salutary remarks and practical suggestions it has had less impact on the teaching of algebra than has Thorndike's corresponding work in arithmetic.

22. Gorman, Frank H., "Some Facts Concerning Changes in the Content and Methods of Arithmetic." University of Missouri, 1931. See also Chapter II in Roy Edgar Adams, *A Study of the Comparative Value of Two Methods of Improving Problem Solving Ability in Arithmetic*. Philadelphia, 1930.

23. Carlton, Frank Tracy, "Economic Influences Upon Educational Progress in the U.S., 1820–1850," Ph.D. Thesis, University of Wisconsin, 1908. P. 135. Reprinted by Teachers College Press, New York, 1965.

**4**

# Conclusion-oriente
# inquiry

THE PRECEDING CHAPTERS make it clear that inquiry can have
good or bad consequences for educational practice, introducing fresh ideas or being extrapolated into irrational
excesses. The process by which the practicing educator
profits from the work of the inquirer needs to be made clear.
Only then will he hold the proper expectations for inquiry and make the proper demands upon the research
community. In this chapter we shall give primary attention to conclusion-oriented inquiry, and in Chapter
5 we shall discuss the operations of decision-oriented research.

The common and superficial conception of investigation and its relation to educational practice is something
like the following: At one end of a sequence are studies of
the nature of man and of society. These studies produce
"findings"—facts and general principles within the fundamental disciplines. The specialist in education then presumably studies those facts and translates them into educational
terms. He next carries out an educational experiment to test
whether the finding holds up in the educational setting.
If he gets positive results, a program of developmental

research is carried out in which teaching materials (or educational methods and systems) are devised, tested for effectiveness, revised, and finally recommended for general adoption. The operating educator then institutes the tested practice in his school. This account is not entirely false, and various examples of educational change appear to confirm it. Thus one might point to the psychologist's discovery that increasing the number of exposures of a stimulus-response combination greatly facilitates rote learning, which led to applied research showing that this generalization holds true for the child's learning to recognize words. This in turn led to developmental studies in which frequencies of words presented in children's primers were adjusted to maximize learning. As primers based on this principle captured the attention of committees adopting textbooks, publishers were forced to design their reading books in the same way (or to claim that they had); and so, for a time, the practice became standard.

This linear sequence, with each stage a rational consequence of more basic work, is a crude description and misleading to some degree. There is indeed a flow of ideas from laboratory to field. But there is also a reverse flow. The eddying current is fed by dozens of other sources, not all of them disciplined. A practical innovation may or may not apply an idea generated in pure research. Most fundamental knowledge, indeed, cannot be "applied"; it does not prescribe a suitable practice. It can only stimulate the investigator facing a practical problem to manipulate some new aspects of the school situation and to appraise effects he might hitherto not have considered. What is tried out in developmental and operational work springs largely from inspirations or hunches; those hunches may be suggested by basic studies but are not derived from them. Conclusion-oriented studies are significant for practice if, cumulatively, they help the decision-maker take the right things into account; they are most unlikely to give the decision-maker the blueprint for an effective procedure, in advance of decision-oriented research.

# *The prevailing view of education*

# *as the guide for practice*

A WIDELY HELD BELIEF SYSTEM underlies the normal practices of every institution. This prevailing view embraces the ends to be sought, the procedures that may be used, the costs it is reasonable to incur, and the degree of success that may be expected. The prevailing belief on a certain point may be disputable. As an illustration, consider whether it is appropriate for a teacher's superior to visit the classroom, unannounced, in order to gain an impression of the teacher's effectiveness. The answer has typically been no, whether the teacher is working in a first grade or a university. Perhaps this answer can be defended, but no one would complain about a general who appears at command headquarters on the battlefield, or a chief engineer who inspects a half-completed bridge. The prevailing view in those fields is different.

The schools of today are not much like those of the turn of the century. Different answers are being given to all the fundamental questions: Who shall be educated? What achievements are of most worth? How shall teachers and pupils work together? Through what governmental agencies, and from what tax base, shall the funds flow? These changes did not come in any sudden revolution; indeed, the "progressives" who tried to overturn the old order in the schools found their movement rejected, although ultimately their ideas, one by one, infiltrated the main body of conventional educational wisdom! [1]

There are nearly constant elements in the prevailing

view; there are slow but steady trends; and there are wild (but usually superficial) oscillations. As an example of the first, one might cite the long-standing acceptance of reading, writing, and arithmetic as "fundamentals" of elementary education. The steady trends are easily illustrated; for instance, the spread of college education at all economic levels. As for oscillations, we may recall many enthusiasms that have captured the attention of educators and perhaps appeared in the typical school for a time: Esperanto clubs, courses in career choice in the eighth grade, and activity programs in elementary social studies.

The prevailing view is not monolithic and it does not change all at once. The teacher of French has a conception of the school that overlaps only partly with that of the biology teacher or the basketball coach. Subcommunities, defined by geography or by specialization, have their own prevailing views; sometimes a subgroup stands opposed to a trend after all others have been converted. The prevailing view within a tightly knit community of specialists shifts before that of the discipline as a whole, and that of the discipline changes faster than the prevailing view in the larger society. It is precisely this anticipatory character of the scholar's reconceptualization that makes him useful as advisor to policy-makers, and as teacher of the next generation.

A strong central trend pervades the community view, however. It is a synthesis or compromise shaped by human nature, political institutions, and the writings of learned men. These forces have been playing upon each other for centuries, and in a stable society opinion reaches a fairly steady state. Events from time to time open the system of thought to radical change; the event may be a depression, an international crisis, the launching of a satellite, or a civil-rights revolution.

# Effect of conclusion-oriented inquiry

How does a conclusion-oriented study modify the prevailing view? Certainly not by a process of direct amendment: The great majority of conclusion-oriented studies pertinent to education speak to questions that do not enter directly into the prevailing view. They may describe taxing practices in postbellum Virginia or analyze whether six-year-old boys learn more quickly when a boy rather than a girl is the model in a filmed lesson. Given the conclusion on either of these specific problems, one could scarcely say whether it is consistent or inconsistent with the prevailing view. Even a study whose findings dramatically contradict the prevailing view will not prompt educators immediately to cast aside the established program. Consider a scientific report that pupils who attend school only every other day throughout the year reach normal levels of achievement.[2] Such a conclusion is too radical to assimilate at once, even on the best of evidence. It is not likely that school-board members or legislators attracted by the potential savings from an alternate-day schedule would insist on a serious confrontation of the question. For a finding to alter practice, it must resonate through a complex communication net, and change conceptions.

A conclusion-oriented study is not performed for the mass of educators; it is performed for the enlightenment of the investigator and the small community of specialists thinking about the same problem. The evidence for a particular hypothesis, or the accurate description of a particular phenomenon, is the harvest the investigator offers his specialist colleagues. His contribution to the prevailing view, which often is in the end a larger contribution than the direct finding, is a by-product that can rarely be planned or foreseen. As investigators discuss their results with colleagues, a restlessness emerges. Findings from different studies seem to conflict. Phenomena are noticed that cannot well be summarized in the available language. Similarities are observed among findings on what were previously considered to be distinct topics. As investigators puzzle over these irregularities, they find themselves assembling what they know in a new way. Some of the concepts so created will influence thought throughout the educational world. Some especially stimulating or clarifying concepts will influence even the views of the public, especially when the researchers come forth to argue their positions in public media.

## Indirect influences of specialized research

There are prevailing views at every level of generality. Pavlov and his colleagues studying salivation modified views the community of specialists held about that physiological process. A broader group of physiologists and psychologists attended to larger implications, and began to think of behavioral processes as controlled by conditioning and analyzable in stimulus-response units. Pavlov had used a strategy of stimulus substitution, for example, substituting a bell for a dish of meat. Soon others were substituting printed words for spoken words as a way of studying human responses. These studies were so far removed from Pavlov's physiological inquiries that they made use of none of his "findings," but his way of thinking had become a model for new and not closely related experiments and theoretical formulations. Pavlov's work, discussed among scientists along with the studies of physiological regulation by Cannon and Sherrington, encouraged investigators to think of man as a machine regulated by external and internal stimuli, which responds through connections built up by conditioning. This orientation led to psychological behaviorism and more recently to so-called cybernetic models of human thought. The biomechanical view favored analytic study of single processes of human action, and tended to discourage studies of "the whole person."

Not all thinkers moved into the Pavlovian camp. Freud's dramatic conception that behavior is swayed by unconscious impulse was equally influential in suggesting subject matter for a science of man. His view appealed to anthropologists, social psychologists, social workers, and early childhood educators who were dissatisfied with the biomechanical model.

Educational thought has been directly and indirectly affected by the Pavlovian, biochemical orientation. One salient example is the current work of the followers of B. F. Skinner, whose studies of animal conditioning are in the Pavlovian tradition. Skinner used conditioning techniques to train animals. In describing the important variables in that process, he arrived at concepts that guide his followers in designing programmed instruction and in treating juvenile aggressiveness. Concepts such as *reinforcement* and *extinction* are too complex to elaborate here; suffice it to say that they carry thinking well beyond the everyday terms *reward* and *forgetting*. These concepts are studied by the teacher in training, and are expected to guide him in the classroom. The Skinnerian concepts are not now truly a part of the community view of education, for they have not circulated very far beyond the psychologists and their students. As concepts flow out beyond the circle of specialists, they are given a looser, somewhat metaphoric application, much as when the Pavlovian studies of salivation gave currency to the metaphor of man-as-machine.

In arguing that research has its impact indirectly rather than directly, and that practical developments emerge from a prevailing view rather than from isolated findings, we are not constructing a special rationalization regarding the field of education. Progress in other fields bears a similar relation to basic investigation, as one may learn from the writings of Price, Schmookler, and Sherwin and Isenson.[3] To quote the last-named authors:

> However important science may be (in, specifically, advancing military technology), we suspect its primary impact may be brought to bear not so much through the recent, random scraps of new knowledge as it is through the organized, "packed-down," thoroughly understood and carefully taught *old* science. . . . What is the process by which science moves into technology and utilization? It is clearly not the simple, direct sequence taught by the folklore of science. . . . The most obvious way in which undirected (i.e., conclusion-oriented) science appears to enter into technology and utilization on a substantial scale seems to be in the compressed, highly organized form of a well-established, clearly expressed general theory, or in the evaluated, ordered knowledge of handbooks, textbooks, and university courses.

Studies on educational matters generally lead to somewhat indefinite views rather than to highly organized theories and tables of numerical constants, but otherwise the parallel is complete. Ideas are used not in isolation but as ingredients for a synthesized conception of the world.

## Studies of education per se

A strictly educational study has both direct products and by-products, and, again, the latter may ultimately be more influential. Thus the Physical Science Study Committee physics course has, as a product, influenced a fraction of the high-school classrooms in one subject. But by capturing the attention of writers addressing educators at all levels, the project became a source of ideology for curricula in many subjects.

The educational experiment may directly follow a laboratory experiment, testing whether the same phenomenon can be observed in the more complex setting and whether the same generalizations hold true. Pigeons in the laboratory were trained to discriminate one shape from another, pecking at a corresponding button and being rewarded with a grain of corn; these studies were forerunners of studies in which children are trained to discriminate one printed word from another, pressing a button and receiving a bit of candy or a token. All that is carried forward is a point of view—a set of working hypotheses—plus a few technical devices. It is possible that conditioning-with-material-rewards can be elaborated into a method for training the unmotivated or the retarded.

An educational study may change the way everyone thinks about learning and education. A conditioning study minimizes the role of explanation and understanding, of curiosity and interest, of interpersonal relations, and of the teacher as critic; it leads teachers toward techniques that elicit desirable, observable responses from the child that can be promptly reinforced. This defines education as a process by which an authority shapes the learner toward a predetermined ideal. But there are competing conceptions, some stemming from inquiries that share none of the implicit biases of the conditioning study. Thanks to plural sets of concepts, the prevailing view is much less radical than the view emerging from a single line of research.

Studies of educational processes originate from a desire to understand the processes more often than from the desire to apply a theoretical conception in a new context. The role of concepts is more to shape the attack and interpretation than to instigate the study in the first place. Studies of practice are likely to arise out of the concern of a professional student of education to understand an educational phenomenon. Thus, when professors training counselors feel dissatisfied with the prevailing conception of vocational choice as a single event taking place sometime during adolescence, they turn to long-term observations of the successive decisions that shape a career over two decades and more. One can scarcely say that they are "applying developmental psychology" even though it illuminates their work.

Conclusion-oriented studies often stem from practical activities. Some newer curricula in mathematics and science lead pupils to induce principles for themselves, rather than stating the rule and having pupils apply it. There has been a certain amount of systematic observation within these curriculum projects, directed primarily toward revising the lessons. This work, done under the pressures of getting new lessons out to the schools, has done little to test the assumptions underlying whatever hypothesis the plan is based on. An untested assumption like that favoring "learning by discovery" has been widely communicated by persons enthusiastic about the new lesson materials, and a person starting a new curriculum project is likely to be influenced by the proposition and try to use it in his work. The scholars concerned with education listen to such general statements made on the basis of practical experience and raise the questions their disciplines have trained them to raise, as exemplified in the psychologists' discussion of "discovery" reported by Shulman and Kieslar.[4] The philosopher will try to develop a clear characterization of what is to be meant by a "discovery" method, because otherwise the phrase becomes a slogan available to drum up enthusiasm for a dozen fundamentally different types of instruction. The psychologist will try to specify just what differences in behavior and attitude result when the same body of subject matter is taught inductively or didactically. The specialist in mathematics education will analyze the curriculum sequence to find the nodal points where the extra time required by the discovery approach is a good investment, for it is evident that the pupil cannot discover everything for himself. The conclusion-oriented workers, then, extract issues from observations of educational practice and formulate them more precisely.

Operational studies in school systems likewise stir up general inquiries about school processes. A city's survey of dropouts, for example, may show that they come disproportionately from certain ethnic or religious groups, after differences in economic level are taken into account. This information may be hard to utilize operationally, but it poses a question to the sociologist who can find out what influences in the home and community make these youngsters different from others with the same economic disadvantages. The understanding from his study may suggest general social changes that community leaders can promote.

There is considerable truth in von Neumann's suggestion that conclusion-oriented research has outcomes of greatest intellectual significance when it arises out of the real world and not purely out of the preoccupations of a discipline, a generation or two removed from the real world. Pure as mathematics is as a discipline, some of its giant strides were made in attempts to think more clearly about surveying, dice games, and the trajectories of cannonballs. As von Neumann said:

> As a mathematical discipline travels far from its empirical source, or still more, if it is a second and third generation only indirectly inspired by ideas coming from "reality," it is beset with very grave dangers. It becomes more and more purely aestheticizing, more and more purely *l'art pour l'art*. This need not be bad if the field is surrounded by correlated subjects, which still have closer empirical connections, or if the discipline is under the influence of men with an exceptionally well-developed taste. But there is a grave danger that the subject will develop along the line of least resistance, that the stream, so far from its source, will separate into a multitude of insignificant branches, and that the discipline will become a disorganized mass of details and

complexities. In other words, at a great distance from its empirical source, or after much "abstract" inbreeding, a mathematical subject is in danger of degeneration. At the inception the style is usually classical; when it shows signs of becoming baroque, then the danger signal is up.[5]

# The role of specialized disciplines

AS OUR HISTORICAL REVIEW showed, research in education has at times been identified exclusively with fact-finding and analysis of quantitative data. Although these types of studies, dominated by models and techniques from psychology, remain important, other types of inquiry can make contributions. In some disciplines the study of education is now quite active, and in others one can detect stirrings that, if encouraged, will become new sources of powerful ideas. It will be useful, therefore, to reflect briefly on the special contributions of some of these disciplines.

## Political science

Political science is becoming an empirical science like psychology and sociology, but with a different perspective and a different tradition. The roots of political science can be traced to the Greek philosophers, and education has always been one of its topics. Insofar as education is arranged by the state to prepare the individual for his place in it, the prevailing view of the relation between citizen and government, individual and society, will have a profound influence on what is expected of the school. The older works on this theme may be classed as political science or philosophy. Utopians, utilitarians, social-contract theorists, and communists—each group has joined theory of government with works defining the desired qualities of citizens and the type of school needed to produce them. The theme of "school and society," which Dewey took as the title of one of his most significant works, is inescapably a topic for the political scientist.

The postponement of the study of education as a political institution in this century perhaps is related to the early efforts of political science to break away from political philosophy, as David Easton [6] has suggested. The empirical political scientists turned their attention to the distribution of power within and between states, and only incidentally were concerned with how education helped one to attain power. Left to political philosophy was the question of fitting education to the current needs of the present social order, a question requiring examination of aims and values. James S. Coleman [7] of the Rockefeller Foundation points out also that the very decentralization of power in the American educational system probably made it a less attractive topic to political scientists than the study of national governmental structures. Today, however, the emphasis is on a study of the political process as a whole, and political scientists must examine how education directly and indirectly influences it. Empirical studies along this line began with the program of Charles E. Merriam and his colleagues in the 1920's (see *Studies in the Making of Citizens* [8]), but it has become a prominent concern of the whole profession only recently.

## Economics

Economic analysis has long had specialized uses in the social statistics of education and in guiding school tax policy. Recently, however, the economics of education has become a central topic in the discipline itself, because of the recognition that knowledge and trained men constitute capital resources. As Theodore Schultz puts it, "Educational activities are a multi-product industry." This leads the economist into manpower studies that classify the labor force, project future needs, and estimate the costs and bases of support required for training programs.

Modern economic analysis radically alters prevailing views. Thus the idea that the taxpayer shoulders the whole cost of education ("because a democracy requires free education") proves to be a myth. One of the largest cost items in both personal and national balance sheets proves to be the earnings that adolescents and young adults forego and the lack of production during the years they remain in school. These costs are less painful than tuition fees because they represent dollars that do *not* change hands; if they were more obvious, they might provide a powerful motive to use the student's time more economically and shorten the duration of his education.

Equally significant policy questions are raised by studies that try to estimate the return from education. To pick a few statements from Schultz' summary [9] of current economic findings: one-fifth of the economic growth of the United States in a recent thirty-year period can be credited to the additional education of the labor force. A dollar expended for elementary education appears to bring a return to the economy, through greater productivity, of $1.30. But, when one looks at effects on farming alone, it appears that a year of added education is likely to convince the farm youth that he should leave agriculture; this loss more than offsets the increase in productivity of the men who stay. One of the prime questions of domestic policy in every nation of the world is "How fast is the economy growing, and how can this growth be accelerated?" Economists are now telling us that dollars invested in education can produce rates of return that are staggeringly high compared to investments of other sorts.

The economist's work is relatively little known to the educator, both because of the technical complexity of the subject and because the economic findings shed light more on national policy than on local decisions. Consequently, economics is sparsely represented in the training of educational leaders, and rarely thought of in discussions of educational research.

## Other empirical sciences

There is no need for detailed discussion here of other empirically based disciplines such as sociology and anthropology, or such tool disciplines as statistics. The importance of these fields has long been recognized. Nor should our concentration on the social sciences imply that the physical and biological sciences can make no contributions. One can only speculate as to how their advances will be relevant.

## Humanistic scholarship

The philosopher, the historian, and others in the humanities are seeking to clarify and interpret concepts. The philosopher's *raison d'être* is logical and conceptual analysis, linguistic and methodological clarification, interpretation and criticism of fundamental ideas and assumptions. Such philosophical activities qualify practice in a variety of ways, but the paths of influence are complex, long-term, and indirect. A philosophical critique or interpretation, even though it has no direct translation into practical maxims or technological design, may deeply affect the intellectual conceptions and the methodological ideals of scientists, professional practitioners, and laymen, and thus may cause a shift in the prevailing view and all that is controlled by it.

Even where a philosophical interpretation simply exposes assumptions, it qualifies further practice by making these assumptions the focus of reflection and deliberation. When raised to a reflective level, assumptions may be transmitted verbally and, more important, may be examined critically. In the course of rational deliberation, they are refined, altered, possibly rejected. Philosophy, in sum, exercises a powerful but indirect influence on practice by facilitating critical scrutiny of basic ideas and assumptions. This influence is particularly great in education, which is concerned with the formulation and transmission of basic intellectual and moral conceptions.

The philosopher frequently functions as a translator, a bridge between research worker and operating educator. He may draw abstract or general concepts out of a work that by itself bears on only a limited question. Often he tries to relate the various special disciplines to one another, or to see their import for issues of practical decision. His training in the tradition of moral philosophy suggests to him the problem of relating scientific facts to moral consequences.

The scientific investigator committed to a school of thought might stay comfortably within its walls, coping with the problems it presents, rather than doing methodological and philosophical battle with another school. But schools such as radical behaviorism (contrasted with phenomenology or other mentalistic psychologies) do contribute conflicting ideas to the common stream of concepts and working assumptions; and unless these inconsistencies are to be resolved simply on the basis of popular appeal, someone has to pit the lines of thought against each other. This forcing of logical debate is a special function of philosophical study.

Analysis is so closely linked to criticism that the two are hard to distinguish. Analysis of assumptions and lines of argument expose inconsistencies, and in that sense they are criticisms. But analysis provides a broader stimulus too. Questions themselves may provide no new information, but a man who offers no findings whatever may nonetheless provoke thought. Socrates is a prime example of humanism in its proper functioning. Deep and systematic questioning stimulates reflection on assumptions and beliefs that have got a grip on practice unbeknownst to us. The "gadfly" is a constant necessity to the health of institutions, even if, as in the case of Socrates, he turns out no publications.

The questioning function suggests, more broadly, the effort to work out the consequences of a theory, a projected action, or an ideological position, and the ability to paint in vivid terms their import. Speculation regarding education requires the ability to imagine the consequences of current social trends in a realistic way. A good deal of social policy is based on this kind of imaginative forecasting in the face of uncertain information. Humanistic scholarship, for example, could reasonably include an attempt to foresee directions in which the ongoing technological revolution in education may lead. Scholars in the humanistic tradition can also provide a certain balance by attempting to understand social policies from the viewpoint of those affected by them.

# The logic of research on social

# processes

THOUGH OUR REPORT is intended to promote inquiry into educational matters, it is not our assumption that social benefits will automatically come from any increase in the amount of inquiry. Some conclusion-oriented studies are much more meaningful than others, and some questions more amenable to the available processes of inquiry. Investigation of social processes is difficult at best, and it is possible for a costly inquiry to yield nothing of value. An examination of difficulties in research on educational topics, and of criteria for recognizing valuable studies, is therefore in order.

## The indivisibility of social systems

The essential difficulty in research on social processes is the interaction of variables. An interaction is present whenever the effect of input A on a system depends on the levels of B, C, D, etc. A teaching method that works for one child will not necessarily work for another. Hold the children constant (hypothetically), and the procedure will work for some teachers and not others. Let a teacher bring to a new school a method that worked for him in a former school, and it may or may not work. Brownell and Moser,[10] studying instruction in subtraction, found that a meaningful presentation of subtraction was ineffective for children who had been taught until then by a rote method; the children simply had not learned to make use of meaningful connections, and the teacher's attempt to explain did no more than add noise to the system. Where interactions are present, it is rarely safe to generalize about one factor considered apart from the others.

Laws in the natural sciences often take the form: "Other things being equal, the relation of $X$ to $Y$ can be expressed by the following equation." Though the law may extend over several variables, the development of law is greatly facilitated by the fact that systems can be almost perfectly isolated. Results are essentially independent of the characteristics of the observer just because systematic methods of measurement rule out observer-process interactions. Results on volume are independent of the chemical makeup of a gas because a material is selected for the container that is chemically nonreactive. The social sciences have had very little success in isolating systems to which strong generalizations apply. To be sure, strong conclusions about subsystems and miniaturized situations are possible. Thus one can arrive at dependable generalizations about learning of animals, where one can bring genetic variation under control by using littermates and can standardize the life histories of the animals up to the start of the learning experiment. But even here interactions require that the generalizations be qualified; e.g., different breeds of dogs rank quite differently, depending on the task and type of training.[11] A simple theory of learning or social behavior evidently cannot have wide applicability, and a theory adequately complex to take into account a large system of interacting variables takes a long time to develop.

Failure to recognize the interactive nature of social processes, together with the myth that practices derive linearly from research findings, leads to an ill-considered emphasis on "information retrieval and dissemination." A favorite complaint of educational leaders is that it takes thirty years for an educational finding to be put into practice, and ingenious enterprises to accelerate this process are continually being set up. When interactions are weak, single findings have meaning in isolation and can be put into practice. If a disease is caused by a specific microorganism, for example, a specific diagnostic test and a specific therapy can be discovered. It makes excellent sense to use high-speed communication devices either to put the finding into every physician's hands or to relay information on the patient to a central agency where experts can evaluate it. But if the disorder is systemic, the diagnosing physician must bring a complete medical education to bear, and then must proceed experimentally by seeing how the patient responds to each of several plausible treatments. A great deal of internal medicine and of psychiatry is concerned with vague and hard-to-locate complaints that cannot be dispelled by "applying a finding." Educational problems are mostly of this sort.

The educator asks many simple questions for which it seems that research files should contain ready answers, but the simplicity is illusory. What can the files tell a principal, for example, who wants to install the best possible system for recording pupil marks and reporting to parents? The files can readily supply diverse examples of forms other schools have tried, and perhaps records of faults and virtues of each. What scheme of reporting fits a given school, however, depends on the aims of the school program, the skill of the teachers, the expectations of the parents, the requirements of schools to which pupils will transfer in due time— and most important, on how the records will be used to guide pupil learning. There are successful schemes in which elaborate anecdotes and test reports go into a cumulative file, ·but such an apparatus is excessive for many schools. At the opposite extreme, a simple scheme that records nothing but "satisfactory" and "unsatisfactory" makes few demands, but then the useful information about pupil progress is lost unless there is a stable teaching staff, intimately familiar with the pupils, who convey the other facts by word of mouth. No plan is right for every school. Conclusion-oriented studies can develop an understanding of marking systems and their functions, but not a universal recommendation. The principal must make an educated judgment in the light of local conditions and the general theory, unless he considers the question important enough to wait upon local research.

There are, to be sure, powerful effects that should be taken into account by all educators, e.g., it is well established that more meaningful instruction gets superior results. However, what will be meaningful depends on the pupil's background; and hence research cannot identify one "best" presentation of a lesson. Another type of strong effect is that produced by technological devices. These devices can be engineered so as to be highly effective in a great variety of educational situations. The fact that they can be standardized gives them much of their power. The engineering and application of these devices, however, is in the province of decision-oriented rather than conclusion-oriented research.


# Uncontrolled variation in social research

When one's research strategy is to seek simple theory by holding some variables constant, one must rely to a large extent on laboratory studies. In a controlled experiment on human subjects one can standardize instructional procedures and some other variables, but one cannot standardize the past history and previous learning of subjects, or the important attitudinal relations between learner and teacher. An educational experiment, even an unusually adequate one, therefore observes a system in which many important factors are beyond control. If their significance is recognized, one can only record them so as to take them into account in interpretation.

Questions about educational systems—about organization of the school staff, tax policy, or the long-term effects on the community of radical changes in the school program—cannot be controlled to hold variables constant. At best, one can reorganize a few school systems and compare their subsequent histories with those of other systems that remain unchanged. But the schools develop within a larger social system that is continually changing; there will be wars, economic developments, new political conditions, and changes in the job market, the nature of the family, and the motivations and attitudes of pupils, educators, and the public. For example, even if findings of a clear difference between two structures for student government in colleges had been established in the 1930's or 1950's, it is most unlikely that the same difference would hold up in a comparison of colleges populated by today's articulate and socially concerned youth.

School populations under study are not likely to be truly comparable. The schools whose administrators, teachers, and communities are quick to accept a new course of study or a new system of organization probably are atypical with respect to financial resources, quality of staff, home backgrounds of pupils, educational philosophy, and quality of the previous educational program. No statistical matching of communities can truly correct for such differences. Volunteering always introduces bias. Only in limited, short-term experiments have investigators been able to assign persons at random to receive different treatments. There is no practical possibility of assigning whole school systems at random to one or another experimental condition; educational change on a large scale must be voluntary.

The very novelty of the experiment is likely to affect the data. There is a certain excitement in being part of something new. The presence of observers and special tests stimulates teachers and pupils. The innovation brings with it extra teacher training. Consequently almost any educational innovation tends to be more effective than whatever procedures were previously carried on on a more routine basis, and even when the experimental data favor the innovation one cannot be sure that it is soundly conceived.

Loyalty to the novel procedure is likely to warp participants' reports on effectiveness. Elaborate controls are instituted to guard against biases in experiments on drugs. Patients are randomly assigned, one to receive unlabeled doses of the new drug while the next receives the drug that is currently a standard treatment or a medically neutral placebo, equally unidentifiable. Neither the patient, the physician who attends, nor the observer on the ward can bias the data. Educational procedures, however, cannot be disguised so that one looks just like another. The pioneers who are testing a procedure may, by their very enthusiasm, become more effective, or they may think that they have. These so-called Hawthorne effects will fade out when the experimental treatment becomes a standard school practice.[12]

CAPITALIZING ON INTERACTIONS The fact that social science cannot readily produce truly general laws or specific remedies is no reason for abandoning inquiry. Interactions, if understood, may be capitalized upon. Skill and temperament interact with task requirements; how well a person does depends on how well the situation matches his traits. This fact allows us to work out a system of vocational choice that affords high opportunities to pupils with different talents. If aptitude requirements were the same for all kinds and conditions of work, every profession would be trying to siphon off the same few men, and the educational system would be asked to cut all its graduates to the same pattern. Similarly, if individuals did not respond differently to various methods of instruction, we would have to relegate some persons permanently to a category of slow learners. Knowing that interactions are present, we can attempt to design distinctive instructional procedures for pupils of different types. Likewise, though it complicates matters to admit that there is no one best formula for getting a school staff to work effectively, the administrator can hope to understand the interactions well enough to fit a leadership plan to his own situation.

Any plan to capitalize on interactions requires effective diagnosis of the system and its elements. One cannot leave to casual intuition the decision that a particular student will learn better if he is allowed to work on materials of his own choosing, or that a particular teacher will work to better advantage with handicapped children, or that a particular objective in adult education is better achieved through neighborhood meetings than through a television series. There are two mutually supporting ways to bring such decisions under control. One is the pursuit of studies in a variety of comparable educational situations or laboratory prototypes of them. Such a research program isolates interacting variables a few at a time; it produces an increasingly valid explanation of the way the forces interact and condition each other; and it suggests what observations are most helpful in categorizing a new situation (person, etc.) so as to decide what response to expect from each possible treatment. Alternatively, one may narrow investigation to a developmental study of a particular system or product to determine what works best in a certain situation—for example, to try out the neighborhood-meeting and television approaches to a single topic in a particular community. The developmental study makes no pretense to generality. The conclusion-oriented study seeks understanding that can guide adaptation as new situations arise, but the guidance is necessarily loose. As we have said, the two methods support each other. The specific study in a single community on a single topic provides data for conceptualization and theory development; and the concepts and conclusions that have emerged suggest to the local innovator what methods he might best try and what data he should collect to reach his verdict.

# Recent progress in research methods

ALTHOUGH THE DIFFICULTIES inherent in the study of social processes will always make systematic inquiry arduous, there has been considerable progress in methodology. The very recognition that simple generalizations are likely to be false is a step forward, because it leads to better questions and investigations.

The work in methodology is facilitated by the emergence of statistical and data-processing systems than can cope with many variables at once. We can thus pose considerably deeper questions than were envisioned a generation ago, when the standard design consisted of one experimental and one matched control group, with a single post-test taken as adequate evidence on the effect of the experimental variable. Today an experiment is likely to vary several aspects of the treatment, to apply the treatment to pupil groups that differ in known ways, and to measure several distinct effects of the treatment, including delayed effects. Such complex designs are far more readily carried out in a laboratory than under school conditions.

Diversified measurement procedures are now available; these cover not only the obviously relevant abilities but also the attitudes and personal styles of pupil and teacher. Although personality and attitude measures have weaknesses that seriously limit their use for making decisions about individuals, they frequently add an important dimension to research conclusions. Methods for studying social systems have likewise improved.

## The computer opens a research opportunity

By producing data radically different in precision and complexity, the computer may open the way to an advance in educational research similar to that which Galileo's telescope opened for astronomy. The computer has many implications for education. Here we confine attention to the possibility that computerized instructional research may remove the placebo effects, volunteer biases, and other distortions that have restricted the meaningfulness of educational experiments. It has already been demonstrated that instruction in some school subjects can be presented effectively through regularly scheduled lessons governed by a computer program. The child goes to the computer room on schedule, is started on a lesson chosen on the basis of his previous performances, and proceeds through a series of explanations, tasks to perform, special explanatory loops when he makes an error, and so on. The computer records each response he makes, so that extraordinarily elaborate data are available for evaluating his progress or judging where the lesson sequence needs revision. Here we are not concerned with the merit or the economic feasibility of regular instruction by computer. Our concern is with the computer as a new type of laboratory.

A Hawthorne effect no doubt operates in computer instruction, but the effect probably operates in all lessons presented by computer, and thus would not interfere with objective comparison of lesson sequences or teaching strategies within the computer mode. Because instruction is individualized, two pupils working side by side can be given entirely different series of lessons. Consequently, a computer system that is providing reading lessons to 100 pupils every day may for the sake of comparison use four or five different methods, each with a different sample of the pupils. Obviously, one would insist that each lesson series be educationally valuable, but in our present state of ignorance there are many approaches that *a priori* seem quite reasonable. Even if one of the treatments proves much superior during the first year and becomes the basis for instruction thereafter, there are dozens of reasonable variations to consider within that broad plan. Hence there is always room for further useful experimentation.

Let us list some advantages of this type of experimentation. In the first place, the instruction is strictly controlled and strictly reproducible, which is not the case when lessons are presented by teachers. In the second place, variation associated with teacher personality and rapport is set aside. (To be sure, what the teacher does during the pupil's hours in the classroom affects his response to the computer instruction, but this effect should not be stronger for one treatment than another.) Third, the pupil is unaware that he is the subject of an experiment (once the computer itself is accepted as a standing fixture of his school). The teacher need not know the details of the lesson plans that constitute the experimental variable, and need not know which child is in which group. Hence the data are fully objective. Fourth, the data can be extensive and complex. In the traditional experiment, data are limited by the unwillingness of teachers to give up class time for thorough measurement of effects. In the computer, every lesson is itself a measuring opportunity, and novel tests can be presented to the pupil as part of regular lessons, so that the anxiety often associated with a test need not occur. Fifth, the investigator is not limited by the readiness of teachers to use a new procedure. Although any experimental lesson sequence must be responsibly chosen, with due regard for its probable effects and its relation to the pupil's regular classroom work, there is no need to convince each teacher of its value or to train the teacher in its use. Consequently, experiments can be set up far more rapidly, and can be chosen without regard to such scientifically irrelevant factors as the teacher's feeling that he is too busy to participate. Because the experiment is simply a controlled variation in the pupil's regular program, it does not require any special time allocations. Sixth, the experiment can be carried out for a long period. Whereas previous experiments in education have been of very short duration or have specified the alternative procedures only in very broad terms, the computer permits a highly controlled procedure to be followed through a year and perhaps longer.

Research by computer will not be easy nor will it lead to sweeping conclusions in short order. Preparation of instructional materials for experimental purposes is laborious; innumerable bits of material have to be designed and fitted together into a complete lesson sequence. This alone makes experimentation by computer costly. An exploratory period will be necessary before the strategy of using the computer as a research tool is reasonably clear. For example, at present we cannot say whether a single year-long experiment is as reasonable an investment of energy as a series of two-week experiments. Many important questions about instruction, notably those having to do with pupil-teacher interaction and the development of the pupil's creative potential, must be studied by other means. Despite all these limitations, it appears safe to predict that the advent of the computer will raise research on instruction to an entirely new level of sophistication and dependability.

# What conclusion-oriented studies

# are most valuable?

IT IS SOCIALLY necessary to direct research funds where they will be most productive, to encourage scholars to investigate matters likely to have greatest significance, and to organize institutions to facilitate such programs. It is not easy to make general statements that can guide the choice of research problems, because an approach that is highly effective in one discipline or in attacking one problem may be much less effective for another. Moreover, investigators have different styles, and the investigation that permits one man to develop his ideas may prove not at all enlightening to another even though their topical interests are similar. The general comments we offer must be read with these reservations in mind.

Alvin M. Weinberg,[13] director of the Oak Ridge Natural Laboratory, has discussed at some length the difficulty of choosing between lines of research activity. He distinguishes between internal criteria, having to do with the quality of the investigation as judged from within the discipline, and external criteria, having to do with the significance of the inquiry for mankind or the nation.

## External criteria for resource allocation

Our whole argument as to the potential of research for educational improvement, and our concern for making use of the several pertinent disciplines, indicate a need for wise resource allocation. To recommend priorities or proportionate allocations among disciplines or problems would be out of place.

THE IMPORTANCE OF DIVERSIFIED RISKS  Any attempt to set priorities among research problems has an inherent danger. A listing short enough to have directing power is likely to have a detrimental effect by discouraging attention to topics left off the list. There is no aspect of education that could not conceivably profit from research attention. The list of topics might very well be too conservative; consensus does not launch bold ventures.

The investigator takes a risk when he commits himself to pioneer a new area. His career will advance rapidly if he reaches an exciting conclusion and will languish if he does sound work but does not stumble upon a new idea. Not every intellectual exploration produces a revolutionary idea, and some yield no ideas at all. Risk itself is a mark of vitality in research.

The person allocating research resources must also take risks. It is wrong for him to attempt to pick a winner with every judgment; indeed, if every allocation turns out "well," the program as a whole is insufficiently adventurous. The only sound position is one that conceives allocation as the building of a portfolio. Distribution of new funds calls for a review of the whole present portfolio, and of the opportunities for investment at a given moment. All too often, a topic is given high priority by some influential committee, and then left unreviewed at the top of the list even after all reasonably competent research on the subject has the support it needs. We would criticize a portfolio most severely for an imbalance that fosters luxuriant development along certain lines and neglects others. Diversification, however, must not scatter resources so widely that no activity can build up momentum. If resources of an agency are meagre, they had better be spent all on one program of study. If small agencies do not flock in the same direction, their portfolio taken together will embody the desired risk.

A brief extract from testimony given by representatives of the highly successful research program of the National Institutes of Health before the House Committee on Appropriations gives some hint of the readiness-to-fail needed in education. The contrast with programs in preschool education is marked; educators tend to go into action on a massive scale before testing their working assumptions and discovering their limitations. Dr. Kenneth Endicott of the National Cancer Institute had just described the current status of work in chemotherapy, including certain difficulties.

> *Senator Hill:* I judge from what you said the chemotherapy program has not quite come up to what we had hoped it would; is that right?
>
> *Dr. Endicott:* Well, of course, I have been so close to that program, I am prejudiced, but I think really in view of the magnitude of the job . . . the program has gone exceptionally well. It is, I think, clearly succeeding and the objective was trying to develop drug cures and we are getting them.
>
> Now, to be sure, we are not getting them yet in the most common forms of cancer. . . .
>
> I think we need no longer speculate as to whether it is possible to cure human cancer by drugs. I personally feel that that is not subject to debate any more.

At this point the then Director of the Institutes, Dr. James Shannon, added a statement that might well summarize a whole philosophy of research management:

> I would like to recall how matters stood at the beginning of the program. When the question was asked, "Is it indeed possible to cure cancer by chemical substances," the answer at the time was "One does not know."

You may recall, Senator Hill, that on a number of occasions over the past 10 years I have pointed out that to answer that question would require a very extensive, very expensive exploratory effort—not a development effort but a direct research effort—and that we should be willing to spend substantial sums. . . . [If] it were shown that one cannot cure cancer by chemical agents, the program would, in retrospect, still have been worthwhile in order to exclude this as an approach.

Fortunately now . . . we have the positive answer . . . that, indeed, you can cure a variety of cancers with chemical substances. The effort has been highly successful in that it has answered the question that was posed.

Now you may think, sir, that a program that costs some [$30 or $40 million] is a very expensive program. Indeed it is. But in proportion of the loss of human life, the disruption of the family. . . . What this program has done is to demonstrate . . . that cancer is a number of diseases rather than a single disease and that these will have to be attacked one by one. Hopefully, out of this will emerge generalizations that can be transferred from one form of cancer to others, but it requires continuous surveillance and continuous reorganization of the programs.[14]

RELEVANCE The scholar advises that inquiry should be free, because no one can predict just where useful ideas will turn up. This advice by itself is a counsel of anarchy. The mission-oriented agency (and any governmental agency or university department spending funds appropriated for educational research is mission-oriented) has the clear duty to make judgments as to relevance. Concern for relevance is not inconsistent with freedom of inquiry.

But the relevance of conclusion-oriented research is not to be determined by asking what product it will generate or what specific educational decision it will bear upon. Neither the conclusion-oriented social scientist nor the philosopher can foresee the new ideas and challenges to the prevailing view that will be his largest practical contribution. Even after Freud achieved success in treating hysterical symptoms, who could have foreseen that the concept of "repression" would revolutionize Western thinking about morals and discipline?

The critical test is not *assured* relevance to education but *potential* relevance.[15] Broadly educated reviewers, some of them practical men and some of them scholars from disciplines other than the investigator's, can comprehend his description of the territory he proposes to explore and the intellectual context into which it fits. Hence they can judge whether there is a good chance of results interesting to those who face educational problems directly. The odds will almost never be favorable to a great intellectual breakthrough in any one study; that is what we mean by *risk*. But some undertakings are more appealing than others, by two tests: Would a new finding on the topic challenge presently held conceptions of the educational process? Is the state of the art such that the topic can be soundly investigated?

## Internal criteria of merit

RIGOR   Certainly studies conforming to the canons of disciplined inquiry are to be encouraged more than work that ignores them. The techniques and standards of a discipline are guards against self-delusion, bias, and conformity to views that happen to be popular. They require objectivity and reproducibility in the development and presentation of conclusions. This means that an observer or experimenter will state in detail what he did with respect to treatment, collection of data, and analysis. The report cannot usually be complete enough to allow a reader to repeat the experiment for himself, but it should be definite enough to communicate clearly; and supplementary documents should be available that would permit literal reproduction of the experiment or a repetition of the observations in similar situations.

Self-criticism enters at the outset, with a consideration of possible counterhypotheses, and collection of data that will at the end of the study give a basis for choosing between possible interpretations. Often the techniques of data collection need to be checked, for example, by employing two or more raters in order to assess the adequacy of the observations. The inferences made from the data will be checked by controlled statistical analysis or, if the study is nonstatistical, by ultimately having independent analyses made by different persons. Finally, the conclusions will be carefully qualified to make clear to what extent they are reports of what was directly observed and to what extent they are extrapolations and speculations. Similar self-criticism and examination of alternative explanations are expected in historical and philosophical studies. Such a study will begin with available records and impressions rather than with observations specially made, but the trustworthiness of these sources will be taken into account and the reasoning that leads from starting point to conclusion will be fully articulated and thereby opened to refutation.

Not all that has passed for educational research has been disciplined to this degree. Investigators rarely control the instructional methods or administrative procedures about which conclusions are drawn sufficiently for the findings to be reproduced by others. Investigators not infrequently frame studies to advance evidence favorable to a conclusion or innovation in which the investigator believes, rather than testing the proposal against reasonable alternatives. The final report is sometimes little more than an essay expressing beliefs held before the study began, embellished rather than supported by the study itself. Even the paraphernalia of statistical analysis may be used to support preconceptions. For example, a writer may emphasize that some experimental procedure produced a "statistically significant" difference and thereby confirmed his working hypothesis, whereas another writer who doubts the hypothesis could as easily stress the small magnitude of the difference and question whether the hypothesis has any important explanatory power.

That educational research is inadequate in quality seems somewhat less discreditable when we encounter the statement by Weinberg that applied research even in atomic physics and engineering has less than it should of the "ruthless interaction and self-criticism" that is characteristic of purer work. Weinberg suggests the inclusion, within any laboratory undertaking applied studies on a large scale, of a group doing "pure" research, on the ground that such investigators will "transfer their standards of excellence both to colleagues working in applied programs and to management."

ENDURING COMMITMENT  The superior research enterprise is persistent. Fresh conceptualizations are integrative in nature, and are fed by investigations that probe into a phenomenon from different angles and in different settings. A single study may assuage curiosity about a tiny question to such a degree that no one is ever again curious to make the same inquiry; but if a study of modest cost fails to be repeated in the course of subsequent investigations of the same general topic, it is likely that the study had little intellectual value in the first place. The repetitions in new settings determine how the effect varies when conditions are altered, and so help to explain the effect.

As an investigator accumulates experience on a topic, his studies take on more meaning for him than they do simply as individual research reports. Too often, the mechanisms of research support imply that the research community is a factory turning out neatly boxed studies, and that if a dozen experiments were set up simultaneously in a dozen laboratories they would make, more promptly, the contribution that the same dozen studies will when performed in succession by a single research team. This is far from the case, since the investigator intimately familiar with the series as a whole sees the problem in an ever-changing light, so much so that it is difficult to conceive of a true research program in which a series of a dozen studies could be laid out and followed as initially planned. The series would only be well underway when the incoming results would begin to arouse curiosity about new dimensions of the problem, to suggest counterinterpretations to be built into the new design, or to identify a methodological barrier to be cleared away before the main inquiries proceed.

Although much can be said about the design and analysis of individual experiments, almost nothing can be said in a general way about the conduct of a research *program*. How thoughts grow, how new questions come to the fore, how an investigator comes to take a new view of his subject and to develop by-product conceptualizations—these can be exemplified from the history of science, but they cannot be reduced to prescriptions. As a consequence, many students get the impression during their research training that the whole of research is carrying out single studies.[16] The management system that makes research grants most readily available for specific studies spelled out in advance, and that weighs the achievements of a scholar according to the number of titles he turns out, encourages this innocent view. Educational research workers often have had no scientific training as undergraduates; they first come to grips with the research process during their graduate work. The person entering the educational field hears so much conversation on current proposals and slogans that he is unlikely to see today's views as the outcome of a long and not entirely straightforward struggle for understanding.

In the natural sciences the observations of a generation or a century past are honored in theories and often are explicitly described in textbooks. The older work is a part of current knowledge. This is much less the case in social science, and not at all true in education. Thorndike's study of mental discipline and a few other historic studies receive honorable mention in current sources, but most reviews on an educational topic stress the past decade and ignore whatever evidence was previously laid down. Educational thinking seems to move by spasms of action and reaction. A writer brandishes recent studies to repel last year's view; relevant work done a generation ago is ignored. Perhaps this disregard of the past explains the shortage of perspective and of cumulative effort in educational research.

We would hope to find a steadily increasing complexity in the papers that emerge from a particular scientist's program. His first papers in a field are likely to be purely descriptive or purely empirical; his later ones, to show a greater degree of deduction and inference. There will also be induction: his statements will begin to bear on matters well outside the territory he has been examining intensively. Most leading contributors in the empirical disciplines and in history remain actively in contact with primary data; but as their experience advances they do more integrative thinking, and use findings of junior associates rather than confining attention to their own data.

A programmatic enterprise requires a substantial commitment on the part of the investigator, but it is more economical from the social viewpoint than the hit-and-miss approach in which every study stands by itself. The very fact that early returns could cause the programmatic investigator to curtail his planned program allows for economy. If the studies were carried on simultaneously, they would all be completed before the inadequacy of the plan could be discovered; and, making their separate way into the literature, it is possible that they would not suggest the same searching reconsideration.

This might seem to argue that all research enterprises should be massive, long-term affairs, but scattered studies also have important roles to play. One is self-discovery. In selecting a line of research, it is important that the investigator know himself. If some types of studies stimulate him more than others, he should select a problem in which he can exploit those idiosyncracies of interest or thought process. He cannot know what these may be except through exploratory work in which he attempts a variety of styles of research and deals with a variety of topics. It is sad to see a young man emerge from graduate school and embark on a lengthy program of research that is only an extension of the research on which his mentor made his reputation a decade before. We would encourage a certain dilettantism in the young investigator that would rarely be appropriate in an older man. Unless he makes self-testing forays into a number of research areas, he may make a premature commitment and invest his best years in studies that, though sound, yield little in the way of new conceptualizations. The older man too must now and then take a fling in a new direction, if he is not to ossify.

The second reason for letting a research program grow out of explorations is that commitment and diligence alone will not necessarily solve a problem. At any given time there are some problems "ready for solution," whereas others are not ready to yield to the most determined attack.

One cannot simply pick a highly important social problem and hammer his way through it. He has to find a point where he can gain leverage with the tools and concepts he presently possesses. To know if such a possibility exists, he must explore. In the course of these exploratory studies his hunch that a lengthy research program would be profitable becomes stronger and stronger, or he decides that his approach is unlikely to get beneath the surface. It is likely that the young man, or the older man embarking on a new line of work, will have several disappointments for every hunch that leads to a successful program. His first investigations may be characterized as scattered and non-persistent; yet it would be a serious mistake to concentrate stubbornly on the problem that first came to mind.

THOROUGHNESS   In general, conclusion-oriented research will make the greatest contribution when it aims at relatively broad, enduring understanding, not confining itself to descriptive questions of the present moment. This is not to exalt "pure" sciences above studies of educational matters. Instruction in reading will have continuing importance; and any study, for example, that helps to explain why some children like to read and some do not is worthwhile. A thorough mapping of interest into demographic segments of the population, however, is of limited value. Knowledge about factors in the home and community that promote interest may well have lasting significance, but a tabulation of differences between ethnic groups would soon be out of date, as social conditions change. Cataloging of children's reading interests was once a popular form of research. The catalog contributes to a cumulative understanding of the child if one digs deep enough to learn how these interests were acquired, but sheer frequency tabulations explain nothing. They do not even tell the writer of children's stories what to write about, because a skillful writer can make almost any topic appealing.

An educational matter can be studied profoundly or superficially. It is one thing to compare outcomes in the classrooms of male and female teachers, very likely finding significant differences, and perhaps recommending policy on the basis of them. But the sex of the teacher interacts with dozens of other variables. A more penetrating study would find out what teachers of both sexes do in the classroom. It would, we suspect, find that male and female teachers who work similarly with pupils obtain results similar in most respects, but that some styles of teaching are more common to one sex than the other. This would force the inquiry back onto recruitment and training to find out why the two sexes tend to differ in teaching style. Other lines of work would try to locate the specific functions that one sex can perform better than the other. This would suggest ways to allocate responsibilities within the school staff. Descriptive studies of present institutions and events are of limited use, we suggest, unless embedded in a systematic attempt to explain similar phenomena at other times and places. The very fact that a conceptual clarification comes slowly argues for stating questions so as to transcend current situations, except in a decision-oriented context.

COMPETENCE OF PERSONNEL   Everyone is aware of the ability of the investigator as a criterion for allocation, but Weinberg draws attention to the equal importance of having excellent research managers when funds are placed at the disposal of large laboratories, projects, and federal programs. Large conclusion-oriented enterprises are new to the educational scene, and there is as yet much to be learned about how to organize them.

No matter how able the persons managing educational research enterprises, the very newness of these operations means that managerial experience in this field is extremely limited. Thus impetuous proliferation of programs requiring managerial excellence should be avoided.

Good management implies appropriateness of size, but the size of a research enterprise is often dictated by the amounts of money available. Increasingly, guidelines written in Washington are announcing that package proposals costing about a certain amount per year will be entertained. These guidelines are not dictated by a wish for economy; they are often dictated by the difficulty of distributing money in modest amounts and by the political necessity of making impressively large allocations to various topical and geographical areas.

Size need not be bad in itself. Some types of research

enterprise, such as a computer-instruction laboratory or an integrated experimental school, require a large capital outlay before research can begin. As the mammoth enterprise needs to be staffed with several layers of excellent investigators, not just with one big name at the top, the test of quality of personnel is a more severe one for the large enterprise.

The significance of an enterprise lies in its freshness of thinking rather than in the volume of facts it collects or the number of preplanned experiments it runs. Size may dilute quality, if only by elevating the ablest thinker to so high a supervisory level that he is far removed from primary data. Size also endangers quality by introducing a subtle need to report "success" to justify having spent a lot of money. We have already quoted approvingly the emphasis of the cancer-chemotherapy program of the National Institutes of Health, which is willing to spend large sums to be sure of what does *not* work; this attitude is not possible when, as in much educational research, the funding agency requires dissemination of results to start almost the day a laboratory opens its doors.

The external criteria for research continually highlight problems that cry out for solution, and mission-oriented agencies are charged with attracting investigators into those fields. This is as it should be; but an offsetting internal criterion is that the investigator should investigate the problems he considers most worthwhile and for which his talents are best suited. If the need to support his graduate students and to help his university balance its overextended budget, or the pressure arising from the current assumption that any really good man will have a grant, leads him to work on a problem where he cannot make his best contribution, both he and the community will suffer. The seductiveness of money is an old story in the physical and medical sciences, and they have built up some defenses. The social scientist and the educator, who have only recently been able to taste the fruit of the money tree, must be especially wary of allowing economic considerations to impair a research program.

NOTES

1. Cremin, Lawrence A., *The Transformation of the School.* New York: Knopf, 1961, esp. pp. 328ff.
2. Something like this is reported in a study recently conducted in farthest Lapland.
3. Price, Derek de Solla, "Is Technology Historically Independent of Science? A Study in Statistical Historiography," *Technology and Culture*, Vol. 6 (1965), pp. 553–568; Schmookler, J., *Invention and Economic Growth.* Cambridge, Mass.: Harvard University Press, 1966; Sherwin, C. W., and R. S. Isenson, "Project Hindsight," *Science*, Vol. 156 (1967), pp. 1576–1577.
4. Shulman, L. S., and E. R. Keislar (eds.), *Learning by Discovery: A Critical Appraisal.* Chicago: Rand McNally, 1966.
5. von Neumann, John, "The Mathematician," Heywood, R. B. (ed.), *The Works of the Mind.* Chicago: University of Chicago Press, 1947, p. 196.
6. Easton, David, "The Function of Formal Education in a Political System," *School Review*, Vol. 65 (September 1957), pp. 304–316.
7. Coleman, James S. (ed.), *Education and Political Development.* Princeton, N.J.: Princeton University Press, 1965, pp. 11ff.
8. Merriam, C. E. (ed.), *Studies in the Making of Citizens.* Chicago: University of Chicago Press, 1929–1933.
9. Schultz, Theodore W., "Some Recent Work on the Economics of Education," *Investment in Capital Series*, Paper No. 65:11. Chicago: The University of Chicago, 1965.
10. Brownell, W. A., and H. E. Moser, "Meaningful *versus* Mechanical Learning: A Study in Grade III Subtraction," *Duke University Research Studies in Education*, No. 8, 1949.
11. Scott, J. P., "New Directions in the Genetic Study of Personality and Intelligence," *Eugenical News*, Vol. 39 (1953), pp. 97–101; Friedman, D. G., "Constitutional and Environmental Transactions in Rearing of Four Breeds of Dogs," *Science*, Vol. 127 (1958), pp. 585–586.

12. Cook, Desmond, *The Impact of the Hawthorne Effect in Experimental Designs in Educational Research.* Technical Report. Columbus, Ohio: Ohio State University, 1967; Scriven, Michael, "The Methodology of Evaluation," in Tyler, Ralph, and others, *Perspectives of Curriculum Evaluation.* Chicago: Rand McNally, 1967, pp. 40ff.

13. Weinberg, Alvin M., *Reflections on Big Science.* Cambridge: Massachusetts Institute of Technology, 1967, pp. 55–100.

14. Hearings, House Committee on Appropriations. Washington, D.C.: Government Printing Office, 1966, pp. 1079–1081.

15. Merton, Robert B., "Basic Research and Potentials of Relevance," *The American Behavioral Scientist,* Vol. 6 (1963), pp. 86–90.

16. Taylor, Donald W. (chairman), "Education for Research in Psychology," *American Psychologist,* Vol. 14, 1959, pp. 167–179.

5

# Decision-oriented studies

WE TURN NOW to investigations carried out to serve a specific practical end, to guide more or less immediate decisions. The excellence of the product being developed or of the institution whose operations are studied should be the ruling concern of the decision-oriented inquiry. We have defined products to include instructional materials, systems for school management, designs for school buildings, and so on. Designing, pilot testing, and tooling up for production constitute a development enterprise, one part of which should be systematic inquiry. Development is distinguished from operational activity by the fact that it terminates when the product goes into production. A design is developed to the point of usefulness, and put into the schools; there the project ends, though it may be reinstated when revisions become necessary. Operational studies, on the other hand, continue more or less steadily. They are developmental in the sense that they help to reshape the educational system and its activities. But, whereas the developmental project is usually framed in time, operational research maintains a steady watch on the ever-changing system. It can have no "final" product.

# Research in the development

# of products

A NEW PRODUCT can have great impact. An intellectual conclusion about education has no effect on the classroom until
teachers have accepted the idea, have decided to use it, and
have made thousands of detailed decisions about its day-to-
day application. A new product can put the conclusion into
practice with much less demand on teachers for comprehension and detailed planning, as it lays out a plan that
less imaginative and less self-reliant teachers can follow. If
the teachers accept the scheme, a certain minimum level
of excellence in the program is thus almost assured, provided, that is, that the product itself has been thoroughly
engineered.

There is an important distinction between mere developmental activities and developmental (product) research.
Design and production can be carried out with no systematic, disciplined inquiry. Indeed, in the course of educational history, most curricula, teaching materials, building
designs, etc., have been brought to final form through no
more than casual tryout. Until relatively recently this lack
of rigor was true of invention and design in all fields of
human endeavor. But one field after another—navigation,
agriculture, manufacturing, nutrition—has taken the steps
forward from folklore to casual empiricism to technology.
Controlled measurement and observation have refined
products and procedures, with correspondingly better results. Education is only beginning to emerge into a technological phase, and there are many problems in the transition.[1]

# Inquiry as an adjunct to development

Development, but not educational research, goes on when the university professor attempts to improve his lectures from year to year. His process is simply one of thoughtful self-criticism. A textbook for the national market is prepared on much the same basis. The scale may be different: the draft material tried in a number of classrooms, and opinions solicited from several critics. But the process is still casual and places little burden of proof on the product.

To design educational materials is a creative, imaginative activity, requiring enthusiasm and spontaneity. The most obvious role of disciplined inquiry during development is to be critical: to ask hard and unpopular questions, to find fault, to certify genuine accomplishment while curbing premature enthusiasm. Any critic can play this role, but the research worker brings to bear especially incisive techniques. Perhaps the very incisiveness of research-based criticisms has caused the researcher to be regarded as a hanging judge. But disciplined inquiry, properly used, teams constructively with imagination. It helps the developers to choose between alternative plans that seem equally meritorious. It tests whether an expensive addition to the proposed program is warranted by its results. It clarifies why students have difficulty at certain points and thereby suggests remedies. The observations required for a systematic study may turn up unexpected treasures—for example, the class whose exceptionally good results can be traced to some innovation by its teacher, which can thereafter be made a part of the regular program. But the essential merit of systematic inquiry is that it protects the developer and the school against self-delusion.

The power of facts to cut through unwarranted enthusiasm is illustrated by an incident relatively early in the measurement movement, when tests of character were applied to youths participating in the "character-building" program of a community.[2] This program, which featured recitation of certain moral principles and awards for good behavior, was highly regarded by its leaders and by the community. It was thought to instill ideals of good conduct. The research staff, however, noted how these youths behaved when given opportunities to cheat, not knowing they were observed. It was discovered that boys who had succeeded best in the program—as judged by the number of awards they had won—were *most* likely to cheat. This reversal of expectation led to drastic changes, because the program was evidently encouraging too much interest in reward for its own sake. Without objective research the fault could not have been detected and demonstrated convincingly to the agency directors.

The power that facts on performance have to guide improvement is perhaps most concretely illustrated by the methods used in preparing "programmed" textbooks. These are designed so that the pupil writes one answer after another to questions on successive elements in an explanation. According to the theory by which most programmers operate, if he makes an error the explanation was unclear in some way, or moved too fast. Classroom trials of drafts are essential to make the text effective. Any spot where errors pile up is a spot to be revised in the next draft; often the nature of the errors shows just what is the source of confusion. Similar but less formal microevaluation can be made of any instructional material in draft form.

Product research was significantly lacking from the historical review in Chapter 2. We saw that developmental *activity* flourished, starting with Dewey's Laboratory School and represented most recently by national curriculum projects in science, mathematics, and other fields. In nearly all these projects, however, data collection has been peripheral and has rarely influenced important decisions. One reason has been the missionary spirit of the usual development project. Only a stoical project director will commission a research staff to be deliberately skeptical. Another reason is that models for product research in education have not been developed, so that no one is very sure what such research can and should attempt to do. (The development of tests is an exception, as we noted in Chapter 3.)

When research is carried on as part of development—so-called "formative research" [3]—there is not likely to be a public report on it. It is conducted for the private guidance of the developer. Insofar as it makes suggestions, these are incorporated in the product without need to report their origin. Where it notes faults no report is to be expected, as these will be overcome if possible and certainly will not be advertised. Without reports to illustrate what developmental inquiry does, the decision-maker does not realize what he can ask of research workers. The investigators themselves lack a realistic picture of the problems and successes of their colleagues in other projects.

The complexity of product research is not well recognized. There is the myth referred to earlier, that development is simply taking a scientific conclusion and putting it into a useful package. There is the myth that describes answering a well-defined question. (This characterizes only research as the conduct of neatly planned experiments, each a small fraction even of conclusion-oriented studies.) There is the myth that one can somehow show that one product "is better" than the next, when results depend on how each is used, and with what students. What is best for one school may not be best everywhere.

Developmental research is untidy. It is disciplined, in that the investigator is expected to be systematic, so that other qualified persons can follow his reasoning. But the process is one of reacting rationally to the unexpected. Though the innovator may be sure what general form his product will take, he will soon find himself deep in problems that call for engineering studies, inventions, or fundamental scientific inquiries.

Sherwin and Isenson,[4] in describing the findings of Project Hindsight, point out that although a new engineering development may double the effectiveness of a piece of military equipment without raising its cost, the improvement cannot be credited to any particular change in design or technology. Rather, the better performance comes from a whole system of changes matched to each other. Even the invention of the transistor could not proceed as a straight application of the semiconductor principle. No less than eight other problems had to be solved with new knowledge or a new engineering concept before efficient devices could be produced.

For the educator, perhaps the best reports on disciplined developmental inquiry are to be found in military training. Psychologists and educational investigators have worked intensively on the improvement of training systems, and have been encouraged to engineer the systems for maximum effectiveness. The military services are accustomed to asking for performance from training devices as much as from weapons, and the results of technical training are clearly observable. Relatively little description of development projects has been published, because engineering studies of a specific training system have little interest to an audience outside the development team, but there are reports that convey a sense of such work.[5]

A sketch of one such developmental enterprise will suggest the types of problems that developmental research can identify and solve, and also illustrates how such investigations differ in timing and character from a program of conclusion-oriented work. The account is based on personal acquaintance with the project; no documentary citation can be given, because most findings went directly into program changes, without writeup, and others went only into file memoranda. Says our informant:

At one point, the Navy wished to train certain men to operate a listening apparatus which generated information to be used tactically. The essence of the task was to detect faint sounds and to classify them as to their probable origin. Recordings were made at sea to represent the range of sounds likely to be encountered in actual operations, and more or less random excerpts from this library of recordings were assembled into a first trial training program. The trainees listened to each selection and each pressed buttons to relay his reports to the instructor. The instructor could introduce explanations, corrections, etc., as appropriate.

A research team was directed to check on the effectiveness of the training and to improve it so that the final package of materials could be sent out for use at various training stations. The first task of the research team was to define the required performance clearly, to catalogue discriminations required so as to determine which ones were being mastered. That is, the complex task had to be divided into its psychological elements. Then tests had to be organized for measuring student progress on each discrimination. Where progress was unsatisfactory, the training had to be modified: by increasing the number of pertinent exercises, by devising specimens that emphasized the feature the men were to learn to recognize, and by devising explanations for use by the instructor. The sequencing of the exercises was also checked by tabulating the errors made and modifying the sequence wherever unexpected errors piled up. While there was systematic data collection, there was no formal research design. A drill was played to a class on Monday morning; the records of class response and the comments of the instructor were tabulated and interpreted before noon. A note of needed alterations was made, followed by a search through the recorded library to find suitable substitute selections. On Tuesday a new drill record was assembled and introduced to the instructor. On Wednesday, data on the new drill were collected in the classroom and if necessary further changes followed. While many of the alterations were designed to remove difficulties, tasks that proved easy also received attention. Often, the implication was that the time devoted to training that skill could be reduced. But on occasion it was found that the skill appeared easy just because the library selections were unrepresentative, and contained "give-away" cues that would not always be present in tactical operations. The systematic tests used in checking out the program served also as a basis for certifying the successful completion of the course, and, ultimately, for reporting to the Navy what the program could accomplish.

All this is straightforward checking on educational effectiveness. Side questions went in all directions. The push-button system originally used made audible clicks, so that students were being cued (sometimes falsely) by their classmates; the equipment therefore had to be redesigned. The display system for the instructor had to be redesigned so that he could take in the information about individual responses. The most interesting problems arose when experienced operators from the fleet claimed to be able to draw certain conclusions about the tactical movement of the target object from the sounds coming from it. It was proposed to add training on this skill, and the first question posed was whether the judgment could actually be made. An experimental test at sea verified the claim that at least a few men could make correct judgments with high probability. But to the untrained persons (including those devising the training course) the sounds of a given target appeared the same, regardless of its actions, and the successful seamen were unable to explain what they heard that led to their judgment. A laboratory project was then mounted to determine how sounds carrying the critical information differed physically; with suitable acoustical equipment a difference was established, and in due time the experimenters were themselves able to judge target movement from the sounds. To develop a subtle and almost indescribable discrimination, it was not sufficient to present drills like those used for grosser skills; men were unable to hold the subtleties of one sound in mind long enough to compare it to the other. The final solution was to translate the sound into a visual pattern; the visual patterns for the two sounds were distinct and an instructor could point to the distinguishing features of two patterns side by side. Then he could train the men to listen for the difference they saw, when a sound was played and the visual pattern displayed simultaneously. Ultimately, the men were able to make discriminations from sound cues alone.

Most developmental research is like this: ever-changing problems, instructional tasks that cannot be described in terms of existing theory in the basic disciplines, solutions arising from a mixture of discipline, art, and cleverness, and a use of observations without a full-fledged "study" leading to a report. To detect and solve some of the problems required little more than an open-minded observer. To resolve others required conclusion-oriented investigation like that in a basic discipline (here, psychoacoustics).

The reader may object that this technological example is not much like the problems of conventional education. There are two responses. First, technological methods increasingly are being seen as relevant for schools. The design of almost any educational film, for example, can be improved by studies of attention, discrimination, and comprehension similar to those described above. Second, even in courses such as history that seem quite different in character from this training course, one can profitably examine in detail the contribution of each element in the educational procedure. To be sure, inquiry is easier where the outcomes are definite and readily measured.

Developmental research rarely is published. Because colleagues in his field of specialization therefore cannot review and criticize his work, the investigator must impose a higher degree of discipline on himself than conclusion-oriented workers do. Moreover, he must forego some of the gratifications available to those whose work is more visible.

## Research to serve the educational consumer

A second kind of product research, sometimes called "summative evaluation," [6] is designed to serve the prospective consumer. Just as the purchaser of a car wants to know how quickly its brakes will stop it and how many miles to the gallon it gives, the school system should be asking what performance can be expected from a teaching device. Even though results obtained in other schools are an uncertain guide to decisions, the administrator cannot reasonably go to the trouble of installing a new system unless he has grounds for believing that its consequences will be good. Evidence from systematic trials is clearly a better guide than advertising claims.

Producers of educational materials have rarely attempted to supply systematic evidence on the results to be expected in representative schools, partly because the educator has not demanded it. This is understandable because factual information means little as long as teachers use the materials differently. As procedures become more standardized, summative evaluations are more pertinent.

A trend toward standardization is seen in curriculum projects of national scope, where integrated packages of texts, films, and laboratory exercises are developed and teachers are trained to use them in much the same way. Programmed instructional materials are even more standardized in their application, and data on their effectiveness are relatively easy to obtain. A committee representing interested educational organizations has already outlined in detail the sort of factual report that should be offered as evidence when programmed materials are placed on the market.[7] The demand for such information will be much stronger when printed programs evolve into computerized systems for instruction, because the great cost of the computer, both upon initial installation and in later operation, will prompt administrators to look hard at competing offerings. Indeed, it is unlikely that computerized systems will be adopted widely unless there is convincing evidence that the payoff offsets the cost.

Evaluative studies have implications of several types. This is seen in the evaluations demanded by the Elementary and Secondary Education Act in connection with its support for compensatory education in preschools. Because programs are administered locally and differ greatly, the investigation must be a local one, with whatever guidance a few strategically located research centers can provide. Hence the study tells the local director and staff how well they are doing. At another level, the collated investigations survey the state and national systems, telling whether the activity is beneficial on the whole, whether it should be continued, and what modifications are needed. The cumulative data, particularly when they allow comparisons of programs having different features, are likely to suggest general conclusions. It would be highly important, for example, to discover that results tend to be better if the child's mother participates in the school a few hours a week.

## What product research is most valuable?

We might well parallel the discussion of Chapter 4 on conclusion-oriented studies with a discussion here of the logic of research in a developmental context. Interactions make it difficult to establish broad generalizations about social matters; they also make it difficult to conclude, from data on one group of schools, that a certain instructional package will serve the next school well. Hawthorne or placebo effects threaten the validity of educational experiments; this caution applies *a fortiori* to tryouts of new curricula, because teachers employing the new material may be specially recruited and indoctrinated.

EXTERNAL CRITERIA FOR DEVELOPMENTAL ACTIVITIES
External criteria have to do with the potential contribution of a project. Because all developmental projects have practical aims, differences with respect to external criteria are

much smaller than among conclusion-oriented studies. In product development, there are two kinds of questions to consider. First, should the developmental activity be launched? Does it deal with educational outcomes one cares greatly about? Is the present educational practice distressingly ineffective? And how plausible is the alternative suggested? Second, assuming that the activity is launched, how large a component of systematic inquiry should it contain? Having some systematic inquiry is likely to make the difference between a product that is only a reasonable approximation and one that is efficient. There is a point of diminishing returns. If developmental research within a project expands indefinitely, it becomes a distraction more than a help. This we shall discuss in connection with internal criteria.

Developmental activity arises from a dissatisfaction. An obvious step is to ask a task force to create a better operating procedure, better equipment, better instructional materials, sometimes even to invent a new institution. But no developmental project is guaranteed to succeed. Developmental effort is a good investment when a substantial amount of basic knowledge about the problem is at hand and when the project is so scheduled that a reasonably adequate answer to the remaining uncertainties can be produced at a useful time. When these conditions do not obtain, one finishes with an inadequate product or no product at all. As good a demonstration as any is the nuclear-powered airplane, which absorbed a billion dollars and fifteen years of effort before President Kennedy faced the facts and scrapped the project. A Congressional postmortem [8] mentions, among other administrative errors, "leap-frogging into developmental aspects prior to the completion of basic and applied research phases," "planning major systems prior to the completion of subsystems," and endless postponement of tests of a prototype, "leaving a vacuum of data by which to evaluate progress and determine feasibility of next steps." Fortunately, there has not yet been a billion-dollar disaster in educational development, but the same faults can be found whenever impatience is the ruling spirit. One educational example (see Chapter 3) is the attempt that was made in the 1920's and 1930's to use aptitude profiles as a basis for guidance before an adequate theoretical foundation had been laid down. Though the evidence is not yet clear, it is possible that the hastily launched Headstart program will be a similar disappointment.

One can sympathize with impatience. The school administrator and the government official are answerable to the public, and the public is much more interested in solutions that will benefit today's children than in superior solutions that will profit only some later generation. But administrators must learn to live with and even to encourage the judicious reluctance of scholars to plunge into development the moment a demand arises. This reluctance has precedents. The young Friar Copernicus declined his Pope's invitation to come to Rome for a task force on calendar reform, though the church holidays and business practices, badly out of phase with the seasons, needed a new calendar. Copernicus held that theoretical matters needed to be clarified before a sensible calendar could be constructed. He did not forget the Pope's question. Late in his life he did turn out practical recommendations on the calendar, but only after his conclusion-oriented work had given a powerful base for suggestions. Just as one asks for potential relevance in choosing among conclusion-oriented studies, so one asks for a potential of successful completion in choosing among developmental activities.

Problems of magnitude and timing are all-important. A strong hunch that improvement in a given direction ought to be possible justifies a developmental effort. It may be necessary to start many small teams off on the same general quest, hoping that one of them will stumble on the needed clues. The less clearly the product is visualized, the more nearly the plan and time schedule must approach the openness of conclusion-oriented inquiry. Where, on the other hand, one has a conviction about the direction along which the solution lies, the focused crash program is probably efficient. But there is a considerable risk in carrying the conviction over into practice without objective pilot testing. The specific form a program takes may be poor even when the basic idea is sound. Operational failure on a grand scale can kill a movement; trouble at the pilot stage can be quietly remedied.

INTERNAL CRITERIA FOR PRODUCT RESEARCH Internal criteria for product studies have much in common with those for conclusion-oriented studies; rigor, depth of penetration, and competence of personnel are surely wanted. Rigor in developmental research is likely to express itself differently than the rigor of conclusion-oriented research, just because there is more improvisation and less design. The leader in educational development must be enthusiastic to hold together a team of volunteers, many of whom have forsaken their usual professional roles to answer his appeal. He and his volunteers can sustain themselves best by convincing each other that their product will truly improve the educational scene. A disciplined and properly motivated investigator can contribute immeasurably to the probable success of a developmental project through his application of benevolent skepticism and an evident readiness to search for still better ways of doing the job.

If leaders of innovating teams are to profit from disciplined inquiry, they will have to discover ways of organizing the team so that the fact-gatherer is neither an intruder nor a threat. The investigator will have to be supported by respectful attention from the project director. Too often, whatever unfavorable findings an investigator working for a project turns up are filed and forgotten, while his supporting findings are advertised. Some project directors, indeed, make it clear that the product in hand is excellent beyond doubt, and that the investigator's task is simply to produce some data that can be used to advertise it. Because a true scholar will reject such a commission, the project director has cut himself off from the possible contribution of disciplined inquiry.

Depth of penetration is a related matter. To ask only, "Is product A better than competing product B?" is to provide information of transient usefulness at best. To identify the conditions under which the product performs best is more helpful to decision-makers and very likely adds to the general understanding of how such products function. A still more penetrating study will ask not about overall merit but about each separate educational effect. A product admirable from one point of view can be detrimental in another respect; although an educator might be willing to sacrifice the second objective for the first, he is denied the opportunity to make this judgment if he is offered only the gross conclusion that A is better than B.

Instruction affects the pupil in many ways. One should know the effects on morale and interest in learning as well as on subject-matter mastery. One should ask how well the pupil is progressing toward independent self-direction; a program that promotes this will very likely not be the one that produces the best scores on a test of pure knowledge. One might collect data on groups of pupils as groups; skills of cooperation and communication are often as much to be prized as knowledge of content. Hence the best research on a product is likely to be wide-ranging in its observations, taking advantage of interviews with pupils and teachers, inviting philosophical analysis of the instructional materials, and measuring pupils in ways not ordinarily considered in classroom testing.

Some projects warrant a larger component of product research than others. Systematic inquiry is slower than intuition. When a first approximation to the solution is available, or when alternatives are clearly identified, disciplined inquiry becomes advantageous. Just as the excessively fluid situation makes poor use of disciplined efforts, so also the excessively crystallized situation makes ineffective use of inquiry. When the shape of a product is fixed, either by the stubborn personality of its creator or by political forces, no effective use will be made of research findings. Research could do little to facilitate plans for desegregation, for example, as long as decisions were being made as much by political power as by principle. Nor can inquiry modify decisions about course content in a curriculum project if the subject-matter specialists who control the project are sure they know what the content should be.

Perhaps everything depends on the project director. If the developer desires hard-headed, constructively motivated inquiry, the effort is likely to be profitable. If he installs the research team to satisfy pressure from outside, only mutual frustration will result. The sponsor of a developmental effort may be reluctant to establish a project that does not employ disciplined inquiry, but a sound climate for inquiry cannot be established by decree. Where a developer does not understand the uses of inquiry, the alternatives are to deny him support, to support him because his creative ideas ought to be assembled in usable form even if not tested or perfected, or gradually to educate him to make use of product research. To insist merely that a fraction of the budget go into "research" or "evaluation" will accomplish nothing.

A concern for rigor in summative evaluation has frequently led to the suggestion that such studies should be conducted by an independent testing agency not identified with any of the products. This "Consumers Union" device has not been tried. Such an approach has some hazards. Any finding will be based on only a partial inquiry, just because there are so many outcomes from an educational activity that not all of them can be systematically observed. In particular, it is hard to get data on certain long-term changes in pupils which may be the special contribution of the innovative program. Unless the evaluator is unusually sophisticated, he is likely to collect data on the most tangible, most traditional outcomes, and not to give due attention to some of the less clearly defined and less measurable outcomes toward which the new curriculum is specially directed. One can be sure that the consumer-oriented agency will check on how well a new mathematics curriculum develops skill in algebra; but if an innovative curriculum is attempting to develop the ability to solve problems intuitively, measurement limited to traditional skills would not provide a fair summative evaluation. Despite all these limitations in evaluative research, the consumer deserves trustworthy studies in his behalf. This becomes vital when giant corporations battle for the school dollar. The only alternative to a consumer-oriented agency is a standard of product testing that allows studies conducted by various producers to be interpreted side by side.

Not the least of the contributions of dependable evaluative research is that it will promote adoption of meritorious educational innovations, even costly ones. The public (including the rank-and-file of the educational profession) can shrug off an educational development supported only by the ritual chanting of believers. If superior effects are solidly confirmed, however, the burden of proof shifts onto the school that does not adopt the new practices. Research findings are not the sole considerations in reaching a decision. But clear evidence of payoff from a new program should at least ensure that the proposal will be considered seriously.

# Operational studies

THE SECOND category of decision-oriented research encompasses the studies carried out by educational systems to guide and monitor their own operations. Some of the studies obtain facts pertaining to a nonrecurring decision; others produce current answers to recurring questions. The investigation may be deliberately superficial, to obtain whatever facts a quick survey can provide, or it may probe underlying causes and conditions. The distinguishing feature of this type of research is its specificity. It is not intended to obtain an answer useful in other localities (though sometimes a local finding will prove suggestive elsewhere or may stimulate conclusion-oriented research).

Operational research is much less entrenched in American education than in industry, public health, or, for that matter, baseball. Certain statistics are routinely collected at the state and national levels, but these facts rarely bear directly on decisions. City school systems usually have bureaus of research, but their capabilities and responsibilities have been quite limited. A number of universities have set up offices of institutional research or the like; but because the professor's classroom is inviolate, the investigators have not generally been encouraged to give thought to instructional activities. The main effort of these offices has been student personnel studies.

It is much harder to form a picture of the extent and quality of operational research than of the other categories we have discussed. Operational research is performed for the guidance of the decision-maker, and often it is properly kept private. If a weakness in the school's program is detected, it is rarely appropriate to publicize the weakness; rather, the responsible persons endeavor to introduce quiet changes that repair the defect. Any report is for internal consumption. It does not find its way into libraries and is not cited. Those engaged in operational research have virtually never summarized their experience or discussed the conduct of such research. Research in higher education is an exception; systematic lectures by experts in that field have been published.[9] Similar accounts of research in state and city systems are much needed. Without them, administrators have no opportunity to assess the potential usefulness of internal research. We note that the perspective-giving publications on research in higher education arose not from the initiative of the research community but from associations of institutions of higher learning. That is, the reports were prepared at the request of the decision-makers speaking through their institutions. Perhaps a similar role on behalf of research in school systems can be played by *their* institutions, such as the American Association of School Administrators or the Education Commission of the States.

The effect of operational research on practice can be immense. The effect is immediate and powerful because findings go straight into the hands of the decision-maker who commissioned them. This is a radically different process from that whereby a scientific conclusion is diffused through the scholarly community, filters into the prevailing view, and ultimately induces subtle change in the classroom. Operational research can also affect the prevailing view indirectly, because striking local innovations are described in mass media and in educational journals.

In recent years, a number of developments have occurred to increase the amount of operational research and its quality. The stronger state departments of education and the Office of Education have helped to standardize the statistical data recorded by school systems. Computer processing has made those data more accessible for analytical purposes. And increasing concern of school administrators with the effectiveness of their expenditures has motivated operational studies. In addition, federal financing of special or innovative programs in schools, as well as concerns of state officials, has brought increased attention to evaluation of school programs. Although these evaluations have been of mixed quality, their existence constitutes a new body of operational studies, and their quality is improving. Altogether, the potential for operational studies is beginning to be realized in schools to an extent greater than at any time in the past.

## Examples from research on colleges and universities

For examples of present-day operational research we draw on reports in the field of higher education, which are open to examination. One line of work stemmed from a nationwide, conclusion-oriented study in a sample of colleges. A particular college applies the techniques of that study to its own student body. It asks, among other questions, what sort of students tend to drop out before completing degrees. The files identify the dropouts, and personality tests that had been routinely administered to all freshmen provide an important part of the descriptive data. A study of this sort may suggest that the admissions procedure is faulty, recruiting students who do not find this college rewarding. It may also suggest that the instructional or extracurricular programs are failing in some way, since students who should be prize graduates are leaving the school.

Illustrative results can be cited from the Massachusetts Institute of Technology.[10] Students with high scores on "thinking introversion," "complexity," and "impulse expression" are believed to be most likely to engage in creative and independent thought. "Thinking introversion" refers to an interest in reflection and imagination as opposed to action, and "complexity" to a tolerance or even a craving for the novel and unpredictable; "impulse expression" is associated with rejection of conventionality and orderliness. The study found that students high on these scales were three times as likely to drop out of MIT as the low scorers. That is, MIT was losing three times as many students who as freshmen preferred to try out new solutions, "fool around" with ideas, and take cognitive risks; it tended to retain the conservatives who seek a well-ordered life leading to tangible goals. The loss of unconventional students was especially great in the School of Engineering; students ready to explore rash ideas evidently were far more comfortable in the School of Science. Such a finding challenges a faculty that sees itself as preparing leaders and innovators. The study does not indicate what should be done to encourage the less pedestrian student; but merely by raising the question, the investigation makes it far more likely that some action will be taken.

A much more elaborate study, also of the dropout problem, was conducted by the Association of American Medical Colleges.[11] This is an institutional study, carried out through a central agency; the facts on each institution were returned for local review. Again, the task was to characterize the dropout and look for hints regarding faults of the program. It is impossible to summarize all the results. Some findings were to be anticipated; for example, dropouts had poor academic and intellectual-test records. But one might equally have expected more dropouts among those with poor financial resources; this was not the case. The negative finding is significant, because it implies that changing the program of financial aid would not solve the dropout problem. Dropouts were conspicuously different in personality: less achievement-oriented, less aggressive, more orderly, and more deferential (almost the opposite of the dropouts in the MIT School of Engineering). A number of factors distinguished schools with high dropout rates from those with low rates; for example, programs in the former made a greater (!) attempt to capitalize on interest and intrinsic motivation. Although all this could be seen as general, conclusion-oriented research, the studies go much further by characterizing each medical school and suggesting actions it can take. Improved holding power in one school was traced, through a combination of statistical and questionnaire research, to a whole series of actions: appointing a strong dean of students, removing geographical restrictions on eligibility for admission, developing channels of student–faculty communication, encouraging faculty studies of the instructional process, and recruiting faculty strongly interested in teaching, among others. In many schools the need to improve student–faculty communication and mutual understanding was emphasized as a source of difficulty. The investigation not only provided a direct service to the schools that participated, but also set up procedures and an intellectual base for similar decision-oriented studies in any other medical school and very likely any other professional school.

## Research in school systems

There are few source materials on public-school research. In many school systems, the research division apparently does little more than fill out forms required by higher authority, manage a routine testing program, and the like. The following paragraph comes from a recent survey report made by authorities who examined the school system of a major city:

This (Research) Division has not been seen or used effectively by the school system as an essential part of its machinery for evaluating present operations or for helping plan improvements. Even when studies have been made, full attention has not always been accorded their reports and the implications of the reports. It is not customary to include the Division in planning experimental programs or to evaluate their results.

It appears that this is a typical situation. Justman,[12] speaking from his experience as a city research director, says simply that school administrators regard research as a luxury; and that within a research bureau it is a luxury to have any time left over for research after other duties are performed.

Davis [13] prepared case studies of research offices in six California school systems that amplify the picture. One school system of intermediate size (90,000 pupils) has one staff member with a doctorate and three with master's degrees. The duties are categorized under the headings of pupil accounting, enrollment trends and projections, evaluation of ability and achievement, surveys of administrative practices, in-service education, and consultation to special projects. It is evident that this division spends far more of its time in facilitating routine operations, largely administrative, than in inquiry about education. The testing activities might reveal needed improvements in the instructional program if the results were reflected upon, but they rarely are; the office's task is to collect scores for use in individual guidance and classification. The projects completed during the year preceding Davis' study are illuminating: a study of IBM equipment for record-keeping in the school, a tabulation of class sizes, a study of building needs, a study of pupil transfers from school to school, a report of committee thoughts on discipline, and a review of the results of a system-wide reading test. The one other study conducted, though modest, is worth special attention as an example of what decision-oriented work can be: a study collating interviews with teachers who had used a new instructional program in mathematics during the year, arriving at suggestions about improving the program and a recommendation as to its continuation. This is the type of constructive study for which an agency concerned with filling out forms, arranging for routine tests, and conducting in-service training conferences finds little time. With time and resources, the study could rise above the level of collecting opinions to the collection of solid data on instruction and learning in mathematics.

Equally instructive is Davis' description of a research agency in a system with only some 10,000 pupils. The research staff consists of a director (who holds a doctorate) and one secretary. Although his duties include the sorts of research outlined for the system described above, a far larger part of his job description is concerned with reports to the press and public, including the direction of a speakers bureau. The first duty of the office appears to be to take responsibility for an annual report to the public, which by its very nature can raise no hard questions. In addition to the usual memoranda of conferences, two decision-oriented studies were reported during the year in question: an analysis of the consequences of closing two old schools believed to be unsafe, and a summary of facts regarding the local need for a technical college. These are precisely the sort of fact-finding inquiries that are indispensable to management, and yet have no generalized value to other systems.

The most ambitious and potentially significant example of decision-oriented research in Davis' survey was from a third system, a high-school district with 5,000 pupils. The research division there had studied ways of better utilizing the staff, starting with a study of the effects of class size on achievement, going on to a tryout of team teaching and schedule modification, and checking on how well students progressed. Questions of this sort can obviously have the highest significance, but one can be certain that resources were inadequate. The total budget for the department was $17,000, which supports a single staff member. While doing this study he was also managing a testing program, preparing statistical reports, and fulfilling a number of administrative committee assignments. Because highly experienced research workers have been unable to arrive at convincing conclusions on the effects of class size and team teaching, one is inclined to praise this school system and its research director for their vision as to what operational research can do, while regretting that the same vision is not found in systems with more nearly adequate resources.

It is interesting to observe the very different administrative structure used by the Air Force to monitor and improve its ROTC program.[14] A planning committee of Air Force specialists and civilian employees took chief responsibility, aided by an expert committee from outside. The plan called for developing a number of instruments for "quality control" studies, some to be applied to the students and some to officers who had been through the program some years before. It also called for intensive studies to follow up on what the periodic surveys disclosed. Instead of trying to develop instruments itself the committee engaged contractors who have competent technical staffs, each to prepare one instrument or to carry out studies on one subtopic. The findings and recommendations of the contractor were reviewed by the central staff in order to take into account other realities which they knew better than the contractor. This then led to a comprehensive plan on which action could be taken. Some of the studies were nonrecurrent, carried out just once in a decade. Some, such as the administration of attitude scales and rating devices, became an annual function geared to detect significant trends as they first become visible.

There is surely a model here for much research in the more typical educational institutions. The staff of the local school system knows much that has to enter into policy decisions. In particular, the local research staff is in a good position to know where research is most likely to be helpful. Only rarely do the local staff members have the time and expertness to carry out rigorous studies by themselves, especially since each study demands a somewhat different kind of competence. A casual consultant cannot provide the help needed. Very likely subcontracting can raise the quality and depth of operational studies; regional laboratories may be able to provide just that sort of service.

## What operational studies are most valuable?

In setting forth criteria for operational studies, we can be brief. We have little to say that does not duplicate what has been said about other types of studies.

With regard to external criteria, i.e., the choice of significant problems, the key requirement is to focus attention on matters about which something can and will be done. Studies should not be commissioned as a means of temporizing with a demand for change. The research staff ought to be a working tool. The research activity should not be reduced to the collecting of facts "somebody might want some day." We do not disparage census-like activity that gives a picture of the size of the educational enterprise, the qualifications of teachers, the obsolescence of school buildings, and many other matters relevant to policy. But collecting standardized information year after year exploits very little of the potential of a research staff.

We would invoke a criterion of distribution of effort. From Davis' study and the earlier report of Liu,[15] we learn that operational research in school systems, insofar as it is disciplined inquiry at all, has been preoccupied with mass testing programs and with research on administrative decisions rather remote from the classroom. Only rarely has the public school brought its research machinery seriously to bear on improvement of curriculum, instruction, and guidance. Often, the most important place to use the system's best research talent is in a project where the researchers cooperate with a small group of teachers in trying to perfect an imaginative idea. They ought to perform developmental studies of instructional innovations imported from elsewhere, to adjust them for maximum effectiveness. No matter how careful the work of the development team that placed a new curriculum on the market, one can be sure that local adjustments will be advisable. Here is a prime opportunity to use research techniques to improve the effectiveness of a change that has already been decided upon. Possibly more important, the research division ought to be a source of initiative, detecting ways in which the school program can be improved.

College research offices have moved a bit closer to instruction than those in the schools, but the conservatism of professors has restricted most inquiry to peripheral matters. Studies of admissions, dormitory life, financial needs, values and attitudes, and uses of closed-circuit television are far less upsetting to the faculty than studies of the effectiveness of the classroom program. Decision-oriented research can get nowhere until the decision-makers have come to value the research program for the help it gives them. On the typical campus, the professors, individually or collectively, make most of the decisions that strengthen or weaken educational effectiveness. Hence a program of research on a college is unlikely to be adequately balanced until faculty attitudes have been modernized.

As to internal criteria, one is willing to settle for considerably less depth of investigation and less precise evidence in decision-oriented research than in other studies, because of the limits on time and resources. In conclusion-oriented research a problem can be left open until a decisive body of evidence has been accumulated. In operating a system one can allow just a certain period for investigation; after that, action must be taken no matter what the uncertainties.

Considerable judgment must be exercised to pick problems of the right size. Some matters are easily studied, and yet the inquiry does little to make the school system better. Others are too large for a meaningful answer to be given. The right problem will be one on which the research department can obtain reasonably dependable facts that will, when in hand, make the actions taken by the school staff significantly wiser.

## Leadership: the critical need

The requirement of adequate management falls especially heavily on operational research because it can so easily be futile. There has been a consistent tendency to skimp on the resources of the research division, keeping the staff small and often assigning responsibility to persons with minimal training. Because of the diversity of problems, the need to improvise techniques, and the need to work closely with many persons, operational research is an especially difficult type of inquiry. Persons qualified to do it are rare, especially because most research training emphasizes conclusion-oriented studies.

It may well be that new institutional arrangements will have to supplant the research office within a single institution in order to obtain work of the necessary quality. There are emerging institutions such as associations of professional schools, regional associations of colleges, regional educational laboratories, educational data banks, and statewide coordination of evaluation for compensatory education. These should be able to provide far better arrangements for on-line research than the local research offices that have hitherto tried to do the job single-handed. Among other virtues, such collaborative arrangements can provide for the critical examination of studies and so maintain a high level of discipline. They can also accumulate experience on which to base a training program.

In this generation the topic of operational research in school systems has been little discussed in the professional community, though the chief officers of state and city research departments maintain some communication with each other. Operational research in colleges and universities has flourished, comparatively speaking, because the process has attracted the attention of university presidents and of university departments training persons for responsibility in higher education. Operational research receives no comparable emphasis in the training of persons concerned with the lower schools. We believe that all educators can afford to take to heart a message A. J. Brumbaugh prepared for the American Council on Education, addressed primarily to university administrators. In quoting it here we paraphrase to remove specific reference to higher education, for every thought is broadly applicable.

Quality is the key word in education today. How to maintain and improve quality under changing conditions and new stresses is a major issue confronting our schools. Boards, administrators, and faculties must make important decisions about goals, policies, programs, operations, and outcomes for the institutions for which they are responsible. To make wise decisions, data that only institutional research can provide are indispensable. In the development of a program of institutional research several guiding principles should be kept in mind. Particularly important are the following:

To be of the greatest service in improving education, institutional research must be planned. To plan well requires that a comprehensive overview be taken to identify the crucial issues, both immediate and long range, with which the institution is confronted. Research projects, immediate and long range, related to those issues can then be formulated. Projects thus formulated should be arranged in an order of priority on the basis of criteria to be agreed upon.

Responsibility for the over-all coordination and direction of institutional research should be centralized. The lack of central coordination is likely to result in wasteful duplication or costly oversight of needed studies. . . . [Brumbaugh was speaking of coordination within the institution; the emergence of valuable cooperative research arrangements in higher education during the past few years adds a further dimension to the recommendation.]

Even though responsibility for institutional research is centralized, provision should be made for wide participation by members of the faculty and administration in planning and conducting projects. An office of institutional research cannot operate effectively in splendid isolation. Participation by the faculty in institutional research not only educates the faculty member to the issues with which the institution is confronted but also prepares him to consider sympathetically the implications of research findings. Time and money spent in institutional research can be justified only in terms of its immediate or long-range impact.

Institutional research must be adequately financed. Boards and legislative committees too often do not understand the importance of institutional research and consequently do not look with favor on a budget item for it. The faculty, likewise, tends to look askance at the use of funds for institutional research which, in its opinion, might more appropriately be made available for departmental use. Nevertheless, institutional research to be fully effective must be adequately supported.[16]

As Brumbaugh clearly saw, decision-oriented research is a creation of the decision-maker. Hence the key requirement for its improvement is that decision-makers understand what product research and operational research can do, so that they will pose questions worth answering and will provide the resources that make the answers attainable.

NOTES

1. Oettinger, Anthony C., "The Myths of Educational Technology," *Saturday Review*, Vol. 51 (May 18, 1968), pp. 76, 77ff.

2. Maller, J. B., in Hunt, J. Mc V., *Personality and the Behavior Disorders*. New York: Ronald Press, 1944.
3. Scriven, Michael, "The Methodology of Evaluation," in Tyler, Ralph, and others, *Perspectives of Curriculum Evaluation*. Chicago: Rand McNally, 1967, pp. 40ff.
4. Sherwin, Chalmers, and R. S. Isenson, "Project Hindsight," *Science*, Vol. 156 (1967), pp. 1571–1577.
5. Stuit, Dewey B. (ed.), *Personnel Research and Test Development in the Bureau of Naval Personnel*. Princeton, N.J.: Princeton University Press, 1947; *Army Air Forces Aviation Psychology Program Reports*. Nos. 8–13. Washington. Government Printing Office, 1947; Glaser, Robert (ed.), *Training Research and Education*. Pittsburgh: University of Pittsburgh Press, 1962.
6. Scriven, *loc. cit.*
7. Lumsdaine, Arthur A., in Lumsdaine, A. A. and Glaser, Robert (eds.), *Teaching Machines and Programmed Instruction. II. Data and Directions*. Washington, D.C.: National Education Association, 1965.
8. *Interagency Coordination in Research and Development*. Select Committee on Government Research. Washington, D.C.: Government Printing Office, 1964, p. 34.
9. Axt, R. G., and H. T. Sprague (eds.), *College Self-Study: Lectures on Institutional Research*. Boulder, Colorado: Western Interstate Commission for Higher Education, 1960; Brumbaugh, A. J., *Research Designed to Improve Institutions of Higher Learning*. Washington: American Council on Education, 1960.
10. Heist, Paul (ed.), *The Creative College Student: An Unmet Challenge*. San Francisco: Jossey-Bass, 1968, Chapters 3, 4.
11. Johnson, Davis G., and Edwin B. Hutchins, *Doctor or Dropout*. Evanston, Ill.: American Association of Medical Colleges, 1966.
12. Justman, Joseph, "Problems of Researchers in Large School Systems," *Educational Forum*, Vol. 32 (1968), pp. 429–437.
13. Davis, James C., "The Functions, Products, and Financial Support of Six Public School District Research Departments," Doctoral Dissertation, Stanford University, 1963.
14. Sawin, E. I., and Major James F. Smith, "Curriculum Evaluation," *Improving College and University Teaching* (Spring 1966), pp. 81–86.
15. Liu, Bangnee A., *Educational Research in Major American Cities*. New York: King's Crown Press, 1945.
16. Brumbaugh, *op. cit.*

**6**

# Improving
# the research effort

## Scope of the
## educational research enterprise

TO ESTIMATE THE FUNDS expended and the number of people involved in research on education is particularly difficult because of the ambiguity and heterogeneity of the classification "educational research." Some activities labeled as research and carried out on funds supposedly appropriated for research are not critical and objective. On the other hand, the usual estimates of the total effort overlook many disciplined inquiries significant for education that are conducted in scattered public schools, within corporations, and elsewhere.

As an example of the difficulty of defining what to count, we may refer to the specialty of demography, where the investigator may belong to a department of sociology and may rely on the disciplines of mathematics, sociology, statistics, social psychology, economics, and anthropology. His predictions are important to educational planners, yet he is probably not included on any list of educational researchers and his funds enter into no reported total of expenditures related to education.

The settings in which researchers work range widely. An individual in a university is testing a scheme for amplifying electrical potentials of the vocal muscles in order to help a reader suppress subvocal responses during silent reading. A local school system is studying the backgrounds of its able students who do not plan to go to college. An anthropologist is studying primates in a natural habitat and recording their early learning activities—and this too may in time alter concepts of education. Data reported in this section are limited to what someone has officially labeled "educational research," and there is no way to evaluate whether a particular total is too large or too small.

## Sources and extent of research support

The current magnitude of government involvement in educational research is unprecedented. From its feeble start with a few clerks and a budget that repeatedly threatened to vanish, the U.S. Office of Education grew to about 1,300 full-time employees at the end of 1964, and to nearly 2,500 by the end of 1966. Some seventy separate programs under nearly two dozen different Congressional authorizations and a budget near the $4 billion mark indicate the burden placed on the Office. It allocates about $100 million—less than 2 per cent of its total budget—to research and research training. Only a fraction of this 2 per cent finances truly disciplined studies of either the conclusion-oriented or decision-oriented varieties, because dissemination and undisciplined innovative activities share hugely in the "research" budget.

Elsewhere in the federal government the Office of Economic Opportunity supports some studies of the disadvantaged, the National Institute of Mental Health supports research in counseling, the Office of Naval Research sponsors studies of computer-aided instruction, etc. These agencies are all mission-oriented, and they tend to emphasize the topics most directly relevant to their missions. Their studies have often been quite penetrating, however, and have had profound impact on prevailing views at all levels.

In addition to the federal funds they expend, state and local school systems support research directly. The states concentrate their efforts on surveys and descriptive statistics, normative data pertaining to salaries, certification, finance, enrollments, and offerings.[1] City research bureaus also compile statistical reports on such matters as enrollment, population trends and projections, salaries, class size, personnel and staff, age-grade relationships, marking-grading practices, promotion policies and teacher load.[2] Increasingly, they are the agencies responsible for reports and evaluations to account for federal allocations to support special programs.

Research expenditures by private foundations have been and are of key importance. Before the Office of Education was allowed to become an active leader, foundations were almost alone in supporting innovation in education. There are 7,000 or more sizable foundations, and nearly 500 new ones are formed each year.[3] It was foundation encouragement, for example, that enabled operational research in higher education to take its first but all-important steps.[4]

Various sketchy figures can be adduced to indicate the magnitude of the research enterprise. The most authoritative are those reproduced in Table 1, from the Office of Education.[5] A certain amount of guesswork goes into most of these figures; the figures for cities, for example, are said to be estimated from budgets of a number of large cities. The decision as to which federal and foundation grants are for educational research is somewhat arbitrary. Taking the figures at face value, one has to conclude that state and local school authorities are still making very limited provision for research. But funds from the Office of Education quadrupled in the period covered, and those from other sources doubled.

**Table 1. Estimated expenditures for educational research in two recent years**

| Sources of funds | 1960 | 1965 |
|---|---|---|
| State | $ 5,766,000 | $11,000,000 |
| Local school budgets | 2,000,000 | 3,000,000 |
| Federal | 19,179,000 | 69,785,000 |
| Foundations | 6,000,000 | 14,375,000 |
| Total | $32,945,000 | $98,160,000 |

A total of one hundred million dollars is impressive. But it is less impressive when we realize that much of the money goes into developmental work, demonstration, teacher training, and inadequately disciplined inquiry. Even if all the money were truly going into research and developmental studies having a strongly disciplined component, the amount is relatively small. According to the National Science Foundation some 3 per cent of the Gross National Product is currently going into research and development in all fields—and the scientific community considers that sum inadequate. In education, something like *two-tenths of 1 per cent of the expenditure for education* is going into research and development, even as that is broadly defined in the Office of Education statistics.[6]

Virtually nothing is known of the extent to which corporations—profit and nonprofit—are carrying on in-house research. Such expenditures have grown markedly since 1960. The greater part of the expenditure is no doubt closely linked to product improvement, but there is also corporate support for longer range, conclusion-oriented studies. For example, one nonprofit institution offering products and services to schools provides a budget of $1,200,000 for conclusion-oriented research, out of a total annual income of about $25,000,000. (Grants received for the conduct of research are not counted in either figure.)

Although these figures show that there is appreciable research activity, there is much less disciplined inquiry than there should be. Humanistic inquiry pertinent to education is nonexistent except in universities, and only traces appear there. Its virtual absence from the lists of grants is conspicuous. With other types of research, the vital problem is to increase quality and significance. The supply of trained investigators is overstretched and institutional pressures and constraints often reduce the quality of production. If all the present resources could be devoted to excellently conducted, reflective, and creative studies (of both the decision-oriented and conclusion-oriented varieties), the research enterprise would be very much healthier.

# Manpower for educational research

ALTHOUGH a single investigator sometimes takes full responsibility for all stages of a study, particularly the planning and the final analysis of results, there are many other patterns of educational research. Some inquiries require a large team, each person concentrating on one aspect of the task and contributing a special perspective to planning and interpretation. This is well illustrated by national curriculum projects that draw upon subject-matter specialists, experienced teachers, specialists in the design of teaching materials, test constructors, and sometimes philosophers and other students of education. It is hard to say which of these persons are properly described as researchers; all of them are likely to make observations and contribute hypotheses, even though few of them have responsibility for formal compilation of data. Diverse investigators, ranging from planners and interpreters at the highest level down to routine technicians, are needed to staff the large research enterprise in education.

In the ensuing discussion, we necessarily concentrate on the research leaders rather than the innumerable types of subordinate personnel. The leaders include chiefs of staff in large institutes, and individual scholars; they include economists or political scientists who turn for a few years to an educational topic, and persons committed to careers in educational research. Statistical reports on educational research, and many of the published symposia, are restricted to the last-named who identify themselves as "educational researchers," but we shall attempt to discuss the manpower problem in terms of our broader concept of inquiry relevant to education.

## Demand and supply

The considerable numerical increase in professional educational research during the past decade is best evidenced by the growth of the American Educational Research Association. That organization had 1,205 members in 1955, 1,774 in 1960, 4,063 in 1965, and 7,900 in 1968. To be sure, this rise is not due wholly to migration of additional investigators into educational work. A campaign to recruit new members, supported by a lively program of service to members, has drawn into the Association many who had long been eligible. It is possible too that the increased prestige of research has led some persons to join the Association even though they are chiefly engaged in nonresearch activities. The hollowness of manpower counts is suggested by the breakdowns in a "census" of educational research workers.[7] The count included about 6,000 persons, but half of these were working one day per week or less on research. After making allowance for the weaknesses of the data, it is still evident that the number of persons engaged in relevant research has been increasing rapidly.

Despite the new recruits, there are desperately large gaps in the research force. Recognizing that one census will differ from the next because of shifts in definitions, one can be sure that the magnitude of the problem is something like that suggested by testimony of the Associate Commissioner of Education for Research, in testimony before a Congressional committee in 1966: "There are now 5,000 educational research positions vacant because there are no qualified applicants. The demand is certain to expand."[8]

Even so, that officer was unable to give priority to training. Pressed to provide funds for competing activities having greater political appeal, he submitted a budget request that allowed for a drop of 15 per cent in the number of research trainees supported by the Office. Such decisions can only be regarded as short-sighted.

The proliferation of educational research activities— national surveys, regional laboratories, research and development centers, centers for the evaluation of preschool intervention, curriculum projects, industrial laboratories preparing educational materials, and so on—creates hundreds of additional leadership positions each year. The expansion of graduate schools, the elevation of researchers to new administrative positions, and other demands create further vacancies for persons with research training. In recent years it has been usual for educational laboratories to have unfilled places on their staffs, for universities to have placed the year's new doctorates in jobs by the end of April, and for work to be done, in the end, by persons whose training or experience falls short of that required to do the work well. The present level of educational research has been straining the manpower supply beyond the limit, yet we have repeatedly noted a need for more and deeper studies in one or another area.

## Recruitment and training

Although every scientific and technical field laments a shortage of investigators, the social sciences face special problems. The necessity for strong and well-supported training programs in the physical sciences has been recognized nationally for nearly twenty years, and in the behavioral sciences the National Institutes of Health have sponsored a healthy improvement and expansion of training. In contrast, there has been very little money for the support of graduate students and the improvement of training programs in the social sciences and education. Moreover, these fields encounter special difficulty in recruiting because young people are unlikely to hear about research careers in social science. Required science courses in high school and college usually draw attention to the work of the natural scientists. The high-school student's only exposure to social science may be a course aimed to promote self-understanding. Only after he is committed to some other line of study, in college, is he likely to learn what a sociologist or economist does. As for educational research *per se*, he is likely to hear of it only if he trains to be a teacher. Few of those who enter graduate study in Schools of Education grew up with the career motivations of a scientist, nor do courses for teachers ordinarily present research as an exciting activity. Few of those who take graduate programs in sociology, psychology, etc., gain any idea of the problems education poses to those disciplines.

The same things may be said about humanistic scholarship. The numerical demand for such scholars is not so great, but support for students in these fields has been penurious, and national policy has been slow to recognize that cultivation of such talents is necessary. Such steps as have been taken have not encouraged the humanistic study of educational problems.

Training for educational research is now supported under the Elementary and Secondary Education Act. The program has not been assigned the deserved high priority. When brought to a proper level of funding it will make possible some of the desirable training discussed below.

Better and more ample training programs come distressingly late. The nation's insistence on radically improved education calls for trained people now. Three years are required for minimal graduate training. And, while the person completing his Ph.D. is capable of independent work, the complexity of education and of the related research techniques means that an investigator is not likely to hit his full stride until he has had another three to five years of experience. Moreover, training is directed predominantly to a few specialties. Statistics, measurement, and general experimental methodology are the most common fields of concentration; educational psychology and research on curriculum also draw a large number of students. Few universities offer training for operational research in education, and only a handful of schools offer substantial training in history of education, philosophical analysis of educational problems, and other nonempirical investigation. This reflects and contributes to the imbalance of Education faculties. Because statistical training has been relatively strong during the past generation, some faculties are strong in the statistical aspects of educational research and have an effective working relation with their colleagues in statistics departments. On the other hand, because few historians of education have been trained in the past, only the rare university possesses a single active historical scholar with an interest in education, around whom a training program could develop.

The number of persons in educational research is inadequate. To discuss their quality and productivity is to strike an even more depressing note. Quality is hard to document, but there is remarkably wide agreement that many persons trained for educational research are unproductive, and that many of those charged with doing research are not qualified for their tasks. A lack of productivity is suggested by the Buswell-McConnell survey [9] of persons who received the Ph.D. in Education in 1954. In the ensuing ten years, only 20 per cent of them produced as many as two research publications. Lack of productiveness of graduates is a complaint in all departments of the graduate school: many a physicist working in industry, many a college teacher of literature has never gratified his instructors by publishing an original study after his dissertation. A person trained to do educationally relevant research who uses his skills in a service role (e.g., managing a testing agency) is socially useful, but he does not have much opportunity to think about education. Many Ph.D.s become teachers, counselors, or supervisors of teachers, producing no research.

In the study cited, thirty-one contributors were selected whose educational research is especially well regarded by their colleagues. Whereas the general pool of 1954 doctoral recipients in Education had published, on the average, just one article in a ten-year period, this selected group had averaged over sixty articles per person in the same time. Seventeen of these thirty-one had taken doctorates in psychology; only six had doctorates from faculties of Education. (The remaining eight were scattered over six fields of training.) The preponderance of psychologists becomes even more striking since, of the six degrees in Education, four represented specialization in educational psychology or testing. Hence, out of thousands of doctorates granted in such fields as educational administration, curriculum, instructional methods, and secondary education, only two persons reached this roster of significant contributors.

RECOMMENDATIONS  The training of educational researchers should not be the undivided responsibility of Schools of Education. This conclusion is reached by many within the educational field. It stands out among the recommendations of the Buswell-McConnell study, recommendations reached after discussion with experienced educational research workers. The fact that several of the discussants had been high officers of the American Educational Research Association, and that others were or had been deans of Schools of Education, eliminates any question of adverse bias.

Certain features are likely to characterize any superior program of training for research on education. These include: (1) full-time study for three consecutive years, preferably at an early age; (2) training as part of a student group individually and collectively dedicated to research careers; (3) participation in research, at a steadily advancing level of responsibility, starting in the first year of graduate school if not earlier; (4) a thorough grounding in at least one academic discipline, together with solid training in whatever technical skills that discipline employs; and (5) study of the educational process and educational institutions, bringing into a single perspective the social goals of education, the bases on which policy decisions are made, the historical development of the curriculum, the nature of the learner, and other factors.

Of these features, only the fifth has been at all common in the training of doctoral students in Education. In the past, graduate faculties in Education have recruited students for research training mainly among the teachers who attend summer sessions. These teachers tend to be interested in practical recommendations and in advancement to higher posts within school systems. When a research worker is recruited from this pool, he may have completed half his graduate study before he starts to view himself as a prospective investigator, with all the change of intellectual style that implies. He may well be thirty-five or older when he makes the shift. Yet in nearly every scientific field it has been observed that an investigator does his most creative work before age thirty-five. In most Schools of Education the doctoral students committed to doing research are outnumbered at least three to one by those who regard the doctoral dissertation as the one piece of research of their lifetimes, as no more than an academic exercise. The graduate student in Education is likely to participate in research (apart from his dissertation) only if hired as an assistant, and then may carry out routine activities designed to serve the project rather than activities that contribute to his development. Education has no tradition of the undergraduate honors work that other fields use to give students an early taste of inquiry. In a scientific or technical field the graduate student almost always enters with an undergraduate major in a science or mathematics. In education, entering graduate students may have no more intellectual preparation for research than the one or two science courses that meet minimum standards for a bachelor's degree. We must not fail to acknowledge the bright exceptions within this gloomy picture. Many Schools of Education have a few young students who enter with top records in undergraduate psychology, mathematics, chemistry, or the like, shifting to educational research because they are challenged by its immediate relevance to the world and its emphasis on integrated knowledge rather than on isolated specializations. No doubt there are ten times as many such students who could be recruited.

To what extent does graduate training in the academic departments have the features we consider desirable? Although departments vary, most faculties follow the first four practices on our list. Where the academic department falls short is in acquainting the student with educational institutions and problems, and with their intellectual and social background. A sociology department may have no course treating the school as an institution. A research training program in child psychology may give no attention to the child-teacher relation or to the psychology of learning to read, vital as those are in the child's total development. Even if the student does encounter research on educational matters, within the context of his discipline, he is likely to gain no sense of the philosophy behind the school curriculum. When and if he does turn to educational studies he is therefore unable to see his problem in perspective, and his conclusions are likely to be injudicious. A related limitation of training within an academic department is that the training may concentrate on idealized problems and so provide little guidance regarding the management of the untidy, ill-formulated problems that abound in education. For example, expertness in analyzing data from an experiment in which subjects were assigned to treatments strictly at random is not a qualification for planning rigorous analysis of data collected in an educational setting where, almost inevitably, assignment of pupils is nonrandom.

Full understanding of educational realities cannot be attained on the campus. To know Education is to know how teachers and administrators, pupils, and parents think, work, and feel. Schools of Education were surely wrong a few years ago when most of them made previous experience as a teacher prerequisite for admission to doctoral work; this impeded some of the most promising students. But in the current eagerness to stress solid methodology and theory, training programs should not lose sight of the value of direct participation in school life. For the prospective researcher who has not been a schoolteacher, this experience can come through various kinds of internship or through observations made as a part of research in the field.

These recommendations seem to call for courses and research experiences for which the Education faculty and the academic faculty of the university both take responsibility. There are universities where today's Education faculty contains a strong group of professors active in a particular discipline, so that a large fraction of the training can be given with the School of Education. In a few other universities one will find an institute affiliated directly with some academic department (sociology, for example) that is intensively concerned with schools and school problems. In such a setting a person trained entirely outside a School of Education can develop an adequate understanding of educational realities. But these are exceptional cases. Only a few disciplines in any given university reach such a standard.

The School of Education, like any professional school, must provide advanced training for practitioners as well as investigators. The would-be practitioner places the highest value on techniques or ideas that seem to have immediate usefulness. He is not typically analytic, nor much interested in theory and research methodology. Historically, the administrators, supervisors, and prospective trainers of teachers predominated in the student body. Partly because of the degradation of doctoral research when it became a prerequisite to professional work, research training in the School of Education has often been a superficial presentation of a bland eclectic mixture of techniques from all known disciplines, and ideas from none. This is evidenced in nearly every one of the numerous textbooks on "how to do research in education."

The conviction of this Committee is that solid training requires concentration; a research method is an interweaving of a philosophical viewpoint about knowledge, a set of concepts, a set of techniques, and a set of critical standards for reviewing results. A solid research approach cannot be apprehended, let alone mastered, when there is an attempt to provide a global, conglomerate training.

But it should be evident that there can be no unitary training program for educational research. If the trainee is to penetrate deeply enough to master one of the disciplines he will have to steep himself in its techniques and theories. Electing a course or two in sociology, for example, by no means equips one to do sociological studies. Hence universities will have to develop an array of largely independent programs, each intended to produce one type of scholar. This is not to argue for narrowness of outlook. Probably the best researchers are hybrids who master more than one style of research or scholarly analysis, and many of the best training programs will incorporate two or more disciplines.

Whereas formerly there were few opportunities for research careers, and few students seeking them, the better Schools of Education now can have enough research trainees to warrant a distinct program. The program needs to be special; adding isolated courses and apprenticeships will not suffice. The research trainee cannot be left to select most of his courses from a catalogue designed for the practitioner. He cannot be left without the continual interaction with other inquiry-minded students that is one of the great strengths of graduate departments. For this reason, research trainees within Schools of Education should be treated as a distinct group and given special opportunities to interact with data, with each other, with experienced research workers, and with students applying similar research methods to noneducational problems. Buswell and McConnell go so far as to recommend a degree-granting institute for research training in education, formally outside the School of Education though sharing some of its staff. Separatism can go too far, if it removes the research trainees from all communication with those who have the practitioner's interests. Through such contacts the researcher can learn about field problems deserving his attention, and the practitioner can gain respect for the research worker's style of thinking. Many different programs can be designed that have the desired characteristics; which structure is best will depend on the field of study, the university, and the individual student.

The movement of the past two decades toward a full-time student body in graduate Schools of Education has brought developments that need to be re-examined. Full-time students are a delight to the faculty, but they have to be supported. The advent of research grants that could pay half-time salaries to students was enthusiastically welcomed, and it was rightly seen that these assistantships provide a training superior to the old mixture of courses and completely independent work. But when funds are granted to carry out a particular piece of the professor's research, the student's interests have to be subordinated to has to be done, he may find himself running subjects or the requirements of the contract. Just because the work feeding data into the computer long after that work has ceased to have educative value for him. (This coin has another side; see page 228.) The proper program will provide the student with the apprenticeships and collaborative experience he needs, but it will not enslave him to a project. Very likely Schools of Education will need to engage non-students with technical skills to carry on the noneducative chores on which a fair proportion of every research budget is necessarily spent.

Positive leadership will be required to develop training programs that make adequate use of the academic disciplines relevant to education, and that leadership will have to come from Schools of Education. Only in isolated cases can one expect another department to take the initiative in organizing training for work on education. It is noteworthy that very few of the research training programs supported by the Office of Education are based in departments outside Schools of Education, though such proposals have been officially encouraged. Leaders within Education faculties will have to learn how the basic fields can illuminate educational concerns, and will have to survey their own campuses to identify departments that are likely to enter into collaborative training. Training programs must spread into disciplines other than psychology and statistics, the two that have long collaborated with educators. The list of conventional social sciences does not exhaust the possibilities that should be exploited. Relevant interests are emerging in economic systems analysis, in linguistics and its subspecialties of psycholinguistics and sociolinguistics, and elsewhere.

These recommendations apply to the student who is going to do any kind of conclusion-oriented research. The person concerned with reading, for example, may find his supporting disciplines in linguistics, or perceptual and even physiological psychology, in sociology, in communication research, or elsewhere. But he must be selective; to try to become expert in all these areas is to guarantee mastery of none. If the student's aim is to investigate the organization of higher education, he may put down intellectual roots in sociology, philosophy, or any of half a dozen other fields. Such proposals depart radically from the tradition of training the reading specialist or the specialist in higher education under a senior specialist in that applied field. The history of that type of training has not been encouraging.

We of course do not advise that the researcher attack an applied problem without informing himself of the traditions and past work in the field. Our position is that the investigator should be a disciplined inquirer first and a topical specialist second; those with experience in his topical area have much to teach him.

TRAINING FOR DECISION-ORIENTED INQUIRY How to train the person who will make a career of decision-oriented investigation is a matter for general statements rather than specific recommendations, as the institutional settings in which he will work are only now being created. It seems likely that he will have to be extremely versatile. He will need to gain familiarity in a variety of methods of research, even at some sacrifice of preparation on the substantive aspects of relevant disciplines. This is not to deny what we have earlier said about concentration and mastery. But the individual taking responsibility for decision-oriented studies needs breadth foremost. Decision-oriented studies require excellence and expertise, but these will generally have to be supplied by consultants and subcontractors. No man can hope to be truly expert over the entire range of research the decision-maker who employs him ought to be seeking.

Surely, most of the managers of decision-oriented studies will come from Schools of Education or the rare departments of social science that emphasize applications. Today, those responsible for decision-oriented research are often trained as measurement specialists or as specialists in survey research. The training programs have been essentially the same for applied work and conclusion-oriented inquiry. This is very likely not the final solution.

It may be that as decision-oriented research becomes better established and models better defined, subordinate positions can be designed for persons not well qualified for Ph.D. training. The emerging research institutions will need technologists (e.g., writers of test items, classroom observers, data processors). Perhaps these individuals can be trained through two years of course work (part of it undergraduate) followed by an internship—but we offer the speculation only to suggest how open the problem is. It seems likely also that research managers, who can judge what services are needed to solve a problem, will come to be distinguished from the specialists with high competence in particular disciplines.

However matters may develop, in the near future most of the brass-tacks training for decision-oriented research will take place on the job or in short-term institutes. Programs of training to be provided in universities will be molded only as the goals of the research and the new decision-oriented institutions take shape.

POSTDOCTORAL TRAINING The need for innovation and expansion in postdoctoral training is at least as great as the need for fresh approaches at the predoctoral level. The current demand is stretching most persons engaged in educational research far beyond their training and experience. It is drawing in persons whose previous careers were unconnected with educational research: teachers of mathematics, industrial engineers, laboratory psychologists, etc. At the same time, new technologies of research and new concepts in the contributory disciplines are demanding continual learning on the part of the most experienced investigator. Moreover, a training experience can inspire in an investigator a fresh and significant interest.

Postdoctoral training must vary with the maturity of the investigator, the art he wishes to learn, and the qualifications he brings to it. Significant training can rarely be incidental to a job. To be sure, a professional can always learn by doing, but work assignments usually call for exercise of skills already developed or for improvisation to satisfy a time schedule. A person who recognizes that his training is incomplete needs to be free from job assignments for a time, which calls for special financial support.

His study may include specific courses, but the most profitable postdoctoral training for most persons will emphasize collaborative work with a qualified investigator. The Office of Education has now established a limited number of postdoctoral traineeships, an important though timid step. Bold designs to improve postdoctoral training are also needed. Postdoctoral training is not at all the same as the fellowship that frees a man to pursue his own projects. There is little tradition of postdoctoral training in the areas related to education. The person who comes to the university as a postdoctoral visitor is often left to his own devices, being offered nothing but a selection of courses designed for less mature persons and a desk where he can work independently. By virtue of his maturity and his survival of a selection process, the postdoctoral trainee merits more personal attention and guidance than the student working on a dissertation, but he sometimes gets almost none. His relationship with faculty members should be, as we said, collaborative, not tutorial. But to take advantage of a necessarily short training period, the interaction has to be far more intense than that usual among faculty colleagues.

Unless universities or research establishments take serious responsibility for each trainee, the experience will fall short of its potentials. The emergence of postdoctoral training as a new type of teaching function has not yet been recognized. What prevails is a traditional hospitality that invites any postdoctoral visitor to use the university in his own way. True postdoctoral training is going to be as expensive, in faculty time and laboratory resources, as predoctoral training. Universities should be encouraged to devise effective postdoctoral experience, and this will not take place unless supporting agencies set aside money to operate the program as well as to support the trainee. As a minimum, the subsidy must match the estimated cost to the university of a student-year of graduate training.

Short postdoctoral training institutes can do much.

Institutes are no doubt the best way to use the training capabilities of the very few outstanding investigators, bringing them together at one place with the young investigators who can most profit from them. These busy men are not often available for a special assignment, but most of them can clear their schedules for an occasional institute. How long an institute should last depends on the depth and breadth of training desired. A two-day institute can rarely do more than advise the participant as to the extent of his obsolescence. A two-week institute can communicate a body of knowledge or a specific technique. A six- to eight-week program allows the trainee to explore his interests with the staff, to shape a new research program and receive criticisms, and to acquire fresh perspectives through leisurely interaction with colleagues. Hence the two-day institute provides orientation; the two-week institute provides well-defined training; the two-month institute provides for intellectual growth.

Institutes have been arranged in recent years by the American Educational Research Association, the Social Science Research Council, and other agencies. These have been sporadic ventures; funds have had to be solicited anew to support each separate institute, and planning has been hurried. The time has come for a stable program of institutes, designed to meet specific needs. Institutes conducted to date have concentrated unduly on psychology and statistics. An important feature of the most successful institutes appears to be bringing investigators having primarily disciplinary interests together with investigators committed to specifically educational problems. Contrasting perspectives are thus brought to bear on the complex educational problem, and, as a significant by-product, a number of the former class of investigators become interested in doing research more closely related to field problems.

# Research in academic settings

EACH TYPE of institution has traditions that encourage certain types of studies and certain attitudes toward investigation. The following section deals exclusively with research by university faculties, with which the Committee members are reasonably familiar. As indicated in earlier chapters, research in school systems, in state agencies, in regional laboratories, and in nongovernmental agencies can perform important functions. Such agencies have not been able in the past to do all that they might; we have made some recommendations for their improvement in Chapter 5. To pinpoint sources of difficulty in agencies outside the university and make more specific recommendations, however, would require an intensive and full-scale study the Committee has been unable to undertake.

On the whole, the university places a premium on conclusion-oriented studies, and, as far as possible, on the sorts of studies we have praised in Chapter 4. This value system prevails in Schools of Education as well as other parts of the university, though not to the exclusion of decision-oriented work. The dominant ethos varies between and within universities. We can only regret the long years in which educational scholars separated themselves or were cut off from scholarship in other departments. Communication has been most continuous with psychologists. Much of the expansion of American psychology in this century was the outgrowth of demand from educators, thanks to the impressiveness of Thorndike, Hall, and Terman. One might almost say that it was the enthusiasm of educators that enabled psychology to set itself up as an independent discipline; even in recent times, many departments of psychology were administratively a part of Schools of Education. The contrast with sociology is striking; except in a very few universities, until the current decade educational sociology was in the charge of persons who had little or no contact with other sociologists. Education faculties have been little aware of what the remaining social sciences have to contribute. Only gradually are the rank and file in political science, economics, anthropology, etc., coming to realize that many leaders in their fields are in fact engaged with educational problems. History and philosophy have from earlier days been recognized as highly pertinent to education, but there has been a grave isolation of those who teach and investigate educational history and educational philosophy. Just in the past decade has the isolation diminished.

On the campus there is still a prejudice against Schools of Education and, among those not on an Education faculty, some reluctance to be seen as doing educational research. But there is a growing rapprochement because of the recognized importance of education, the relevance of its questions to key interests of the disciplines, and the greatly improved quality of the student in Education. Relations are still far from close enough, and communication is still inadequate. Schools of Education have not learned as much as they should about what is happening outside their walls. They have not taken enough responsibility for promoting effective campuswide concern with understanding education. The School of Education should be charged by its university to be a catalyst—and should eagerly accept the challenge.

With the fascinating problems the School of Education can present for attention, it should be able to enlist scholars of all kinds, who can contribute much even if only by thinking about matters pertinent to education in the course of their own conclusion-oriented investigations. The interest of some of those scholars can be enlisted for an attack on specifically educational problems.

Though faculties hold a high ideal regarding the pursuit of understanding, subtle influences dilute this ideal. There is, for example, a tendency to reward novelty. The person who is exploring a new idea or method, even a relatively trivial one, may attract more attention, receive earlier promotions, and get better job offers than a person following a line others have pioneered. There is not much enthusiasm in social science and educational research for replication of inquiries. In other fields of inquiry even those who move on to new aspects of a question include in their work a return to the original sources, or set up experiments with the original apparatus and substances so that an independent check on the older findings is built into the new work. Educational scholars are far less likely to look again at what a predecessor has reported on, and yet the presence of interaction effects makes the repetition of an inquiry in a new place even more important than in those sciences that can better control phenomena.

Doctoral training seems to reinforce this tendency. The doctoral thesis should be construed primarily as a solid training exercise that includes a strong emphasis on thoughtful interpretation. The training of researchers would proceed more efficiently without the strain to be novel. The candidate should not learn that it is dangerous to submit a finding that contradicts his initially stated hypothesis or a finding that simply provides a sounder basis for accepting what had already been believed on weaker grounds. Too often the student is encouraged to focus on the topical and the "urgent," rather than try to achieve more general insight.

University practices also put a premium on early results. It is not until the young researcher or scholar has published papers that he begins to receive the fringe benefits of being known. Whatever his doctoral thesis, he is under considerable pressure to publish his findings and get on to studies that, like the dissertation, can be quickly completed. This situation is understandable in view of the number of people in the academic world and their geographic scattering. Early recognition in the profession cannot easily be based on first-hand personal acquaintance with a young researcher's quality of mind and soundness of performance; publication is the substitute. Publication constitutes, then, a kind of publicity directed at a large and distant audience whose professional favor is required for advancement. The net effect is a reduction in the readiness of the young investigator to embark on long-term, uncertain investigations. Gamesmanship advises an effort to get something—anything—into print.

Education has this disease in a virulent form. We believe that not more than one-tenth of the doctoral dissertations in Education and not more than one-tenth of the work published in the less-well-edited journals, even today, are respectable works of serious inquiry.[10] The rest have had their function as training exercises and as tokens required for professional stature, but they have degraded the term "contribution to knowledge." Moreover, because the profession has not scrutinized new work and combined it into successively better-informed syntheses, most of the publications have made no conceptual contribution. David Wilder, for example, finds it all too easy to document a muckraking treatise on inquiry in the field of reading.[11] Jeanne Chall's reflective synthesis in that area represents a kind of scholarship and quality of endeavor that is painfully infrequent in education.[12]

There are additional deterrents to extended investigation of a topic. Throughout his career, a research worker is fearful of being caught in a rut, and is constantly attracted to growing areas of his field. Many, perhaps most, scientists thus make major shifts in their lines of research at least once each decade, and in some cases, as often as every third year. Though such change enhances his general mastery of the field and increases his value as a teacher, it tends also to keep him from sustained and concentrated effort that may lead to deeper and more fundamental understanding. Considering also that research productivity tapers off in middle age and that there is an increasing drain on scholars to meet nonresearch demands, the net effect may be a decrease in the depth and intensity of the whole research effort.

There is a need to devise methods of reducing the pressures for novelty and early publication, and methods of encouraging sustained investigations, replications, and long-term risk inquiries, and, above all, methods to raise the intellectual quality of investigations. Arrangements other than publication are needed to extend recognition and opportunity to able young researchers. For example, a faculty making a new appointment can examine materials that have not been formally published, a practice that is followed by some European universities. This would give proper weight to file memoranda showing imaginative thoughts not yet ripe for publication, and to memoranda written for decision-makers that reveal too much about individual institutions to be given wide exposure.

## Risks of overextension

We have already lamented the shortage of trained investigators. The management of large projects requires senior researchers to divert their efforts from execution of research to administration. As they spend more and more time in distant committee meetings and site visits, they are diverted from thinking, from writing, from developing their own data, and from training. Perhaps thought should be given to the use as research managers of senior faculty who are no longer directly interested in research.

An influx of funds such as that recently experienced in-

creases the risk that faculties will undertake more enterprises than can be managed effectively. There is an evident
need for restraint. The academic profession has nothing
*distinctive* to offer society save a critical spirit. Any valid
criticism requires concentration. All too often on the campus, as a senior man enlarges his empire, he devotes less
and less time to disciplined aspects of the enterprise conducted in his name. The sponsors who believe they have
engaged his talents are actually supporting studies in which
graduate students are *de facto* the principal investigators.
As the senior investigator moves deeper into research management, this reliance on younger men may be a good
thing; but the character of the arrangement needs deeper
and more explicit analysis than it has yet received.

Fiscal policies sometimes distort programs. Departments able to attract grant funds have tended to grow
disproportionately, other areas being relatively starved.
Faculty members have been encouraged, directly and indirectly, to supplement their academic-year earnings with a
summer salary from a grant or contract. The study for which
support can be found may in `some instances divert the
man from work more suited to his talents. In many departments, it is becoming psychologically difficult to do unsup-
ported, spare-time research of the sort considered highly
desirable a generation ago when the total research effort
was smaller. Grant-supported projects tend to develop
existences of their own, with little relationship to the life
of the host institution and sometimes without adequate
concern for the training function.

Institutions should encourage the professor to stick to
thoughtful work on the problems he judges most significant
for his intellectual development. Getting a grant is too
much taken as an achievement in itself, the ability to "bring
in funds" too much a criterion in new appointments. There
needs to be approval for the individual working on problems *not* currently "in the air." The faculty should neither
have to dream up contract proposals for graduate students

to work on nor have to cope with an overload of students taken in to provide hands for some massive project.

University administrators, faculties, and grantors need to re-examine programs and policies. There is, in every institution, some limit on the size of graduate student bodies and research budgets that the institution can properly handle. The institution that overloads itself can change its character inadvertently.

These remarks, and other critical remarks to follow, should be read in context. We applaud the very substantial intellectual and scientific achievements of the system of graduate schools and research support of the federal government and big foundations since the end of World War II. These massive efforts in research and research training are unparalleled in the history of universities in the Western world. The procedures of grant and contract awards have been of central importance in this buildup, and the overall quality, as well as quantity, of research in American universities is surely incomparably better now than it was before 1940.

Perhaps, since this report is being openhanded with advice to high authorities, we may dare also to advise our academic colleagues. Getting that next research grant is not the key to existence. To be sure, there are always promising youngsters one wants to support. But a proper policy of direct training grants would remove the pressure to invent a "project" to keep the youngster from starvation, a project that diverts the senior scholar from proper continuation of his thinking. To be sure, a grant frees one from the need to teach an uninspiring summer class and pays for a trip or two. But a grant is not the *sine qua non* of intellectual production, and it may be, as the jargon goes, "counterproductive." When a grant provides stilts from which a man can see further, it is a magnificent investment for society and a boon to the investee; when a grant (more likely a "contract") bends a man down beneath deadlines and reports-to-file and plans-that-must-be-followed, it is crippling. To go a year without a grant may be to spend a year in the desert. If that does not mean starvation for students, the net result is likely to be totally good. *Contemplation* is a word not much in fashion in a generation where *now* is on every tongue. The academic man has some responsibility to ignore fashion.

Neither the presence nor absence of federally supported research is fundamental. What is fundamental is to create a climate that is favorable to first-class intellectual endeavors and hostile to the second-rate. In some situations the failure to obtain grants has simply been used as a convenient reason to get rid of an unproductive scholar. Genuine scholarship is rare enough in Education or other disciplines to make it doubtful that many serious intellectual efforts have been summarily cut off because they were not grant-supported. Rather, the presence of a grant has too often been taken as a sufficient reason for faculty and academic support of a second-class scholar or research project.

If the university is to retain the momentum of leadership, it must not become the handmaiden of external agencies having funds and goals of their own. The faculty program should follow from its own judgment as to proper distribution of emphasis in research. Its activities should fit its conception of proper training for research students. Otherwise, its training and research functions are dictated by the uninformed, though well-meaning, judgment of granting agencies, and its processes of decision are corrupted. Public support of research is a fine thing, but it must be accepted in a discriminating manner by universities.

## Special problems of Schools of Education

Schools of Education are more like colleges than like departments. Education faculties are diverse in background and experience, not unified by disciplinary affiliation. Research models and styles within such schools are drawn from the social sciences (inclusive of psychology), from history and from philosophy, from regional or area studies, and from "field," "clinical" and "applied" studies as well. The result is that there is serious confusion as to the nature of proper studies or investigations within Schools of Education.

There is a tendency for standards to drop when people from different disciplines have to judge work together. A scholar may more easily overlook shoddy work from another discipline. If a colleague were to criticize the investigator, the comments might be useless to him when they come from a strange perspective. When there are only one or two representatives of a discipline within an Education faculty, the normal, continuous, qualified reiteration of disciplinary standards is largely absent. A scholar within a School of Education, speaking to tolerant colleagues as sole (or almost sole) representative of his discipline, tends more often to speak in generalities and to be more insulated from criticism than his fellow scholar in a department. He is elevated into the local authority, not kept at the level of an honored but fallible servant of the discipline. The isolation of Schools of Education within the university aggravates this lowering of standards. To the extent that the scholar does not make everyday contacts with disciplinary colleagues, he is prevented from benefiting from either "in-group" candor or inspiration.

It is highly important to develop friendly commerce between the Education faculty and the other faculties of the university on a regular and continuing basis. Functional joint appointments are one important mechanism, and they may be essential to recruit an Education faculty of high quality. The special and ambiguous role of such faculty is often not sufficiently realized. A young recruit from a discipline to an Education faculty is expected to retain his disciplinary standards and to contribute to its progress, while developing lateral relations to colleagues working on professional aspects of education or studying it through disciplines other than his own. He is expected to do whatever those in his home discipline are doing, and in addition to do a creative job of a different order. Moreover, he needs especially high ability and much personal security. High-quality graduates of doctoral programs in a discipline normally prefer to take nonambiguous positions within disciplinary departments. Special effort must be given to developing the challenge and promise of a position in Education for qualified people, and special incentives and freedom must be allowed them on the job. Otherwise, a lower quality of faculty is recruited and the vicious cycle of isolation continues: the Education faculty cannot hold its own with colleagues in academic departments; joint efforts dwindle: the Education professor drops in campus esteem; and a still lower quality of person is attracted for the future. The upgrading of educational research requires attention not only to research procedures but to fundamental conceptions of the Education faculty's job and to the recruitment and development of faculty members.

As to research quality, we have already noted the need to toughen publication standards. Much of what is now published is of modest significance and quality. A few journals are making an effort to raise quality by having all manuscripts reviewed by qualified referees. Editors of *The Journal of Educational Psychology* and *The American Educational Research Journal* inform us that three-quarters of the manuscripts submitted to them by research workers have to be rejected. (There is evidence that this is not simply to be explained as an imbalance between the number of manuscripts and space available.) This observation appears to support a strong recommendation for adoption of referee systems by all journals reporting research on education. The editorial pattern of the *Harvard Educational Review* follows that of the law-review journals. A committee of graduate students is chosen on merit by the faculty and charged to edit a journal of high quality, soliciting appropriate, thought-provoking articles. Strengthening of publication standards, of course, must allow for diversity in style and paradigm of research. Imperialism of methodology must not be mistaken for improvement.

Because criticism plays a crucial role in inquiry, the critical standards in the educational community as a whole need to be raised from their present low level. Findings now are hailed and re-echoed without critical examination of the data and logic behind them. There is a ready audience for the research that supports whatever happens to be currently popular in education: creativity, structure, team teaching, who knows what next. There is a prevalence of self-fulfilling hypotheses. It often seems as if educators are less interested in the intellectual warrant of educational doctrines than in their currency. This situation clearly needs improvement, which can only come from the professional groups, journals, and especially from the institutions where scholars in education are trained.

There is useful and important work to be done in education that is not research, strictly speaking. Pressure for everyone to do research is unfair, and is undesirable when directed against the work of specialists in, for example, teacher training. It is unrealistic and frustrating to them. In the long run, the demand that everyone do something called "research" tends to stretch the notion of research to the point of meaninglessness. Better to recognize as legitimate and important the craftsmanship and experience displayed by educational clinicians and program directors, than to force them to claim that their contribution is research.

THE EDUCATIONAL RESEARCH BUREAU    A School of Education often establishes a bureau as an armature for research activities. Bureaus have tended not to be self-sustaining, because the problems that a fixed staff can pursue over a period of time tend to be routine and dull.

If the bureau is a mere bookkeeping device to free some professors to do more research than they otherwise would, it is not a genuine institution. Historically, each bureau has had a high point under the direction of a man with a fresh and significant view to exploit, and it has tended to decline when his idea has run its course or when his directorship has terminated. A bureau may sometimes form an ideal training center, providing contact between faculty members interested in research; but bureaus are no panacea for improving research in Schools of Education.

There is a natural tendency among planners wishing to make a speedy attack on a problem to think in terms of change in the organizational structure of the research-and-development enterprise. The change is generally in the direction of establishing a large organization. What organization will be most productive, however, depends on the task to be done, the state of knowledge about the problem, the temperaments of the best-qualified investigators, and other factors. Also, a particular organizational structure that has exhibited great effectiveness may not be very effective when transferred to another setting or when placed under a different director.

Some who write on educational research seem to be infatuated with the big institution as a panacea. There is, for example, the belief that bureaus within universities, by virtue of their coherence, will produce studies on education that have greater quality and significance than those of investigators operating outside such a structure. Hodges [13] investigated this question by submitting about one hundred published studies of educational problems to an intensive rating of quality. There was no difference between quality ratings of studies produced by bureaus and studies produced by investigators outside bureaus. There was a weak trend that Hodges calls an "intensifier" effect: in universities with good reputations for quality of scholarship, bureau products tended to be superior; in universities of less distinction, bureau products tended to be inferior to those of individuals.

Research-and-development centers constitute a new form of enterprise, and the picture is as yet too unsettled for sensible evaluation. Initially, they have had a variety of purposes, probably too ambitious. We have lately seen a desirable decrease in emphasis on dissemination, and an increasing emphasis on training, linked to the general training functions of the host school. Centers may come to have either the strength or the weaknesses of the traditional bureaus. Vitality of leadership is critical. A holding company for a variety of small disconnected research projects is not worth the investment of administrative time. Centers must be able to concentrate efforts over a substantial period on thoughtful and penetrating work. They should be truly integrated with the work of the School of Education. Housing an independent research agency on campus—especially one charged to produce practical techniques in a hurry—can have more bad consequences than good ones.

Schools of Education have typically attempted to serve the community. They have varied in the emphasis placed on service, and such diversity is to be welcomed. In general, however, their main functions should be research and research training. Other agencies can be developed to carry out service functions on a large scale, but they cannot take over the fundamental research and training functions of the university.

# Funding

## Governmental support for educational research

The federal government is increasingly significant as a source of research support. An effective educational system is essential to the missions of many agencies, and as a result there is support for educational research in parts of the government far removed from the Office of Education or its parent department. An indication of this diversity of interest may be culled from the hearings on a possible National Social Science Foundation.[14] Witness after witness appeared before Senator Harris and his colleagues to explain the use his agency is making of social science and the studies it is supporting through in-house or contract research. The list includes:

1.  *Office of Manpower Research, Department of Labor:* Skill training and utilization, motivation to enroll for training, training of social misfits, etc.
2.  *Office of Economic Opportunity:* Planning and evaluating preschool programs for disadvantaged children, school attendance of the poor, economic studies of human resources, social attitudes of and toward the poor, etc.
3.  *National Science Foundation:* Projects in psychology, sociology, and other fields; curriculum development in science, social science and mathematics.

4. *U.S. Information Agency:* Comprehension of films, magazines, etc., by various audiences.
5. *Peace Corps:* Studies of recruiting, training (especially in foreign languages), effectiveness of educational work abroad, etc.
6. *Department of Defense:* Measuring human capabilities, selection and training, including computer-aided instruction and educational television.[15]

Funding agencies are swayed by political realities. The pressure to disperse funds geographically, for example, will remain with us. It can be constructive, if genuinely excellent centers develop in regions where talent has been less concentrated. If "equal shares" becomes the dominant note and excellence is not the test, however, we will see only harmful consequences. A good man is unlikely to flourish in isolation. There is need for a concentration of talent to support a sound research, development, and training enterprise; and there are not enough excellent persons available to sustain the recent pace of a dozen new centers each year.

The central problem for federal agencies is to make sure that their funds support work of high quality. Review of proposals has been handled in different ways by different federal agencies; because various patterns have worked, one cannot readily generalize. National Institute of Mental Health, using panels of highly competent external reviewers, has achieved great respect for its decisions. Decisions in the Office of Naval Research and the National Science Foundation are made largely by the staff, aided by written opinions from the field. The staff decisions have been well accepted in the field; the officers are competent scholars and have spent considerable time talking with the research community in terms that the community understands. They have discussed concepts and findings emerging in research, rather than the agency mission alone.

PRIORITIES AND ALLOCATIONS    All federal agencies

face the problem of topical priorities. Some agencies and programs have been able to enlist scientists to collaborate with administrators in thoughtful planning. Even at best, this process of assigning priorities involves elements of lobbying, because no investigator can be impartial. The efforts made in the physical and health sciences show that this is a difficult reflective process requiring unhurried consideration, calm examination and cross-examination, and the strategic view rather than the tactical one. Such thorough review of opportunities has not happened in education, in part because expansion has been so rapid.

Often a push in a predetermined direction is uncritical. Thus one group of reformers decided that since medieval music is aesthetically valuable, it should be in the third-grade curriculum; this decision was made without examining the response of children to such music as compared with other equally good music, and its net effect. Such over-determined projects rush forward to dissemination without disciplined inquiry into the basic hypothesis.

There is a tendency to expand on a scale beyond the capabilities of the research community. Evaluation intended to check on the effectiveness of innovative programs for poor children, while an excellent idea, was a new one. Persons and agencies with the experience and training to do it properly were lacking. Before launching the program there should have been two or three years of pilot evaluations by inventive teams. Instead, there was a legislative requirement for annual research reports from all participating school systems. This simply spread out the best-qualified persons as advisors having to make guesses from inadequate experience. In three years the evaluation program has been unable to rise above the makeshift level because every evaluator has been too busy to think.

There are difficulties in organizing research. The administrator wants a focus that will reassure Congress and the public that it is getting someplace, but he knows the danger of unduly restricting creativity and of establishing unwieldy programmatic enterprises. As Clark Kerr said to a Congressional committee in 1965:

> Some hard choices must be faced. The decentralized project approach of the last two decades has much to recommend it. It is selective on merit, flexible in accordance with quality of performance, and responsive to national goals. The universities and their scholars retain substantial freedom. But such dominant reliance on the project approach is no longer likely. In fact the project is already less the chosen instrument than it once was. Productive anarchy is no longer such a politically viable solution.[16]

Perhaps a solution is to coordinate problem-oriented research through decentralized "invisible colleges," that is, through institutionalizing the existing networks of communication among persons sharing common interests and a common set of intellectual criteria. Two agencies of this character can be noted as examples.

Project Literacy, supported by the U.S. Office of Education and directed by Professor Harry Levin from his home base at Cornell University, has functioned since 1964 to stimulate and integrate studies of reading. A moderately large grant permitted Levin to visit research centers, to assemble investigators (including beginning researchers) so that they could exchange and criticize ideas and plans, and to support small-scale studies that might later develop into projects for separate support. This achieves, intensifies, and disciplines work on reading without concentrating specialists in one center and thereby draining the rest of the country. It serves as a means of postdoctoral training. And it accelerates the critical and imaginative processes of the discipline.

A more elaborate mechanism is the National Laboratory in Early Childhood Education, a collaborative enterprise established in 1966.[17] Research teams at six universities, each with its own interests and approaches to research, collaborate through a central agency housed at the University of Illinois. The Laboratory studies emerging ideas and investigations, communicates them, and encourages new research as promising lines open up. There is a strong base of research skill in the child-development area, and the Laboratory is strongly led. Although it is much too early to pass judgment on the scheme, it appears likely that the teams in cooperating universities will be able to make considerably better use of their funds by virtue of the communication network and the central review. There is an obvious danger in centralization of which the administration is aware; because the major support for research on early childhood is to be disbursed through subcontracts from the Laboratory, any retreat from the present willingness to encourage diverse and even mutually contradictory lines of exploration could lose the prime advantage of the scholarly process.

This and other regional or national laboratories are still in a trial period, and it is too early to attempt any assessment of their merits and shortcomings. The suggestion of earlier committees that there be one highly visible central agency for educational research, somewhat comparable to the Clinical Center of the National Institutes for Health, has been outdated by the development of powerful —but more specialized and less centralized—institutions. A dispassionate examination and appraisal of the various institutional devices that have burst on the scene in the past few years will be very much needed two or three years hence. As the experience gained from the recent expansion ripens, it should be possible to learn a great deal about what makes novel institutions effective or ineffective, and about what problems seem likely to be neglected unless there are further structural innovations.

Although Congress has been willing to put massive resources into investigations in the social-behavioral sciences as well as the traditional natural sciences, and although scholars have shed new light on the hard problems the national community faces, the partnership is not fully harmonious. The scholar is pained when legislators do not place the value he does on the scholarly work whose end-goal they do not understand. The legislator is equally pained when straightforward queries about the way money is allocated and spent are interpreted as mistrustful. The Congressman wants to know what payoff to expect, and he is happier if the payoff can come into sight before the next election. The time perspective of the scholar, if not eternal, is a long one. He hopes his efforts will contribute to humanity, but he knows that much of the past investigation that has proved to be most significant paid off in unforeseen ways, after a long chain of developments. We have already quoted Lederberg on this mismatch between the outlook of the scholar and that of the public, and have suggested that the soundest policy is research investment that, seen as a portfolio, has a promise of relevance even if the specific payoffs are unpredictable.

The executive agency, mediating between Congress and the investigator, is caught between two systems of values. Its own operating constraints introduce additional sources of friction. Operating on a year-to-year budget inhibits an agency from supporting far-sighted programs. It tends to call for more frequent reports and evidences of practical accomplishment than it would if a budget hearing were not in immediate prospect. Federal agencies differ greatly in their administrative practices, even when they seem to be carrying out rather similar missions. Some agencies specify what research shall be procured much as if they were buying new issues of clothing for the Army; this aggressive leadership has in a few instances been carried to the point where investigators protest that a proposal is judged not on its merits but "on whether it fits the Plan of the Week." At other times, sometimes within another unit of the same agency, the policy is pure *laissez-faire*. Funds are spent simply by choosing from among volunteered proposals.

# The Office of Education
# as a granting agency

At the center of any governmental concern for education is the Office of Education, now an astonishing giant among federal agencies. As a major review of the Office by a Congressional committee makes clear,[18] its expansion in the 1960's has been phenomenal, whether measured by the number of legislative programs assigned to it or the number of dollars appropriated. Although it is just one unit within the Department of Health, Education, and Welfare, it administers a budget larger than that of eight cabinet-level departments. (Its expenditures are three times those of the Post Office Department.) Within the overburdened Office, research is only one small program in the midst of giants; even so, the Office has a greater actual and potential influence on the contribution of research to education than any other agency in government or out.

This report, then, cannot out of respect and sympathy pass over the fact that relations between the Office of Education and the community of investigators concerned with education are frequently unhappy. Many investigators—especially those interested in fundamental research—are reluctant to apply to the Office for research support if they can hope to get the funds they need from NIH, NSF, or ONR. This might cause little concern, because the project, if meritorious and broadly significant, will be supported by one of those agencies and the conclusions will become available to all. But there is a subtle way in which this preference holds back educational research.

A research worker who obtains support from a mission-oriented agency finds his thinking shaped by that contact. He includes in his application a statement regarding the relevance his studies promise to have for the mission of the agency, and in his final report he may well trace out some implications of his results for the sponsor even though his study was not aimed toward "practical" conclusions. He is likely to be invited to meet with other investigators supported by the agency in related research, which he is usually eager to do; but the group with whom he meets will include a sprinkling of people who share the sponsor's interest in practical consequences. These contacts also tend to lead his thinking to questions relevant to that particular field of application. Although no agency requires an investigator it supports to do any more than carry out his study, loyalty to the sponsor develops, and the investigator willingly helps the agency when it requests some small service: reading proposals, advising it regarding a new development in his field, or sitting on a committee to develop policy. Three significant consequences derive from this tie between agency and investigator: (1) the agency that attracts and supports proposals from excellent investigators uses them as aides in developing its own program; (2) the investigator's thoughts migrate toward topics, tangential to his original interest, that are of particular relevance to the agency; and (3) the prestige of the field, and hence its ability to attract additional investigators, grows as men of good reputation demonstrate their respect for the agency and its mission.

That the U.S. Office does suffer from an unfortunate reputation is indicated strongly by the information compiled for the Reuss committee.[19] Harold Orlans, who directed the staff, submitted various questions to experienced investigators and in addition culled the recent literature for comments on social research supported by many federal agencies. The report as a whole shows strong support for such research and for each of the agency missions, on the part of the social scientists questioned. But serious questions were raised about the direction of the programs and the administrative procedures. The general reputation of the Office of Education can be judged from a tabulation of responses to two questions posed to the respondents. (The responses are scattered through Part III of the report.) As can be seen in Table 2, one question invited favorable

**Table 2.   Responses of social scientists to questions about quality of agency research programs**

| Agency[a] | Which one or more federal agencies would you cite as sponsoring social research of exceptionally high quality? | Which agencies now sponsoring social research should curtail or redirect that research because it is poorly conceived, administered, or utilized? |
|---|---|---|
| National Science Foundation | 16[b] | |
| National Institute of Mental Health | 12 | |
| National Institutes of Health | 8 | |
| Office of Naval Research | 6 | |
| Department of Defense | 4 | |
| Department of Agriculture | 3 | 1 |
| Office of Education | 1 | 5 |
| Department of Health, Education, and Welfare | 1 | 1 |
| Office of Economic Opportunity | 1 | 1 |

[a] Various other agencies, not closely related to educational research, were mentioned by a single respondent.
[b] Each figure is a tally of the number of times the agency was mentioned.

references to agencies, and one invited unfavorable references. The questions were open-ended, and the respondent was free to mention a small unit or a superordinate agency at the Cabinet level. Though the data are clearly unfavorable to the U.S. Office, the picture does not suggest that the situation is irretrievable. The question as worded is concerned with the quality of the research and as such reflects on the investigators being supported as well as on those who provide the support. Some part of the criticism, then, has

to do with the perceived inadequacy of research in education. As we go on, however, it will be evident that the
responses also reflect opinions on the research management of the agency.

Another kind of evidence comes from publication
statistics. If research is taken seriously as a contribution to
a growing body of knowledge, it is published in a scholarly
or technical periodical where it can readily be scrutinized,
challenged, and reinterpreted. Only a fraction of sponsored
research in education is exposed to review in this way. A
technical report may be filed with the sponsor, with a
central repository, and in a few libraries. Speeches embody-
ing the conclusions or recommendations are likely to be
made. But, as another of the illuminating Congressional
inquiries [20] tells us, only 11 per cent of the technical reports
based on U.S. Office of Education projects appear as regular
journal articles. Almost no other government agency concerned with research reports so low a figure; compare these
representative figures: Department of Agriculture, 48 per
cent; NSF, 95 per cent; Veterans Administration, 45 per
cent. The fault, let us emphasize, is not the failure to
"disseminate" findings; the fault is that reports do not
appear in scholarly journals or monograph series, do not
receive critical review, and hence are not strengthened by
disciplinary debate.

Not all findings about the Office are negative. There
is at least one Congressional inquiry in which it fares not
at all badly.[21] Whatever social scientists may think of the
agency, the spokesmen for the institutions receiving contracts give the Office of Education a respectable rating; this,
one gathers, is a view of the agency from the university
business office. A Congressional committee asked universities and colleges to score each of twenty-two federal departments, services, and other agencies as "excellent,"
"reasonable," or "difficult" with respect to red tape, reporting requirements, budget details and negotiating, time
required to reach decisions and fairness of the process of

selection among project proposals. The judgments rank the U.S. Office at the median or slightly above in every respect. Very much higher ratings are given the National Science Foundation and the Advanced Research Projects Agency (about 50 per cent of the ratings score them as "excellent"), and the agricultural research program (68 per cent, compared to the Office's 35 per cent), but NIH rates no better, and the Department of Defense and NASA rate considerably worse.

The persons quoted in the Reuss report range from long-established educational research workers to scholars from other fields who have only recently begun to work on educational matters. The number in parentheses after each quotation here is a page reference, but we make no attempt to cite all references on a point. Statements are made about development work and innovation "prematurely or inadequately funded" (135); inadequately qualified reviewers of proposals (110, 160, 204); poor coordination with other agencies (113, 136); frequent shifts in topical areas chosen for priority support (118, 143); and inadequacy of staff (116, 121, 137). The interested reader is directed to the full symposium, and to Orlans' summary.[22] The problems of staffing are critical, because the quality of research supported will in the end depend on whether Office personnel make good judgments. There is considerable testimony that the Office has been flooded with responsibilities at a rate perhaps four times as great as it has been assigned staff to do the work,[23] and is further handicapped by the fact that highly responsible positions cannot be filled, because of the same manpower shortage we have bemoaned elsewhere. Nothing could be more eloquent than the statement of the director of a research center at Harvard (p. 46): "The people we know at the Office of Education are delightful, capable individuals: the problem is that they must move at a steady dogtrot, if not gallop; and then as a result of one reorganization or another, they seem perpetually to be engaged in a game of musical chairs. In short, gentlemen, the Office of Education people strike us as competent, but nowhere numerous enough."

There has been a national mobilization to remedy social problems through education, but at the headquarters, regulations and political constraints from a sleepier generation still prevail. Each program administrator flounders through a paperwork blizzard, never having time free to read the substantive reports that tell what the research he supervises is discovering or the leisure to be forward-looking. There is indeed the need the Congressional Subcommittee on Education points out,[24] for a "thorough, component-by-component study of (Office) personnel needs, both for the present and for the future." The research programs of the Office can benefit much if such a study leads to action that will match responsibilities to staff qualifications and available time.

The U.S. Office evidently has a somewhat insecure position vis-à-vis the Congress and the Bureau of the Budget. This has made its staff members reluctant to simplify administrative procedures. Even in its earliest days the agency was under attack from Congress for its failure to perform miracles, and Congress has been continually on the alert to criticize the Office for any "interference" with local education. Consequently, administrators and legal officers of the Office lean toward conservative rulings.

This is seen, for example, in the fact that the Cooperative Research Program has adhered to the contract system of research support, although scholars generally recommend the grant system for conclusion-oriented studies and most agencies with superior reputations in the academic community follow the grant procedure. The distinction, as represented in a House report,[25] is illuminating.

Where the Government desires to engage the services of an educational or nonprofit organization for the conduct of a specific piece of research directed toward a specific problem, the use of the contract form is obviously in order. On the other hand, where it is the desire of the Government to stimulate and support fundamental research in a given field, with the perimeters of inquiry limited only by the curiosity and creativity of the scientific investigator, the use of the grant form has several marked advantages.

First, the psychological relationship between the recipient institution or individual and the Government is more in keeping with the concept of maximum freedom of action for the scientific investigator. Second, the problem is avoided of endeavoring to adapt detailed contract regulations designed primarily for the procurement of hardware to the support of creative, fundamental research. Third, advance payment of the grant can be made without the vouchering of expenditures and accompanying "progress reports" or other "proof of work"—both of which exercise a deadening effect upon the initiative of the scientist.

Although the Cooperative Research Program has had grant-making authority for several years, it has only occasionally chosen to exercise it.

One example of conservatism is the insistence of the Office on prior review of data-collection instruments employed on any research it supports. (This is not required by the law on the subject, as a statement from the Office of the Commissioner [26] makes clear.) This intensive review appears to be intended in part to protect subjects against invasion of privacy and in part to forestall any conceivable Congressional criticism. The review is a nuisance to all concerned. Attention may be drawn to the Surgeon-General's statement as to why his agency has preferred a quite different plan that keeps responsibility in the hands of the academic community. [27]

The traditions of the Office do not seem flexible enough to enable it to cope with its new responsibilities, despite the vigor of recent leadership. One critical problem, from which much other trouble flows, appears to be a desperately low proportion of administrative funds to funds disbursed in the various programs. Many operations are short-handed, processing of applications is delayed to the point of absurdity, and administrators are unable to make needed visits to the field. The spend-funds-or-lose-them principle in federal budgeting favors the application that comes in the day the cash drawer is full, rather than the best proposal. New programs burst on the scene with short notice; the urgency of committing funds sometimes makes it necessary to accept inferior proposals which, once supported, become continuing institutions. Slow phasing-in, with ample use of planning and developmental grants on a modest scale that helps a new group to show their wares, would aid the Office to develop a more effective program of funding.

The decisions of the Office of Education regarding allocations of research funds are much criticized in the scholarly community. Panels, when used, have sometimes been overloaded to the point where panel members were unable to make informed decisions. In other instances panels have felt that the staff was overimpressed by the social significance the work would have if successful, and did not understand the reviewer's reservations regarding the quality of the proposed work. Staff members involved in the review process have generally been in poor communication with the academic sector, showing more interest in the topical urges of the moment than in the solid development of knowledge. This is in part a reflection of pressure from elected officials and the schools, in part a symptom of staff overload, and in part a problem of staff recruiting.

Congressional pressures on the allocation of research funds demonstrate a misunderstanding of the research process. We have urged one cardinal principle for research support: *a study is worth undertaking only if it will be truly disciplined and hence capable of giving solid results.* But we find a Congressional committee urging that the Bureau of Research assign a far larger responsibility in the review of research proposals to consultants employed in elementary and secondary schools. With all respect for the contributions such individuals can make to the knowledge of the

Office about current problems of the schools, we cannot equate this with a competence to review proposals. In the course of service on panels of the Office, several members of this Committee have tried to make use of reviews by educators in the field to whom research proposals were sent for comment. Such educators make little contribution to proposal review because they do not discriminate between immediacy and relevance; considerations of discipline, depth, and long-range significance are neglected.

An overemphasis on immediacy is seen also in the Congressional concern [28] that the research projects to which funds are allocated are not in one-to-one correspondence with the action programs of the Office. An action program to help poor children or to improve foreign-language teaching or whatever is legislated by Congress only when some problem rises to the crisis stage. Action, once decreed, is mounted with a rapidity that leaves no scope for proper conclusion-oriented research and all too often leaves none for orderly developmental research. If research is to make a major contribution, it must begin long before a crash program is authorized. Hence there should be a positive effort to identify problem areas that are still below the horizon of legislation and action, rather than for an allocation policy that instructs research workers to bring up the rear after the action starts. To be sure, research should go on in areas where there are action programs, but a good deal of that research should be aimed to provide insights that will be useful in mounting second- and third-generation programs, rather than to provide hasty and partial answers to the questions of the current year.

Credit can be given to the Bureau of Research for efforts to identify problem areas that are outside current fashion. There are serious risks in a policy of "directed research" if a central agency channels research effort without a well-developed sense as to which problems are likely to yield to disciplined inquiry. On the other hand, the agency is not doing its duty if it does not call the practically salient problems to the attention of scholars, so that the scholars will seriously consider whether their techniques of inquiry can and should be turned into those channels. The allocation of resources must in the end be a joint effort of the community of investigators and the mission-oriented agency. Neither can "direct," but both can lead. The negotiating process should be a mutual education, so that all participants will see the final allocations as both sound and potentially relevant.

Perhaps the most important recommendation we can suggest to the Office of Education is that it find better channels for frank communication with the scholarly community. Many communications that come from the Office suggest a lack of understanding of the values and thought processes of the academic world. This gap persists, despite the fact that a reasonable proportion of the staff members have fine academic qualifications and experience (usually, however, limited to Schools of Education). Something in the institutional pattern seems to isolate them and distort their language. Most applicants are hesitant to criticize a potential source of funds, and persons holding contracts feel diffident about acknowledging their troubles to U.S. Office monitors who have failed to establish a colleague-like relationship. Consequently, the Office does not know which of its rulings, policies, and practices alienate and impede the investigator.

## Private foundations

Private foundations have special roles. Some have seen the role as one of enlisting the researcher to promote a pet enthusiasm of the foundation rather than to probe and report frankly. This flaw, however, does not detract from the general picture of the private foundation as imaginative, ahead of its time, and getting greater value for its money than the federal government does. Much of this has been inherent in the spirit of placing one's money on the roulette wheel and accepting profit or loss with equanimity. The foundation seeks the good man and the live idea, knowing that it is in a high-risk enterprise. It does not burden the man with calls for interim reports, detailed accounting, and the question "What have you done for us lately?"

The foundations have conserved their resources by providing only initial capital, rarely making a commitment beyond five to ten years. This allows enterprises to die, which is both good and bad. A lack of coordination of funding from various sources interferes with the natural transition from the tryout phase of a venture to a permanent stable phase. Too often an institution that proved its vitality during the initial phase of foundation support must struggle for inappropriate short-term contracts to hold its staff together in the ensuing decades.

The relations between the foundations and the academic community are excellent, in large part because the staff members of foundations continue to be men of thought rather than turning into pure administrators. They appear on professional committees with some frequency; and when they do, they pull their own weight in substantive matters. Perhaps because they have so simplified their own administrative procedure, they are able—unlike their counterparts in some government agencies—to keep themselves very well informed and, on occasion, to produce integrative works of scholarship.

## NOTES

1. Froelich, G. J., in Harris, Chester W. (ed.), *Encyclopedia of Educational Research*, 3rd ed. New York: Macmillan, 1960, p. 1157.

2. *Ibid.*
3. Walton, Ann D., and Marianna V. Lewis (eds.), *The Founda-tion Directory*, 3rd ed. New York: Russell Sage Foundation, 1967.
4. Cowley, W. H., "Two and a Half Centuries of Institutional Research," in Axt, R. G., and H. T. Sprague (eds.), *College Self-Study: Lectures on Institutional Research*. Boulder, Colo-rado: Western Interstate Commission for Higher Education, 1960, pp. 1–16.
5. Simon, K. A., and W. Vance Grant, *Digest of Educational Statistics*, Washington, D.C.: U.S. Office of Education, 1967, pp. 18, 122.
6. *Ibid.* The total expenditure for education is $48,000,000,000 (p. 18). The latest figure for educational research is just short of $100,000,000. The ratio is 1 to 0.002. A confirming figure comes from the New York City schools, where "less than one-quarter of one percent" of the total educational budget goes to research. Justman, Joseph, "Problems of Researchers in Large School Systems," *Educational Forum*, Vol. 32 (1968), p. 430.
7. Phi Delta Kappa Census, *A Directory of Educational Research Agencies and Studies*. Bloomington, Ind., 1966.
8. Bright, L. L., Testimony. Hearings on HR 14745. Subcommit-tee, Senate Committee on Appropriations. Washington, D.C.: Government Printing Office, 1966, p. 342.
9. Buswell, Guy T., and McConnell, T. R., *Training for Educa-tional Research*. Berkeley, Calif.: Center for the Study of Higher Education, University of California, 1966.
10. This estimate is supported, for example, by Michael, W. B., "Teacher Personnel: A Brief Evaluation of the Research Re-viewed," *Review of Educational Research*, Vol. 33 (1963), p. 443; by Bloom, B. S., "Twenty-Five Years of Educational Research," *American Educational Research Journal*, Vol. 3 (1966), pp. 211–221; and also by Chall, Jeanne S., *Learning to Read: The Great Debate*. New York: McGraw-Hill, 1967.
11. Wilder, David, "The Reading Experts: A Case Study of the Failure to Institutionalize an Applied Science of Education," unpublished doctoral dissertation, Columbia University, New York, 1966.
12. Chall, *op. cit.*
13. Hodges, Caroline S., *Measuring Educational Research Quality and Its Correlates*. New York: Bureau of Applied Social Re-search, Columbia University, 1967.
14. *National Foundation for Social Sciences*, Subcommittee on

Government Research, Senate Committee on Government Operations. Washington, D.C.: Government Printing Office, 1967, p. 39.

15. Diverse as this list is, it is not exhaustive, as the absence of the National Institutes of Health makes obvious.

16. Kerr, Clark, Testimony in *Federal Research and Development Programs,* House Select Committee on Government Research. Washington, D.C.: Government Printing Office, 1964, p. 1024.

17. Hjelm, Howard F., and Marian B. Sherman, "The National Laboratory on Early Childhood Education: A Model of Educational Research and Development," *Journal of Educational Research and Development,* Vol. 1 (1966), pp. 39–45.

18. *Study of the United States Office of Education.* House Special Subcommittee on Education. Washington, D.C.: Government Printing Office, 1967.

19. *The Use of Social Research in Federal Domestic Programs.* Research and Technical Programs Subcommittee, House Committee on Government Operations. Washington, D.C.: Government Printing Office, 1967.

20. *Documentation and Dissemination of Research and Development Reports.* House Select Committee on Government Research. Washington, D.C.: Government Printing Office, 1964, p. 37.

21. *The Administration of Research and Development Grants.* House Select Committee on Government Research. Washington, D.C.: Government Printing Office, 1964, p. 50.

22. *The Use of Social Research, op. cit.,* Part II, pp. 4–8.

23. *Study of the United States Office, op. cit.,* p. 3.

24. *Ibid.,* p. 71.

25. House Report 2640 of August 15, 1958. 85th Congress, 2d session. See also *Study of the United States Office, op. cit.,* p. 225ff.

26. *The Use of Social Research, op. cit.,* Part IV, p. 465. The procedures are defended by H. S. Conrad of the Office on pp. 187–216.

27. *Ibid.,* p. 221.

28. *Study of the United States Office, op. cit.,* p. 209ff.

# 7

# Some paths
## for future inquii

THIS REPORT would not be complete without a somewhat extended list of the problems that should receive scholarly attention, of a vigor and depth not given them in the past. Although we can confidently commend these topics to attention, they do not make up an exhaustive list and we have not arrived at them by a systematic survey of any of the fields, nor have we attempted to represent every relevant field. Rather, this list exemplifies the kinds of questions we consider important.

# Economic aspects

One set of problems has to do with economic aspects of education.

1] Human capital is accumulated mainly through education. Studies are needed of the relation between the theory of the accumulation of human capital and international trade, and also between the accumulation of human capital and the personal distribution of income. Perhaps most important, human capital and physical capital should be more systematically integrated in a theory of economic growth.

2] Studies of the efficient allocation of investment resources to the educational establishment and within the educational establishment are needed.

3] The relation between labor market discrimination and the effects of this discrimination on the motivation of students in schools, especially as related to students' perceptions of their occupations and their place in the labor market, needs systematic investigation.

4] Studies are needed of the economic competition for teachers. Such an analysis should include an attempt to assess the nonpecuniary attractions of the work and their strengths in relation to pecuniary attractions. In other words, we need a deeper understanding of the money equivalents of working conditions for various types of schools and positions.

5] Studies are needed to clarify the pattern and causes of teacher mobility, including movement into and out of the teaching profession.

6] Studies are needed of how we may better utilize present educational plant capacity, teacher capacity, and student capacity. As yet, cost-benefit analysis of alternative uses of resources in education is relatively primitive. The rational allocation of funds among school activities has only recently begun to be seriously studied.

7] The income productivity of learning in different disciplines and professions needs further analysis. It would be useful to have studies comparing the differential costs of education for various careers with the lifetime income differential that can be expected.

8] The economic effects of the age of leaving school have received recent attention, but further information and analysis are desirable. From an economic standpoint, is it desirable to have community pressure to stay in school despite the individual student's dislike of school and the waste of his time? Would it be desirable to have the minimum age for leaving school at about fourteen or fifteen, or make the choice of continuing school easier by offering a more varied curriculum, including a more relevant program of vocational training? What would be the economic effects of such a change in age? Are there any sound economic arguments for accelerating the curriculum to permit students who leave school at age fourteen to have learned enough for gainful employment, or from an economic standpoint is such a policy contrary to all the long-run tendencies in the society?

# Historical aspects

The history of educational institutions, practices, and conduct needs to be studied.

1] We recommend investigation of the changing emphasis in the institutions contributing to and responsible for education of children. How is the role of the family changing? What will be the effects of the new educational concern of churches, museums, and other institutions, such as the military services, which we have not historically associated with education? It is particularly desirable to assess both the past and the present relative importance of schools, as opposed to other institutions like the family, in determining the actual educational level and direction of the young members of our society.

2] Studies in the history of ideas are needed that will deepen our understanding of the development of key notions about education, both in the philosophical tradition and in educational theorizing.

# Philosophical aspects

Philosophical examination of education is needed in a variety of areas.

1] Needed are related philosophical studies concerning educational aims and how they are determined and formulated. To what extent is a statement of explicit educational aims actually effective in the determination of educational programs and policies?

2] How far can empirical research in education, educational psychology, and related disciplines resolve problems in educational theory? That is, what aspects of educational policy have to depend upon normative conclusions and not directly upon empirical findings? And what are the limits of empirical procedures for estimating the "benefits" or "effectiveness" of educational programs?

3] The concepts of justice and equality that are latent in much of our educational policy need to be brought out and analyzed in more detail, particularly their relation to factual data on the presence or absence of equality in schools and in educational opportunity. The factors that determine the presence or absence of democratically desirable arrangements need study.

4] Analytic studies of central educational concepts are needed, concepts that figure in describing educational processes and also in formulating policies for educational institutions.

5] Applications of philosophy to areas of the curriculum are needed, i.e., philosophical studies of the foundations of each subject should be related to problems of curriculum organization and selection in teaching.

6] Methodological analyses are required that address themselves to characteristic problems of educational research, and research in related areas bearing on education. Especially needed are analytic studies of methodological issues in applying science to practice.

# *Psychological aspects*

Education will profit from the work of psychologists who address themselves to the following concerns.

1] More intensive studies of the impact of early experience on later predispositions to learn are needed. Studies of the ways the mass media and schooling interact with each other are especially required for a better understanding of the early years of life. Each socializing influence aids or inhibits the child's subsequent learning, but little is known about such effects.

2] Studies in learning, memory, and attention, as they relate to the organization of curriculum and the subject-matter learning of students, have recently received increased attention in psychology and these efforts should be encouraged.

3] The psychological foundation for dealing with individual differences is as yet unsatisfactorily developed. Theoretical and experimental work at an intensive level is much needed, particularly efforts directed toward serving children who enter school with various kinds of handicaps.

4] We are still far from a thorough understanding of significant motivational variables, and of how we may control these variables in order to increase the efficiency of learning.

5] It would be desirable to review the failures of previous psychological research to lead to a significant educational technology, ranging from such topics as child development to the teaching of reading. We need to understand better how psychological research may contribute to the efficient use of society's technological resources in the organization of schools and the training of students.

## *Sociological aspects*

Another set of problems calls for the combined thinking of the sociologist and the educator.

1] The administrative organization and control of education needs more intensive sociological study. Consideration should be given to the levels of administration, the interaction between local, state, and federal decisions, and the impact of this apparatus on methods for bringing about change in education. The relation of educational administration in practice to political and social pressures should be analyzed.

2] Additional work is needed on the social psychology of the classroom, the mechanisms of teacher control, the structure of attention, the varying roles played by the teacher in relation to the students, and the peer-group relations between students.

3] Work needs to be done on the relation of trends in adolescent roles and adolescent behavior in relation to educational problems. For example, we particularly need a better understanding of the phenomena of student alienation, the withdrawal of youth, and the old and new forms of rebellion.

4] It seems desirable to have a deeper development of

dynamic models that describe the flow of students through the educational system and also the flow of administrative and teaching staff. The dynamics of social change in our educational institutions from the standpoint either of students or of teachers and administrators have not yet received much quantitative analysis.

5] Given that there will almost certainly continue to be large expenditures for new school construction, and great pressure for changes in school organization, there is an urgent need for research on the effects of various modes of organization on students and the effectiveness of their learning. The basic research leading to recommendations for educational parks, decentralization of control, change of classroom organization, and so forth, is as yet in a very incomplete state.

6] As a follow-up to the Equality of Opportunity report, there need to be careful studies examining the factors that affect achievement in school. There should be quantitative studies that take account of variables not previously studied in connection with the level of school achievement.

7] Sociological analyses of the relationship between school systems and other social systems in metropolitan areas of the country are desirable. The extent to which the character and impact of school systems is determined by surrounding social systems and social structure needs investigation.

8] Analytical and systematic studies of the total school environment and organization are needed. Pressing problems in this area include the interactions between the formal school organization, pupil-teacher relationships, the structuring of the curriculum, and the structuring of students according to age and ability.

9] What are the characteristics of innovations that are likely to be adopted? What are the most important parameters to be controlled in instituting change in the school organization?

# *Other aspects*

There are many further serious problems of educational practice which demand the attention of skilled investigators with various kinds of background.

1] We need to study how to organize the work-loads and careers of teachers in order to facilitate their continued development, and also to promote better utilization of them. What are realistic projections for the extent and depth of continued education that will be required of teachers over the next fifty years? What kind of long-term changes can we expect in the composition of our population of teachers?

2] Millions of dollars are spent annually in activities designed to bring about change and, presumably, improvement in schools: consulting services, workshops for teachers, after-school courses, and so on. But we know little today either about the effects of these or, more important, how to bring about comprehensive educational change. Planned strategies, drawing upon studies and findings from related fields, need to be laid out, and their success needs to be traced systematically to gain knowledge about factors resisting or facilitating change. Further questions have to do with the characteristics of those innovations having unusual salience for practitioners and the personal characteristics of educators who support (or resist) innovation.

3] Promising studies are at present trying to work out

efficient learning sequences in fields such as reading and mathematics. But most grade placement of subject matter is justified only by custom. Fresh studies might very well find that major topics or even fields traditionally reserved for grades or levels of schooling are learned more readily at some other level.

4] Studies of motivation, reinforcement, transfer of training, and other concepts need to be moved into the classroom. Laboratory work should be succeeded by naturalistic studies. One might well classify classroom rewards, for example, and observe their effects. The ultimate goal would be to understand classrooms and schools as social systems.

5] It is particularly urgent to improve the education of children who come from families that are economically and socially deprived. For a variety of reasons, intensive scientific study of the environment of these children and the effect of that environment on their success in school has received attention only recently. We do not understand these children and their relatively high rate of failure in school. Because we cannot immediately change the environment that produces them, we need to understand the school variables that can be changed so as to benefit their performance. Major unanswered research questions exist in almost any direction. For example, what approaches to reading will maximize the probability of success of a child from a deprived environment? In what way can the organization of the school be changed so as to maximize the motivation and interest of such children in schoolwork and even in attendance at school? Changing the educational achievement and ambitions of these children is not simply a matter of spending large sums of money. To spend money effectively requires a deeper understanding of the factors that contribute in a significant way to their present high rate of educational failure.

# In conclusion

TO SUMMARIZE A REPORT such as this is not easy. The Committee undertook to set forth what the nature of disciplined inquiry into educational matters might be and to look at the extent and significance of present research efforts. We went on to examine the institutional settings in which inquiry takes place, with an eye to forces that stimulate good scholarly work and forces that inhibit it. Although the discussion contains hints as to actions that might be taken by schoolmen, universities, individual investigators, and sponsors of research, our intention has not been to produce a set of Commandments that, if followed, will bring educational inquiry into the Promised Land. Rather, we have sought to initiate a discussion as to what constitutes quality in inquiry, and how change in educational thinking derives from inquiry. If sponsors, producers, and would-be consumers of inquiry come to comprehend the interplay between research and social processes, they will be in a position to redirect their funds and energies, and to ask the sorts of questions that take advantage of disciplined inquiry. Rather than list recommendations, then, we propose to summarize a few of our main concepts regarding disciplined inquiry in education.

1] The main function of conclusion-oriented inquiry is to gain a better understanding of some educational process, or of some aspect of the nature of man and society. The research that has the greatest long-term significance is that which produces new concepts, rather than that which attempts to use the delicate apparatus of science to hammer out an immediate solution to a current problem.

2] An attempt to solve an immediate problem can also capitalize on inquiry, first by using the available knowledge and concepts to work out a sensible plan, second by using direct decision-oriented inquiry to guide day-to-day decisions as the plan is put into practice, and also to determine how well the final scheme works.

3] The two kinds of inquiry which we have referred to as "conclusion-oriented" and "decision-oriented" are carried out with different time perspectives and often require different techniques. Indeed, they may require different kinds of investigators and different kinds of research organization. Hence it is important to distinguish the two functions, and to call upon each type of inquiry for the kind of service it can best render. Decision-oriented studies are studies in the service of a decision-maker, and they will be useful only if the decision-maker truly understands what they can contribute and demands that kind of help. Conclusion-oriented studies are in the service of the whole educational community. They are generalized, their broad conclusions and new ways of thinking are intellectual resources for educators, scholars, and laymen, but they do not give a pinpointed answer to the problems the decision-maker faces today.

4] It is a mistake to press the conclusion-oriented inquirer to arrive at generalizations that the practical educator "can apply." Even in highly technological fields, basic understandings gained through fundamental research are not directly applied; there must be additional conclusion-oriented research to understand the practical problem, and then there must be decision-oriented design studies and tryouts to produce a practical solution for a particular situation. Enlightenment gained from conclusion-oriented studies helps the designer to know what to take into account in his plans and his evaluations, but it never dictates the shape of the practical solution.

5] Significant changes in thinking about the purposes of education, the curricular content and instructional procedures, and the organization of educational institutions are often brought about by scholarship that is far removed from the educational scene itself. Indeed, some of the most basic changes in educational thinking during this century derived from investigators who were not concerned with education. (We have referred to Peirce, Freud, and Pavlov as notable examples.) Their ideas, filtering into the prevailing view of the nature of truth and the nature of man ultimately altered what the community expects of the school and what procedures it considers reasonable.

6] The range of scholarship that can contribute to a sounder view of education is enormously varied. Inquiries that are self-consciously directed toward education can be as excellent in rigor and interpretation as any inquiries in the more traditional fields. Inquiries of a nonexperimental sort can raise as many questions about practices and ruling conceptions as can the empirical studies that have held the center of the stage during this century. Philosophers, economists, and many others contribute to thinking about education, and they may do so either by addressing themselves directly to educational topics or by clarifying fundamental concepts that enter into the thinking of policy-makers.

7] Disciplined inquiry has a contribution to make, different from and sometimes superior to the contribution from other kinds of thinking. The distinctive feature of disciplined inquiry is the texture of the argument that is developed. The investigator submits his thinking to the skilled and assiduous review of his colleagues, who have special training in such criticism. A special warranty attaches to the conclusions that emerge from the serious debate of scholars. For a number of reasons discussed in our report, studies of educational matters have not generally been subjected to this intensive disciplinary critique, and their conclusions have sometimes lacked the solidity that is the chief justification of systematic inquiry.

8] The most critical problem is the shortage of excellently trained investigators who, together, can form a self-critical scholarly community. New kinds of training, properly supported, will be required if we are to have a supply of investigators proportionate in number and variety to the current demand for better ideas about education and more efficiently operated institutions.

9] Many current institutions and traditions grew up under historical circumstances that no longer pertain. Historical circumstances decreed that education as a field of study should split off from the remainder of the scholarly community, with deleterious effects. The breach is now being healed, but slowly. A true integration of educational scholarship with scholarship in other pertinent fields is necessary to strengthen the educational scholar and to enlist in the search for better education the resources within the traditional academic disciplines. The same historical circumstances have pressed the student of education to carry out studies intended somehow to determine what professional educators should do. That demand distorts the process of inquiry; it foreshortens the time scale of inquiry, fosters dramatic claims rather than sober conceptualizations, and tends to encourage inquiry into overly complex problems about which sound generalizations cannot be made.

Likewise with respect to decision-oriented studies, historical forces have shaped institutions and expectations so as to lose much of the potential of the investigator. The investigator serving the decision-maker has been asked to tackle problems of enormous complexity, with miniscule resources, and simultaneously has been assigned so many trivial duties that he has no time for thought. If systematic inquiry into local and current operations is to serve the educator with anything like the payoff it has for the industrial manager and the public-health officer, new ways of carrying out operational research in education will have to be devised, and new types of persons trained for those roles.

There has been a grave tone to our discussion of the present situation in educational research. Demands are being made for which scholars, individually and collectively, are unprepared. Some of these demands are ill-conceived and divert resources from better inquiries. Some are demands that scholars would like to satisfy, but cannot either because resources are too limited or because the state of the art dictates that progress will be disappointingly gradual. Our grave evaluation is not, however, to be mistaken for pessimism. It is our view that a frank recognition by everyone of difficulties and limitations will make the research community vastly more useful.

We hope that educators and policy-makers will learn to ask of researchers the sorts of questions that scholars can answer dependably. We hope that they will acquire the patience to support persistent, long-extended inquiries into the truly fundamental questions. We hope that educators and researchers together will invent institutional arrangements whereby systematic inquiry can play a major role within developmental projects and day-to-day management of educational systems. We hope that a greater number of scholars will come to feel the challenge of educational questions, and extend their competence so as better to cope with these challenges.

The improvement of education will never be an easy task. No magic bullets will dispel ignorance and apathy. No amount of educational technology will reduce the value of wise and sympathetic teachers. Educators, laymen, students, and scholars are unanimous, however, in their belief that every aspect of education can be improved. Purposes, content, and procedures are steadily being modernized, steadily coming closer to the requirements of a new kind of world. The conceptual fruits of disciplined inquiry have played a major role in this reformation.

As more inquirers turn their attention to education and the underlying processes, and as the community of inquirers collectively raises the standards of such inquiry, we can expect a clearer understanding of educational processes to emerge. In the field of medicine we are a century or less from Pasteur, Osler, Koch, and Semmelweis, yet our capacity to prevent and cure illness is already miraculously greater. If scholarship of the same order arises in education, and is used with equal intelligence by practitioners, education in the twenty-first century will pull ahead in the race between civilization and catastrophe.

# Appendix

## Abstracts of studies on educational research

Buswell, Guy T., McConnell, T. R., Heiss, Ann M. and
Knoell, Dorothy M. *Training for Educational Research.* Center for the Study of Higher Education:
University of California, Berkeley, 1966. (Cooperative
Research Project No. 51074.)
This report, based on questionnaire returns from 818
recipients of the Ed.D. and Ph.D. degree in Schools of
Education during 1954, records the variables related to research productivity in the ensuing ten years. Questionnaire
returns from 1,750 doctors receiving degrees in 1964 were
also examined for shifts in amount and direction of change
during the decade in factors associated with training for research. Dissertations of doctors in the 1964 sample were
analyzed for research methodology used, problem areas investigated, sampling, and statistical techniques.
Academic and institutional correlates of the productive
researchers are presented. Recommendations for training
future researchers in education are made to universities
and the U.S. Office of Education.

Hodges, Caroline S. *Measuring Educational Research Quality and Its Correlates.* New York: Bureau of Applied
Social Research, Columbia University (dittoed manu-
script), May 15, 1967.
This author documents the development of an instrument for assessing the quality of educational research in
order to compare the educational research completed within

research bureaus with that done by independent scholars. Underlying the hypotheses that investigations by bureau personnel are of a higher quality than the work of an independent scholar are the assumptions that the bureau has a greater pool of talent to be used and a facilitative structure for useful interchange of ideas.

On the rating instrument used by nineteen judges for sixty-one articles from bureau based researchers and sixty-one matched cases from independent scholars, no difference in quality of research done by the two groups of researchers was found on any of the quality scales. However, when school reputation was held constant, affiliation with a bureau showed an intensifier effect on the relationship between school reputation and research quality. The greater the school's reputation, the more likely was bureau research to be of higher quality than the research of the independent scholar. The study found a strong positive relationship between research quality and private control of the university. Moreover, it appeared that a School of Education had to be twenty-five years old or older to produce significant percentages of articles which were judged high in quality.

Those articles rated by judges as highest in quality were found to come from a greater percentage of authors who 1) specialized in psychology; 2) were female; and 3) were students rather than professors. The author speculates about the reasons for each major finding in the study.

Lazarsfeld, Paul F., and Sieber, Sam D. *Organizing Educational Research.* Englewood, N.J.: Prentice-Hall, 1964.
    Sixty institutes of research in thirty-six universities provided information about their organizations. The history, relations with the university, internal organization, service functions, etc., were assessed. Problems identified included the fact that research in education is geared to improvement rather than the understanding of education; local clients rather than the field at large appear to be served; the career lines of education appear to be unique in higher education. Often, teaching or administrative experience before the advanced degree is required and the degree itself is seen only as a means to professional advancement; the climate of re-

search in Schools of Education appears to be detrimental to the production of quality research and researchers.

Recommendations include: The establishment of communication with and studies of educational problems by social scientists; the strengthening of the relation between the independent research agencies and the universities; the improvement of the research training programs; the establishment of field testing and demonstration centers apart from basic research organizations. Appendices include a breakdown of specific research activities performed by the research organizations.

Sherwin, C. W., and Isenson, R. S. *First Interim Report on Project Hindsight.* June 30, 1966. No. AD 642–400, Clearinghouse for Federal, Scientific and Technical Information, Springfield, Va.

Project Hindsight is the study of the role that research played in the development of weapon systems between about 1945 and 1962. The Department of Defense, spending around 25 per cent of its $300 million to $400 million research budget on basic or undirected science, sought to evaluate the return it was getting for this expenditure. These authors tried to provide an answer to that question. In addition, they sought to determine what management pattern led to research utilization and what contributions were made from in-house laboratories and those of contractors.

The method of analysis was comparison of a successor system with a predecessor system, identifying those key contributions, or "events," which were instrumental in improving the system. Each identifiable event was traced to its source and classified as a technology event, an applied science event, or an undirected (nonmission-oriented) science event. Twenty systems, from night vision scopes through ballistic missiles and computer systems were analyzed by thirteen teams of investigators, resulting in 710 documented events.

The analyses showed that 0.3 per cent of the events were from undirected scientific efforts. Almost all the other events were motivated by Department of Defense need. However, the authors point out that for the twenty-year time span studied it was to be expected that basic research would show little effect on weapon systems whose conception takes place ten years or more before development. They conclude that the potent contribution of basic research is in the "packed-down," thoroughly understood, and carefully taught old science of handbooks, textbooks, and courses.

The process by which basic science moves into technology and utilization was not found, but clearly it was not the direct sequence which the folklore of science fosters.

Sieber, S. D. *The Organization of Educational Research in the United States.* New York: Bureau of Applied Social Research, Columbia University, 1966. (Cooperative Research Project No. 1974.)

Information on the organization of educational research was obtained from those institutions which granted a doctorate in Education for the year 1963–1964. Included were responses from 68 per cent of the deans of department leaders, 82 per cent of the directors of faculty research programs, and 90 per cent of the research units associated with those institutions. The methods used in data collection were questionnaires, field trips, supplementary documents, content analysis of school catalogues, research proposals and historical data. Areas of interest to the author included organizational resources and their allocation, value climates, behavior and interactions among participants, attributes of participants, and institutional outcomes.

Recommendations based on the author's previous contact with leaders in educational research, his personal judgment, and the survey results, include: descriptions of the organization and role to be played by research units if they are to optimize their potential; ways to reduce the service/research tension that exists since multiple roles are called for by most Schools of Education; practices to be followed to incorporate the arts and sciences into an educational research organization; potential training programs for educational researchers; and some proposals to improve the working relationship between scholar and bureau to the Office of Education.

Storer, N. H. *The Social System of Science.* New York: Holt, Rinehart and Winston, 1966.

This analysis of science seeks to define the relationship of professional recognition to scholarly creativity and analyzes science as a social system whose basic exchange commodity is creativity.

The norms of science as reported here are objectivity, generalization, organized skepticism, communality, emotional neutrality and disinterestedness. These norms are related by the author to the exchange commodity. Science is then viewed as a system in which the fruits of investigation are placed before a professional audience in anticipation of a "competent response." This analysis is said to hold for humanistic studies as well as empirical research. Although in fields not requiring empirical studies the nature of verification of a scholar's work differs widely, his creativity is again the exchange medium which, when made public, seeks from others a competent response. The disciplined scholar operating under these norms is viewed as doing his research because he selects to, not because he has to; thus adherence to the prevailing norms is quite strong and modification of the norms occurs quite slowly.

This description of the scientific community is used to analyze problems of the system, such as the ability to distinguish quack from genius and the status differential between applied and basic researchers. Hypotheses about the ability of the norms to survive are offered in light of the growing number of scientists, the expansion of knowledge, and the demands of society for ever more applied studies.

# Index